Co

Prologue

Chapter 1 - In which we remind you who we are and what we do and Steven mutilates a pop star's sex-toy in the name of art.

Chapter 2 - In which we both do some growing up, Steven steals a cake and Kevin loses his virginity to a 1930s swing classic.

Chapter 3 - In which we tell you about our College teachers, Steven preserves Rachmaninov's dirt and Kevin acts as a pillow for his comic hero.

Chapter 4 - In which we talk about being gay in 1990s London, living in the shadow of AIDS. Steven meets Princess Diana, and Kevin gets mugged wearing rainbow trousers.

Chapter 5 - In which Kevin hides from a conductor and sets fire to his employer's eyebrows. Steven nearly makes it into the *Big Brother* house.

Chapter 6 - In which Kevin establishes a Bohemian commune, falls in love and turns down an offer from Sidney Poitier.

Chapter 7 - In which a night of drinking leads to us forming our double act. We launch in a fabulous venue, go on our first cruise and run the gauntlet of American immigration.

Chapter 8 - In which we thoroughly enjoy ourselves on Cunard's Queens. We are surprised by armed police in a public toilet and Kevin has an encounter with a chocolate cake in Kenya.

Chapter 9 - In which we move to Scotland, Steven suffers a loss and we come to a realisation about fine wine.

Chapter 10 - In which we are represented in court by a pantomime villain, confess to smuggling honey into Australia and accept some free drinks through mistaken identity.

Chapter 11 - In which we become friends with a superstar, hang out with the Botox ladies of Tramp and Kevin plays at an unintended recital for the homeless.

Chapter 12 - In which we tell you about the exotic places we have visited. Steven attracts some attention in Costa Rica and we both risk our lives on a wet rope-ladder in the Faroe Islands.

Chapter 13 - In which we star in a Canadian play in Austria, and endure a weekend with an American deity.

Chapter 14 - In which we move into the world of mobile phone apps and spend hours deleting nude photographs of men.

Chapter 15 - In which we get involved with a trouser-dropping impresario and decide not to be Two ***** on a Stool.

Chapter 16 - In which we are deprived of our rights and learn a lot about stagecraft from The Great Soprendo.

Chapter 17 - In which we remember some characters we have met on ships, fail to recognise several people and experience a buttock-clenching half-hour.

Chapter 18 - In which we start running up huge legal bills, Steven finds us lots of new friends and we come to a new arrangement with the cruise lines.

Chapter 19 - In which we tell you about the Edinburgh Fringe Festival, create a marvellous deception and are deceived ourselves.

Chapter 20 - In which we talk about how we each approach performance, about some of our favourite places to play, and explain why you haven't seen us on *Britain's Got Talent*.

Chapter 21 - In which we choose our three favourite performances, and we return to the beginning and Kevin's birthday party.

Chapter 22 - In which we somehow get through lockdown, help to make Mr. Trump famous and look forward to new opportunities.

Epilogue

Prologue

It is Sunday March 1st, 2020. A lovely bright spring morning welcomes us as we arrive at The Brighton Dome. Inside and out, this is a magnificent place. It is astonishing to think that this huge oriental looking building was originally designed to stable the Prince Regent's horses. Now the exquisite art deco interior is absolutely perfect as a concert hall, and we are so happy to be back here preparing to play at the most fabulous music venue we know.

We have been rehearsing for months. This is the one concert that we have been really looking forward to - perhaps more than any we have done in our career. Of course it isn't our first time on this stage: but last time we were playing with the Brighton Philharmonic orchestra. Today we have the honour of being invited back for a matinee concert of our own. No sharing the limelight with an orchestra and their conductor. This one is all about us.

There have been performances to big audiences before: Edinburgh's Usher Hall, the Cadogan Hall in London and we are not long back from a whole month of sell-out shows in Cape Town and Johannesburg. But this is one of those occasions that really matter.

We have the same nervous feeling you had as a child about to start school, as a teenager before your first kiss, or leaving your parents' home to live on your own. It is the tentative step towards adulthood, or in our case finally making the grade as a big venue act. Playing the Brighton Dome on our own, feels properly grown-up.

It is also Kevin's birthday. Our closest friends and family have made the trip down to Brighton to be with us for this big event: some of them have come all the way down from Scotland. For once we have decided to stay at a decent hotel, not the usual budget hotel or Ibis. So often we have seen the look of disappointment on the faces of the theatre staff when they ask:

'Are you staying at the Grand?'

and we reply:

'No, we're at the Travelodge.'

This time though, we slept in plush beds and had a decent breakfast, and are arriving in good shape ready to set up for the afternoon ahead. We make sure the huge background screen is in place, and the camera we use to project an image of our hands playing the piano keys is working. And then we run through a sound check. Sometimes the technical part of our show can cause problems, but today it all goes like a dream, and within thirty minutes we are satisfied that everything is going to work as it should.

There is nothing quite like the smell of an old theatre: a faint dry-dusty perfume in the red velvet seats, a damp mustiness below ground. It is a scent-memory of years of entertainers readying themselves in the run-down dressing rooms: bygone acts whose photographs and posters cover the walls of the foyer and the staircases.

As we leave the auditorium to make our way to the main artists' dressing room via a maze of corridors in the depths of the building, we bump into an eccentrically dressed lady who asks us, in a very posh accent:

'Where on earth am I?'

There is a temptation to reply: 'The Brighton Dome', but instead we ask what it is she is looking for. She says she has been searching for the downstairs dressing rooms, so we ask her to follow us and talk to her as we try to disguise the fact that we're not sure we remember the way ourselves. We get to the room we have been allocated and offer her some water or a cup of tea.

'I'm actually looking for Worbey and Farrell' she says.

Her face lights up when we tell her 'That's us!' and when she says she's here to review our concert and that she thought it would be nice to meet us beforehand, we're secretly relieved we've been nice to her so far. The three of us sit down and chat for a while, and then we realise that time's getting on and we need to head back up to the stage because some members of the audience are coming in early.

We have agreed to sit at the piano for a while and play for a group of visually and hearing-impaired people. It is to give them an opportunity to feel their way around the piano and get an idea, through touch and vibration, of what the actual concert will be like in the afternoon. We notice an elderly couple sitting in the middle of the stalls, a few rows back, who don't seem to part of the group so we go over and greet them, and they tell us that they just want to hear us play something, as they aren't allowed to be at the performance.

'My husband is currently having chemotherapy and our doctor has told us about a strange virus taking hold in Brighton. Apparently it would be too much of a risk for him to be around so many people,' the lady explains. 'It's such a shame because we so much wanted to hear the *Warsaw Concerto*. We managed to persuade the staff to let us in for your rehearsal. We hope you don't mind?'

So we play the whole concerto to them with as much drama and romance as we can muster, and as we do so our special guests are gently feeling their way around us, even putting their heads under the lid to experience the vibrations. One lady sprawls awkwardly in a heap underneath the piano, a grin spreading across her face, which we both find hilarious. When we hit the final cadence the old couple both stand up, clapping, with tears in their eyes. It is a great start to the day.

The concert has sold very well. The feeling of nervous excitement standing backstage is hard to describe; at the same time it is both the worst and the best thing in the world. It's like teetering on the edge of a cliff with our fingers crossed, waiting to jump. We know our material backwards of course; all the work we have done in preparation is the trampoline at the bottom which will allow us to bounce to safety but if we don't stay focused and give the audience the very best we can, we could just as easily crash.

The announcement is made, the doors open and we stride out to thunderous applause. Many in the crowd already know us and what to expect - we can sense their excitement, and we are thrilled that so many of our friends and family are here to witness it. We welcome everyone to the show, do the opening lines of our patter and then the first laugh rings out around the hall. It is all going to be fine. We guide the audience through a range of emotions and build towards the interval. Normally we would finish the first half with something fast and dramatic, but on this occasion we end with our new arrangement of Nigel Hess's composition Ladies in Lavender from the film of the same title. It is a beautiful piece, and we can feel everyone is swept up in the moment. A warm silence seems to have descended on the hall.

The second half is loaded with our most technically difficult works and by the time we get to the end of Rhapsody in Blue we are exhausted. The audience has been with us all the way and we could not have got any more from them. The final piece is greeted with a standing ovation; something that is not easily achieved in our country; people in a British audience don't want to draw attention to themselves by standing up. Taking the applause, we allow ourselves to look out and see familiar faces – there is Kevin's schoolfriend, the film producer Jules Hussey in the front row, there is Lady Colin Campbell and there is Steven's sister, Dawn...

We perform an encore and then we make our way back to the dressing room, clutching our champagne and flowers courtesy of the Brighton Philharmonic, and collapse onto the sofa. Quite emotional, we hug and congratulate each other that we 'got away with it again', and then prepare for the real work of meeting our public face-to-face in the foyer.

Later, we are in the bar of the pub we have hired to celebrate Kevin's fiftieth birthday. It is a wonderful evening and such a diverse set of friends are with us. At one table The Great Soprendo and several glamorous drag queens are chatting with a member of parliament and a famous QC. A transvestite and a madame from an Earl's Court brothel are deep in conversation with a rent boy and a lady of the realm. There are lots of Kevin's school friends and family in the room and everywhere you look there are church bellringers. To anyone else this might be a strange dream, but to us this is where we belong.

It has been one of those days that you never forget, and we feel on top of the world. We stumble back to our hotel rooms, looking forward to what we believe is going to be our most successful year yet. We have more concert and theatre dates booked for 2020 than ever before. There will be international tours, private concerts, cruises around Alaska, Russia, the Middle East, and four more weeks performing in South Africa.

We just can't wait for the rest of the year. What could possibly go wrong?

Chapter 1

In which we remind you who we are and what we do and Steven mutilates a pop star's sex-toy in the name of art

'Welcome to the stage – Worbey and Farrell!'

And welcome to our world! We are Steven Worbey and Kevin Farrell - a four-hands one piano double-act - and our mission is to reveal the fun to be had in classical music. This is the story of our lives cheering up piano recitals together, and how we like to enjoy ourselves when we are not performing too. Quite a lot of drinking and debauchery (sometimes with some well-known people) has contributed to our story over the years, but we wouldn't want you to think of us as gratuitous name-droppers, and we certainly don't want to offend anyone. Unless they deserve it!

This is the story of both of us, and perhaps the story of many other people that chose to go into the world of show. We want you to read this book in the same way as you would listen to us playing the piano: as a duet telling a story. You can't pick out which of us is playing an individual note in our music, and for most of this tale you don't need to think about which of us is carrying the melody.

However, sometimes one or other of us will get up and address you directly, and (just as happens when we are on stage) we can't resist indulging in a bit of chat between us. We hope it isn't too confusing; if it is, let us know after the show.

[STEVEN: We will probably be in the foyer lapping up the love and flogging our merchandise.

KEVIN: And after that we will be in the bar!]

If you haven't seen our show already, you may have never heard of us. On our publicity posters we describe ourselves as 'internationally acclaimed concert pianists with a wicked sense of humour' because it is important for people to understand that we are really quite good and we don't dumb down the quality of our playing, even while we are having a laugh. We are a Steinway accredited ensemble with reputations to uphold. We have played with symphony orchestras, achieved millions of hits on YouTube, and entertained people in over one hundred and fifty countries around the globe. We quite often get invited onto the BBC's classical channel, Radio Three and we have appeared on television many times in lots of different countries: in the UK, in Portugal, Germany, Austria and South Africa.

And if that gives you an idea of what to expect from us, let's start by ruling out some of those things straight away. Richard Beck from Broadway Baby wrote a nice review of one of our performances saying:

'They are cabaret artists who don't do cabaret; they're concert pianists who don't play a concert; they're stand-up comedians who don't even stand up'.

We could add to that: we both play the same piano at the same time, but we never do duets, and even though we live together, we have never been together.

The most obvious difference between us and other concert pianists is that we chat to our audience. Most piano soloists just don't. They walk on looking mournful, as though their cat has just died, play the piano beautifully and then walk off again still looking miserable. We simply don't believe that all the enjoyment has to be taken out of music – especially so-called classical music - so what we do is a piano concert delivered in a fun way. We want people to enjoy their whole evening, so we give them a selection of music played to the very highest standards, and in between we tell a few stories to make them laugh. We really like to make friends with our audiences.

We mix classical and popular music, orchestral works and film and television music, ragtime and boogie-woogie; there is nothing wrong with playing *Bohemian Rhapsody* after Rachmaninov. After all, if the music is good, it really doesn't matter who wrote it, or where it came from. And we like to demonstrate that some familiar popular music was originally written as a classical piece.

Although our approach may be unconventional, we think it helps music achieve its full glory. If it's obvious that we are having some fun up there playing the piano, then with any luck our audience will too.

[S: One woman in Buxton told us she laughed so much she had to put her teeth in her handbag! That one went on the poster!

K: The best thing to hear after a show is when some old bloke comes up to us in the bar, and says (usually in a Yorkshire accent):

'Oh, bloody hell, I was dreading t'night. The wife dragged me along here, and you two came on and I thought – I wonder what these bloody Charlies are going to do. But I really enjoyed it.'

S: And then, strangely, the wife will join in: 'Do you know, I was determined not to enjoy myself, I was determined, but I suddenly found myself clapping!']

That kind of reaction happens quite a lot, particularly on cruise ships where people will have come along just because we are the entertainment for the evening. We are proud that we have been booked to entertain people on some of the world's best cruise liners, but we often have to remind ourselves that the audience aren't there specifically to see us. They haven't paid for us - they've paid for the cruise. Many meander into the theatre just to give the act a try, to see if it's their best option for the night, and they think nothing of just walking out from the front row if they don't like the look of us. We've seen people claim their spot ninety minutes before the performance, and then as soon as we bounce onto the stage, before we've even said 'Hello!' or anything, we hear a loud voice ring out:

'Come on, love. It's not for us!' and off they go.

There's still an air of snobbery around classical music and it's hard to know just how this has come about. After all, many of these pieces were composed by people who really liked to have a good time and shared that with the people who came to hear them. The film Amadeus isn't exactly a documentary, but there's no doubt that Mozart was every bit the party animal that it makes him seem. As soon as he left the stage, he would hit the bars, carousing and drinking with little care for how he would feel the next morning. And quite often, we do the same.

In fact, Mozart wrote some funny and very vulgar songs which hardly anyone knows about now. There's a six-voice canon (K 231) called *Leck mich im arsch* – 'put your tongue up my arse'. And there's another song where he included some innocent Latin words which, when sung in a Bavarian accent by his friend sounded like the German for 'It's not easy to lick my arse and testicles.' Arse-licking seems to have been quite an interest of his.

When we were growing up it was quite normal to see people like André Previn and Daniel Barenboim performing on the main channels on television (this was when there were only four channels in the UK). Classical music was quite familiar to our working-class households. Morecambe and Wise could only do a sketch based around Grieg's piano concerto if millions of people knew enough about the music to be aware that Eric was playing 'all the wrong notes'. So many adverts used classical music then. For decades *Bach's Air on the G String* was known as the 'Hamlet Cigar music', and Old Spice used Carl Orff's *Carmina Burana*. No-one would have been able to sing Tchaikovsky's *Danse de Mirlitons* if you asked them to, but they knew 'Everyone's a Fruit and Nut Case' from the Cadbury's advert. We were all exposed to a lot of classical music in those days.

Over the years since then classical music has disappeared from the popular channels and been side-lined onto specialist radio stations or cable channels where it is dealt with in one of two ways: either it is played seriously and surrounded by snobbery, or (and as a reaction to that) it is treated as 'reassuringly' frivolous. Rarely is classical music just allowed to be good fun.

It wasn't exactly normal for children to go to classical concerts when we were young, but it certainly wasn't as unusual as it seems to be now.

KEVIN

My parents loved classical music, and my Grandfather played the violin. My Mum listened to a lot of music, and I was introduced to the joys of the records that Richard Baker used to bring out based around his radio show *These You Have Loved*.

Mum was a hairdresser and one of her clients was a funny woman who lived in a caravan near us. I had developed quite an enthusiasm for music at a young age, and she gave my mother lots of records for me to listen to. She also tried to explain music to me. For instance, she told me that Tchaikovsky was gay and that you could hear the torture in his music.

I was probably only about nine at the time, and a child of that age certainly wouldn't be trusted to hang out with an old eccentric like her nowadays. She really knew her stuff though, and her record collection introduced me to so many classical performers. I adored Beethoven, and the very first album I bought for myself was a recording of his second piano concerto. I found it exciting listening to these amazing gems. I couldn't believe the feelings I got from first hearing Rhapsody in Blue.

I vividly remember going to a concert with my Uncle David to hear Michael Tippett's *Child of Our Time*. When we got home my Mum was doing my aunt's hair. She used to cut everyone's hair in the family.

Mum said: 'How was the concert?'

And he said: 'Bloody awful!'

But I loved it!

STEVEN

Something similar to your experience with the caravan lady happened to me. There was a local doctor who found out that I was a pianist when one of his daughters was about to marry my uncle. I was quite young, but this man used to take me to along to the Nottingham Concert Hall where they had a classical concert every Friday night.

He would pick me up outside the house in his expensive car (he was from a very wealthy family) and all the neighbours would be twitching their nicotine stained net curtains to see what was going on, and I would climb in the back and off we'd go to these classical concerts. My family couldn't afford anything like that, and anyway my Mum and Dad wouldn't be interested in going to hear anything other than UB40 or Bryan Ferry.

It was a wonderful experience for me to hear an orchestra live. I think it really gave me my enthusiasm to become a professional musician. And then later, I was seduced by his other daughter, who was rather gorgeous.

Quite recently our friend the classical pianist Artur Pizarro was playing a Beethoven piano concerto at The Queen's Hall in Edinburgh. We took along a young lad we know to see and hear the performance. He had never been to a classical concert before and was quite affected by it. In the third movement he found something in the music funny and started laughing at it – it was a spontaneous and natural response, really lovely - and it quite impressed us. But it didn't go down well with some pompous members of the audience around us, who probably hadn't heard what he had. It is often the case that people are watching the performance rather than listening to it. Just being there in the concert hall is more important to some people than engaging with the music itself.

For the most part, concert and festival organisers seem quite keen to keep elitism in music. Perhaps they believe that if they give the impression that classical music is out of the reach of the ordinary person, the public will perceive what they provide as being something a bit special, and worth paying extra for.

Just about the only time each year that you see an orchestra and an audience being encouraged to let their hair down and become a bit raucous is at the *Last Night of the Proms*. What is so good about that concert is that the music is presented in a friendly and less elitist way. Everyone still has the utmost respect for the works, and for the skill of the performers, but the whole atmosphere is lighter, and clearly everyone - audience and performers alike – are enjoying themselves.

We try to emulate that feeling in our shows, and by using a little humour, we hope we can get people to embrace music that they might otherwise avoid. But we suspect that some festival organisers see shows like ours as a threat. They are so anxious to maintain a high-brow image of music that they don't want to be seen to be turning to the dark side.

There's nothing nicer than seeing someone responsible for booking performers for a festival really surprised that an event has gone down much better than they ever thought it would. And when we have sold more tickets than their Shostakovich event, and everyone is going home with a smile on their face, they'll say to us:

'Well, that was nice, but we can't do that sort of thing all the time. We can only have fun and let our hair down on one night in the season.'

A music and arts festival booked us recently as the 'debunking act', as an antidote to everything else, the equivalent of the *Last Night of the Proms*. Introducing us, the Artistic Director hadn't done his homework and didn't realise that we are actually a four-hands-one-piano performance, so he walked on stage and told the audience to

"Look forward to all those wonderful Brahms duets, and the like."

He wasn't expecting us to perform arrangements of orchestral pieces and was really surprised by the show and the reaction we received. There was a bit of eating humble pie afterwards, but he was nice enough to be congratulatory, and quite apologetic.

Another thing that amuses us is the pretentious language that is used in programme notes produced for concerts. You will see rubbish like:

'The recapitulation of happiness in Tchaikovsky's violin concerto, the development of themes of joy...'

Surely, the public would be more interested in knowing the truth about what was going on in a composer's life around the time they wrote the music. Some historical context would make for much more interesting programme notes. On Tchaikovsky's violin concerto they could say:

"Having been forced to marry a nymphomaniac when he was gay, he was reported for having sex with his nephew. The Russian government found out what he had done and gave him a choice between being arrested for sodomy or committing suicide. He finished the concerto, and then decided to kill himself, but failed."

Although all of that is factually correct, we may be going a little far there - but you get the idea. Academics endlessly analyse music and deliver theses about musical construction that the composers may have had absolutely no awareness of. Often, how a piece of music came into existence, was not the result of careful crafting as the academics claim. Bach, for instance, was writing music as a job; he had to compose to survive financially, so he just produced a lot of what he was good at.

Stravinsky came up with a series of pieces of music, put them on a washing line and then chose an order for them to emerge as *The Rite of Spring.* The ground-breaking bassoon theme at the start of the ballet was originally written in a later part of the work, and Stravinsky then decided to go back and fit it into the opening. So, when people talk about the development of a theme from the opening throughout the work, it really happened the other way round.

STEVEN

One of my Professors at the Royal College of Music, Phillip Cannon, said something on that subject when he was teaching one of our harmony classes and it has stuck with me ever since. He told us:

'I'm teaching you about the way all these pieces are constructed and although the way they are built with such genius is fascinating, it is actually none of our business. The composer didn't want us to look into how they were put together; he just wanted us to enjoy the music.'

Phillip was a wonderful man, and he was also very funny. We got on very well and spent a lot of the lesson talking about my fellow students getting drunk. He would give me harmony homework which I never used to do because I was out at night. But then I'd copy my boyfriend's, and Phillip would give me higher marks!

He was also almost always tipsy.

KEVIN

I heard about him from another student, probably the first week I was at the College. My friend said:

'I've just had the strangest lesson with Phillip Cannon. He got me to go to the College bar and get him a large glass of wine and a drink for myself.'

Apparently when he went back to the table, Phillip was appalled that he was drinking coke.

'But I've put a couple of vodkas in it!'

'Thank f*** for that!'

So, now you know that we are not music snobs, and we despise pretentiousness. But when we say that, people assume we are in favour of, or engaged in, dumbing-down classical music. In fact we hate that even more.

STEVEN

There are some hideous vomit-worthy things being done in the name of music now, especially on Classic FM's website. They will have a woman ruining a Chopin piece and she's half-naked as though she's on some tacky soft-porn channel. Or there will be a ripped and muscled male singer in a castle in front of a wind machine, long hair flowing, singing *Nessun Dorma*, also very badly.

Classic FM started out with a mission to bring classics to the masses, and their style is intended to reassure the audience that classical music really isn't as difficult as they have been tricked into thinking. The listener doesn't feel threatened by familiar voices who have drifted there from another form of entertainment – people who used to read the news, or introduce hymns on television, or gardening programmes. But that presentation reduces the music to the level of the products that are being advertised in between pieces. A voice will tell you:

'On a hot day like this, what better way to cool you down than to play you *Winter* from Vivaldi's *Four Seasons?*'

We used to do a sequence in our show where we had some fun with that simpering kind of delivery. We called it: 'Relax with the Classics'. We would play short excerpts from well-known pieces and then announce:

S: A lovely piece by Debussy there. His wife shot herself because she couldn't stand him.

And then play another:

K: A marvellous work by Tchaikovsky, written while he was contemplating s**gging his nephew.

Followed by:

S: A classic piece from Schubert who died of syphilis.

And then we'd go through a few short pieces, breaking out to give the same comment.

K: Schumann. Syphilis.

S: Scott Joplin. Syphilis.

We would work through several composers who died the same way, so that the audience got the idea and were calling out as soon as the piece finished. There is something very satisfying about hearing the word 'Syphilis' ring out around a concert hall as you finish playing.

But then we got to the *Moonlight Sonata*.

S: Beethoven. Died of...

And the audience in unison would shout 'Syphilis!!'

K: And we would look at them in horror and say: 'No! Cirrhosis of the liver.'

S: Then pause, and say: 'And syphilis.'

There aren't many people giving classical performances like that, and so it's not easy for festival organisers to promote us by making comparisons to other performers. Nobody knows how to categorise us; nobody knows how to package and sell us so that people will know in advance what they are getting. We don't want to dumb music down, but we also don't want to be pretentious about it. We are absolutely serious about the quality of our performance of the music, and at the same time we want the audience to have as much fun as they possibly can.

The Deal Music Festival used something like this:

'Did you love Victor Borge? Did you like Hinge and Bracket? Well, come and see Worbey and Farrell!'

We let them put that in the programme, but we're not like either of those two acts. We are two concert pianists who play the same piano at the same time, and we play it in a very unusual way. Some people call the way we perform a duet, but we've moved a long way from what that normally implies. Although some duettists also play together on one piano, with them it's always two hands on the left, two hands on the right and never the twain shall meet.

The pianos we use are always the very highest quality grands – usually a Steinway - and they aren't modified at all. We both sit on the same stool and although we play the keyboard together at the same time, we are actually playing different parts of the score independently. This means we get ourselves contorted into all sorts of strange positions, reaching over each other, standing up and running around to the other end of the keyboard, and sometimes we even go inside the lid to get at the strings. You won't have seen the piano played the way we do! Traditionally concert pianists have never wanted to embarrass themselves, but we know we look silly anyway, so we don't really mind how daft it looks if we can get the effect that we're after.

[K: We often tell people (as a joke) that Steven plays the black notes and I play the white ones.

S: And I say he is never allowed near the pedals because he can't drive.

K: I was asked to give up by my first driving instructor, when I was seventeen. Think of all of those lives I've saved!]

As an instrument, the piano has seldom been pushed to its boundaries. We think there's a lot further it can go. Sometimes pianos have been used to create theatrical sound effects on film and television, and we demonstrate some of those in our shows. We show how the familiar noise of the Tardis dematerialising *in Doctor Who* was just the sound of the lower strings of a piano being strummed. The strings inside can also be played to sound like the guttural noise of a didgeridoo, or even an acoustic guitar.

Albeniz's *Leyenda* is a beautiful guitar piece that Segovia used to perform, and by experimenting we found that we could produce a wonderful effect if we dampened the strings inside the piano while they are being played. The best way to do this is to simply lay the palm of the hand quite firmly across the strings.

STEVEN

It is really effective, and the sound is incredibly like a guitar being plucked. Kevin reaches right under the lid while I play the piece, but of course it means he can't play while he's doing it. It would work even better if we could use four hands on the keys instead of just two, and yet still have the strings dampened. We can't bring another person on to stick their hand under the lid, so for years we tried everything we could think of to lay across the strings that would have the same effect as the skin on Kevin's hands. It needed to be long enough to cover a couple of octaves, heavy enough to stay in place and stop the normal vibration of the strings, but also have the same texture and softness as the flesh on the palm of the hand.

We tried pieces of wood and metal of different thicknesses and weight, but they didn't have the same softness as flesh. So, then we tried working with bags of rice, courgettes, bananas and other pieces of fruit, even a pound of sausages one time, but they weren't heavy enough and wouldn't stay in place. Nothing worked. If you got the right weight, you couldn't get the right texture, or vice versa.

Finally, we found the one thing that does work perfectly, and it was something that had been lying around the house for years. It has exactly the right balance between soft and firm, it has the texture of skin, and it is just heavy enough to do the job.

A very large pink sex-toy.

The story behind how we came to have this object in the house is quite interesting. I didn't buy it myself (honest!), and it wasn't a gift. I kind of inherited it because it was left behind in a room in a house in Ealing that I moved into when I was a student.

I had been looking for somewhere to live and there weren't many places that could take me with the two pianos that I owned back then, and there were even fewer landlords who were willing to put up with the noise of me practising all day long. Eventually a friend put me in touch with the owner of a nice house who was quite happy to take me in.

When I moved in, Jimmy Somerville of The Communards and Chris Lowe from The Pet Shop Boys had moved out. I don't know for certain but I think it was Chris that had been living in my room. When I got there

I found lots of 'personal' possessions had been left behind, including this large and accurate reproduction of a man's bits. Clearly whoever owned it didn't want it anymore, so I just put it in a box and forgot about it. And when eventually I moved on, it came with me along with everything else.

We had been carrying it around for years. Every time we moved to a new house it was in the bottom of a box that hadn't been unpacked from the last time we moved. Quite by accident we came across it again, realised it was the right size and weight, and tried it out on the piano strings as our silent assistant for *Leyenda* and it worked absolutely perfectly.

We are not afraid to be different but even we knew that it probably wouldn't be acceptable to produce something like that in the middle of one of our shows, especially as it is incredibly realistic, so I said to Kevin:

'We need to try to disguise it somehow'.

[K: The problem was also that we needed the surface texture so we couldn't cover it with material or anything when it was in use. Maybe we could have kept it in a bag, but it wouldn't have looked good if I'd dropped it or I had been seen doing the unsheathing]

I decided the only answer was to modify it, so to speak. So, picture the scene; there I was in the kitchen with a big knife, and then a hacksaw, sawing through this thing, wincing all the time. I managed to get the end off quite easily, but the bottom was a bit of a challenge. Eventually it came away in my hand and I was left with just a cylinder.

But, looking at it, I realised that the designer had moulded the outside so well that, even without the more sensitive bits, it still looked like what it was meant to be. But now it was actually worse because it seemed to be modelled on the victim of a horrific mutilation.

[K: It certainly gives us the desired result, but can you imagine getting caught flying into Dubai airport with it, and having to claim it is essential for our art? We just have to enjoy the effect it has in the privacy of our own home]

The pianos we use on stage always survive the experience intact; we're not in the business of trashing any instrument.

Actually we did vandalise one, but it deserved it. Highcliffe Castle booked us two years in advance and then phoned up the week before to say they had a 'slight problem'. They didn't have a piano.

They managed to get hold of an 1890's Broadwood from somewhere that looked like an old MFI table. The keys were jangling when we started, and we'd demolished it by the time we finished. We did the music world a big favour.

The exciting thing for us is to see how we can get the piano to sound like an orchestra. We take a well-known orchestral score and then rework it for the piano. The bottom octaves become the lower strings (double bass and cello) or the timpani, the horns and other deep brass instruments. The middle of the keyboard gives us the string section and then to the right we have the flutes and piccolos. In some of our programmes we explain and demonstrate this principle while playing John Williams' *Love Theme from Superman*.

Everything we perform is either our own arrangement or our own composition. We don't use the great piano works because although it would be possible to rearrange a Chopin Prelude or Nocturne for four hands, doing so would spoil the piece. So, starting with the sheet music, we work on the different components of the music together and try to mimic the different instruments on the piano to create the mix of sounds that would normally be heard. This isn't a gimmick; we really are trying to recreate the experience of hearing a full symphony orchestra, by using just the sounds that a piano can produce.

For instance, we spent over fifteen months working on Gershwin's *Rhapsody in Blue*. The piece was originally composed for piano and band, although it's often played with a full orchestra. In our arrangement we had to make it clear when the piano was playing on its own, when the orchestra or band were playing, and when everyone was involved together. It is so complicated that it still scares us to death every time we play it.

[K: It's good to be scared! The first time we performed it was live on a Radio Three show. I asked how long we had to rehearse, and the presenter said 'Ten'. I thought he meant ten minutes but then realised he was counting us in: 'Nine, eight, seven...'

S: My heart is thumping every time we start it, even though we've been playing it for a couple of years now.]

Playing a piano normally, the right hand does very different things compared to the left hand. You wouldn't play melody with the thumb on the left hand for instance. If a deeper note instrument has been used for a melody by the composer then it needs to be the right hand of the pianist on the left that's playing it. At the same time, the accompanying band might be playing in the same octave or below, which means whoever is on the right has to reach across to get at the keys they need. Sometimes, to get the textures and colours of the different orchestral instruments, we open the lid and pluck or stroke the strings on the inside.

Traditional concert pianists don't need to worry about how they are moving around the keys, but for us our performance is often as intricate as a ballet. When we are working on an arrangement, we need to concern ourselves not only with who is playing which part of the piece, but also how they are going to get to where they want to be on the keyboard. Neither of us is very tall, so quite often someone needs to stand up to reach a key, and there are times when we have to swap over and one of us jumps up and goes to the other end of the stool.

[S: American audiences always find that astonishing. We quite often hear them call out: 'Ooh – did you see what he did there!?']

These are things we need to choreograph and rehearse repeatedly: which of us reaches over or under, what happens when split-second timing requires one of us to lift off a key to allow the other to use it. There would be no point in writing our arrangements down for another duo to try; so much of our movement together is intuitive, telepathic even, and a simple musical score couldn't cover it.

Towards the end of *Rhapsody in Blue* the piano and orchestra are playing precisely the same notes, so we end up with our fingers literally on the same key. Working like this has become second nature to us, to the point where we are surprised when people find it interesting, but accidents do happen occasionally.

[S: I got my little finger caught in Kevin's cuff recently, and missed a few notes.]

Once we've decided who is doing what, how and when, then we can work separately on our own parts – although usually we rehearse together.

[S: I'm quite good at working on my own, but Kevin doesn't really like it. We're quite different types of pianist. I play in more of a classical way.

K: And I'm more of a composer-pianist.

S: So, if I go wrong when we're playing (which is rare, fortunately), then we're completely stuffed.

K: And if I go wrong, I can usually improvise my way out of it. In a concert on the Isle of Man recently I completely ballsed it up! It just kept getting worse and worse, and I was having to do more and more improvisation to get us back on course. I don't think anyone noticed. The applause was amazing at the end of it, but I was shaking and completely drained.

S: We were arse over tit for about two minutes, but you covered it very well. If that had been me, it would have sounded awful! Actually, the worst thing about that was you were dripping sweat everywhere, the keyboard was like a salty swimming pool.]

Our whole act was developed at Steinway Hall in London. They have four or five rehearsal rooms with very nice pianos down in the basement of their building on Marylebone Road, and they charge quite a lot of money for people to go in and use them, but since we've become a Steinway ensemble, they have let us use them for free.

KEVIN

They'd started letting us in for free anyway because they found what we were doing quite refreshing. The technicians and engineers that worked there would come in and find us playing *The Simpsons* theme tune, or something by Quincey Jones and they found it all rather amusing. They were used to famous concert pianists going in and playing Bach and Chopin and Beethoven, but they got a bit of entertainment from what we were up to.

One afternoon we were down in one of the basement rehearsal-rooms at Steinway Hall. We'd had an idea to try playing some of the great piano concertos that were written in minor keys, but convert them to the major key, just to see what would happen.

We were having a go at Rachmaninov's third piano concerto shifting it from D Minor to D Major. We found that it takes all the drama out of the music and it sounds very odd, but it does fit beautifully for a transition into another well-known piece. It absolutely melts into the German national anthem.

We noticed a man kept appearing at the window of the rehearsal room. We assumed that he was a technician we hadn't seen before, but then he burst in through the door chuckling at what we were doing and very keen to shake our hands. It turned out to be Tamas Vasary who is one of the best pianists in the world and most famous for his performances of the Rachmaninov third concerto, the exact piece we were tinkering with. It was very embarrassing.

He must have thought we were taking the piss out of him, but he was quite delighted with it.

STEVEN

To become a Steinway accredited artist, officially you need to be a bona fide Steinway owner, but we couldn't afford to buy a new piano from them. The London office were quite keen to have us though, and said they had a clapped-out Steinway Model K which we could have if we paid to have it shipped up to our house, so we handed over one penny to make it officially ours and paid for the transport. Actually, although together we are a Steinway Ensemble, only one of us could be a Steinway accredited artist. They asked which one of us it should be.

[K: I said: 'Well, it's obvious, isn't it?'

S: So, it's me! They send me a birthday card every year!]

Getting the accreditation had to go through head office in Hamburg and the office in New York had to give their approval as well. They needed us to write testimonials about why we liked their pianos so much – which wasn't difficult. It took several months for Hamburg and New York to investigate us to make sure we were good enough -they did a lot of research into our concerts - but eventually we got a call to say that we were accepted. There was also an invitation to Steinway Hall to collect a gift they had for us.

We were led through rows and rows of fantastic pianos, and we were thinking: 'This is unbelievable' and then our guide stopped us in front of a wonderful instrument.

'There you are! This is for you!'

We thought he was pointing at this beautiful piano, but in fact he was showing us the stool. A very nice stool, probably worth a couple of hundred quid. But just a stool nonetheless.

We are quite often asked why we only use one piano stool for the two of us. The short answer is that it's what we have always done, but it is also true that we think it helps with the telepathy that we need if our bodies are pressed together. Our style of playing really depends on us thinking as one, and somehow that just doesn't seem to happen if we sit apart.

[K: I would get lonely if I had a stool to myself!]

We don't shy away from the really big orchestral works. The pieces we have arranged include Tchaikovsky's *1812 Overture*, Saint Saens' *Carnival of the Animals*, and Elgar's *Pomp and Circumstance March No.1*. Bach's great organ work, *Toccata and Fugue in D Minor* is one of our trickiest arrangements and probably the most difficult piece we've ever done, as it's so exposed. With it being so linear and contrapuntal, if one of us makes a mistake it's very difficult for the other to play along and correct it. Put simply: if it goes wrong, we're really in trouble.

The only people who are doing something remotely similar to us are two American concert pianists called Anderson and Roe. They also do a four hands piano act (sometimes they also work together on the same piano, but as often as not they have two instruments), and they too create their own arrangements of pieces that were not originally written for piano.

They are fantastic players, and their arrangements are brilliant, but their act is much more atmospheric and dramatic. They make elaborate videos of themselves playing, dressed up in gothic costumes with theatrical camera shots, so like us there is more than just the music. But they don't interact with the audience at all, and they're not funny, so if we described ourselves as 'like Anderson and Roe', or they described themselves as 'like Worbey and Farrell', the audience would definitely get the wrong idea.

When we adapted *Bohemian Rhapsody*, the comment we heard most often from audience members was that although people were listening to our piano, in their heads they were hearing Queen performing it. That's really what we wanted. Make a mistake in that piece though, and everyone in the audience could hear it immediately: If we wanted an easy life, it would be much easier to stick with Rachmaninov.

[K: I never liked *Bohemian Rhapsody* before we started working on it.

S: We didn't want to do it, did we? It was because we were doing a show entitled Rhapsody, and friends thought the audiences might expect it.

K: I actually loathed the piece until we started dissecting it. But by the time we had finished arranging it we'd fallen in love with it.

S: We realised how good it is. It's a masterpiece.

K: I wasn't very keen on doing *Peter and the Wolf* either but then when you take these things apart and put them back together you find out just how good they really are. They're all pieces I really love now. We've made *Peter and the Wolf* a little bit more cheerful too. In our version the duck survives.

S: Imagine ending a wonderful story like that with the death of a poor duck! It wouldn't go down well with kids' parents if it were written these days.]

Performing that piece presents the additional challenge of us having to multitask. At times, the narration continues over the music, so we have to recite at the same time as we are playing. We decided that each of the characters in the story has to be distinct and have a different voice so, to make it a bit easier for ourselves, we've relocated the story from Russia to Doncaster; the local accents are a bit closer to our own.

There is sometimes a tension between tackling something commercial or well-known, and doing a work that we love but most people wouldn't normally hear. We have to be careful with balancing what we choose to perform. Put *Carnival of the Animals* or *Rhapsody in Blue* on a poster and people will buy tickets but if it says *Ma Vlast* by Smetana no-one's going to come along unless they really know the piece.

One mistake we made was titling a show *Warsaw Concerto* because, although the music is quite well known, people don't necessarily know what it's called, and the name sounds a bit grim. The music was written by Richard Addinsell in 1941 for a film called *Dangerous Moonlight* in the UK - and *Suicide Squadron* in America. The film was never as popular as the music has become. The story is that the Director wanted Rachmaninov to compose something, but he was told by RKO that they couldn't afford him, so Addinsell was asked to write something in the same style, but to keep it cheap. We love playing it - it's like having a bath in syrup - and the audiences really enjoy it, but the title isn't well enough known to use it as our headline.

We do aim to deliver some music in each show that people wouldn't normally listen to, but generally ours is a concert suitable for all shoe sizes. Of course, you can't please absolutely everyone. One time when we were on an American ship a woman came up to us as we were selling our compact discs after the show.

'What's on the CD? Is it the music that was playing before you came on?'

She was very disappointed when we had to admit it was just recordings of us playing the piano. It was awful to think that our show had ruined her enjoyment of the canned muzak broadcast over the ship's tannoy.

People are never shy about telling us what they think of our performances, good or bad. They sometimes let us know, even if they haven't watched us play.

STEVEN

A case in point. We were on a P&O cruise ship called the Aurora, relaxing and enjoying a couple of beers after the show in one of the bars. A woman came up to us and said:

'Here. You two. I didn't see your show.'

I said: 'Did you not? Never mind, perhaps you'll catch us on another cruise somewhere.'

'No. I don't think so.'

'Are you not planning any more cruises then?'

'No. I'll be at home, looking after my cat.'

We didn't know where this conversation was going, so I just said:

'That's nice. What's your cat called?'

'Pansy. No offence.'

Sometimes I think I should have said: 'We've got a dog. She's a bitch. No offence.'

But of course, I didn't.

Chapter 2

In which we both do some growing up. Steven steals a cake and Kevin loses his virginity to a 1930s swing classic.

We started working together in the spring of 2003 but we had known each other for many years before that because we both studied at the Royal College of Music in London. By a strange coincidence we both occupied the same bed in our first year at the College. Not at the same time of course: we arrived a year apart.

[K: I was a year ahead, studying composition.

S: I was a year behind, studying classical piano.]

Although there were several to choose from, we were allocated to the same hall of residence, to the same room (room number 16) and took the same bed, the one next to the window.

We both grew up in the middle of England - our childhood homes are only about forty miles apart - and so we have quite similar accents. Both of us have been obsessed with playing the piano from a very early age and thousands of hours were spent at the keyboard as teenagers, before we even got to the College.

STEVEN

I grew up in a little town in the English Midlands called Burton-on-Trent. It's famous for its breweries and the Marmite factory, so it is quite a smelly town.

My parents were very young and inexperienced and they really didn't have much money when I was young. Mum was only seventeen when she had my sister Dawn and only nineteen when I was born so we lived mostly with my grandparents and they played a huge role in the lives of my sister and me when we were growing up.

My granddad Phillip was a very fine professional jazz pianist before the Second World War, touring with Len Nash's Dance Band and several others. Then he was called up into the army and was involved in the desert battles against Rommel, and when he came home he had rather lost his zest for life and his love of music. He stopped performing professionally and became a painter and decorator, and would only occasionally play as a background accompanist. It may also have been that he just couldn't make enough money from being a musician.

I think I must get my talent from him and his three brothers who were all musicians. I used to go and visit two of them who lived together like an old married couple, bickering with each other. I suspect now that they were both gay. I liked to hear them play violin and piano sonatas together in the evening. The younger of the two used to have very long fingernails and his talons clicking on the piano keys would make more noise than the instrument.

The last of the four brothers was a cellist and he died only recently, aged 102. I have a picture of him playing the cello nearly sixty years ago at about the same age as I am now. He looks so much like me that I could easily fool people into thinking I can play it.

I've really no idea how they all became so musical. I suppose it must have been handed down from a generation or two before them because it is definitely a genetic thing, having a musical talent. Their grandfather had the splendid name of Buster Hyman, but that's all I know about him. My parents weren't musical at all: music completely missed out their generation, and missed out my sister too.

Someone asked me when I was little what I would like to be when I grew up. I said I wanted to be either an ice cream man or a swan. My sister thought it was very funny that I wanted to be a swan and used it as an excuse to throw stale bread at me, so that plan quickly lost its attraction. Dad said that if I was an ice cream man I would have to drive a van, so I decided instead I would be someone who plays the piano like my grandad.

Grandad had a little Hammond organ on which I learned to play tunes like *Oh! I Do Like to Be Beside the Seaside* and *Spanish Eyes*. Those Hammond organs have an amazing sound and they are now collectors items. Eventually he bought a Challen baby grand second-hand from the BBC, which he kept in his chilly front room and on which he taught me the *Moonlight Sonata* by rote.

[K: It's not – it's by Beethoven!]

He went through it with me, note by note. It took us ages but eventually I got it perfectly and I played it to everyone in junior school. And when we went on holiday to Blackpool when I was about six or seven I had a go on the mighty Wurlitzer organ. Somewhere there's a film of a tiny me playing *Spanish Eyes* at the Blackpool Tower. Apart from that we didn't play together much and he died when I was a teenager.

I didn't have my first proper piano lesson until I was twelve. I didn't have a piano of my own until I was fourteen so I learnt to play everything on that Hammond organ. My first piano teacher assumed that I could already read music because I could play pieces quite well but I didn't even know that the top clef is different to the bottom clef because Grandad had never shown me how sheet music works. It's still not something I do well; he was always a much better reader of music than I've ever been.

Often when I was practising my Mum would say:

'You've played that bit! You keep playing the same bit over and over!'

And then she'd get the hoover out and run it round about me, between my feet and bashing into the piano legs. She didn't get music at all, but she was proud of me and loved to hear me play. Sometimes, when she had been out for an evening and came home late at night, she would wake me up and get me to go downstairs in my pyjamas and play for her drunken friends.

'Just come down and play Revolutionary Shtudy!'

And I'd be thinking: 'Oh no, she's been on the Diamond White again. It's three in the morning. I've got school tomorrow!'

Chopin's *Revolutionary Etude* is a rather fast piece and it was always her favourite. Usually, when I'd played one piece I had to play another, and another, because she really liked to show me off.

I became completely obsessed with the piano: I would be doing eight hours of practice a day if I could, especially at the weekend. Through the week it was harder to fit in but I would never go outside at breaktime at secondary school. I would always just go along and practise in the music block. It was an ordinary comprehensive school in Burton-on-Trent called Wulfric (although it's now known as the de Ferrers Academy) and is a very good school indeed. Whenever it was raining at lunchtime I became something of a star attraction; kids would stand and watch me and I'd try to teach some of them little pieces as well.

Playing so much during the break times (and being the funny boy at the back of the class) got me through school. I was picked on by bullies a bit because I was a rather girlish, and I did used to get called 'poof', but I was safe in the music rooms and they mostly left me alone. But it wasn't easy being a young gay boy at school in the Midlands in the 1980s and I envy the kids of today living in more tolerant times.

In those days there was very little acceptance of homosexuality. From the age of around eleven until I was eighteen, I pretended to be something I wasn't. I kept my real self a secret from everybody including, in some ways, from myself. I had girlfriends because that was what was expected of me. That wasn't difficult because I got on with the girls so much better than the boys anyway.

It wasn't my fellow pupils that brought about the most damaging moment in my school years though. That involved a religious education teacher whose lessons were supposed to be about learning life-skills by studying bible stories, but much of the time it was him pushing his own beliefs and condemning other people's morals.

He was an amateur musician, but he never showed me any encouragement and I had the impression he didn't like me. I remember sitting at the back of the class sometime around 1987 when Aids was all over the news. The whole lesson seemed to be directed at me and me alone. He gleefully told us that he had known for years that God would bring punishment on homosexuals and now the time had finally come. My stomach was going into knots when he said those words and I was convinced I was going to die of Aids.

I'm sure I will not have been the only child who had been subjected to that kind of treatment by him over the years. Untold damage was done by people like him to young LGBT schoolchildren; such trauma often leads to suicide. He was also strongly anti-abortion. One day he brought in a glass jar containing what he claimed was a real pickled unborn baby that had been aborted. He said he'd had it locked away for years, and it had to be kept a secret between him and us. His behaviour was just like grooming, only in this case he was luring us into bigotry. People in such positions have a responsibility to look after the mental health of the young minds in their care, but he was filling us with fear.

That event hung over me for a long time. After I left school, and when I had settled into college in London and began feeling confident and secure in myself, I got the courage to write a letter to the headmaster of the school, and I told him in detail about both of these experiences. I knew he was a reasonable man and I trusted that what I said would not be ignored. Not long after, I heard that teacher had taken an early retirement and I do hope my letter might have been part of the reason.

In every school there will always be one boy that scares people to death, and when I was twelve and thirteen the one that frightened me the most was a lad called David-Joseph Brown. He always seemed to be in a fight with someone, and one morning, after I'd been playing the piano during assembly, he cornered me in the playground.

I thought: 'This is it, it's my turn: he's going to attack me.'

Unexpectedly he just said that he admired my piano playing, and he wanted to learn to play. So for a while after that, he sat with me in the music block and I taught him some little tunes. Then he got his own piano teacher and he became a very good player in an astonishingly short period of time. At the same time he completely transformed from being the school bully to one of the best students in school.

We became good friends and spent quite a lot of time together. He lived close to me, so in the evening he would come round, and we would sit and listen to Chopin and Rachmaninov in my room and discuss concertos into the early hours of the morning. We fantasised about our bright futures as concert pianists: not normal behaviour for teenage boys at all but, looking back, it was so inspiring.

I was playing the piano a lot, but it wasn't my only teenage hobby. One day when I was about fourteen, not long after my Grandfather died, I was just sitting having my dinner on a tray at my Nan's house when I looked up and saw someone who looked like an old tramp trying to get in through the gate at the end of the garden. I watched him struggling to get it open and eventually he trudged up the path and knocked on the door. My Nan answered it. I could hear him say to her in a gruff voice:

'I believe you have a young man living here.'

'Yes, that'll be our Steven'.

'Would he like to come bell-ringing with me?'

And my Nan said: 'Course he would. Steven, get your coat!' And off I went!

[K: 'These days they'd be phoning the police to get him locked up!']

We got into his old Hillman Minx and without really saying much he drove me up to the church. When we got there we parked, but before he got out he reached over and picked up a little pot from the dashboard and took out some pencils with novelty rubbers on the tops (ones shaped like bananas, and cars, and fruit) and proceeded to show them all to the church tower one by one. I remember thinking it was all a bit odd. And then he put them all back and we went up the tower into the belfry, and he taught me how to handle a bell-rope.

The next time I went my very best friend John came along too and the two of us became quite addicted to this new hobby. It isn't just getting a bell to make a noise: there is so much more to it than that. It's a strange mixture of music, a team sport and a mathematical puzzle. Every time the ringers pull their rope they change the order in which they are ringing the bells, so everyone needs to know what position in the sequence they are going to be next to avoid two bells ringing at the same time or leaving gaps in the music. It's a feat of memory in the same way that a musician remembers a score without reading the sheet music and it appealed to me, perhaps for that reason.

For months, up to five nights a week, John and I would go ringing bells somewhere in the area. I was neglecting schoolwork and some of my piano practice. And then at weekends we would join in with other ringers on what was called a 'tower-grab', touring the area trying to ring at as many churches as we could in a day, visiting sets of bells we hadn't rung before.

This old man (he was probably only in his mid-sixties) was called Derek Jones. He was a fascinating man, and apart from the bellringing he taught us so much. As we drove along in the old Hillman he used to tell us about the local geography, about science and the architecture of the buildings we were visiting – just really interesting stuff to pass the time.

He did have some strange eccentricities that we got used to though: the pencil rubbers featured quite a lot in his life. Whenever he saw something remarkable like a church he hadn't visited before - a lunar eclipse once - he would get these rubbers out one by one and make sure they had seen it too. Another time he stopped the car on a main road to show his pencil rubbers that the odometer had just clicked over to 200,000. His house was full of old cardboard boxes of rubbish because he could never bring himself to throw anything away, and he kept pigeons in his shed. There were about sixty of them which I used to feed when he was away.

[K: Were they clay pigeons, or real ones?']

We went all over the country, ringing bells in different churches. He even drove us from Burton to Edinburgh once to ring at the cathedral, all the way there and back at about 50 mph. While we were in there we went up to Fettes College, a huge gothic school that had five little bells in a turret. There seemed to be no-one about so we let ourselves into the building, found the bells and rang them without asking permission. When an angry woman came up to find out who was making all the noise Derek just said:

'It's all right, we're going. We've grabbed the tower now'.

Another time he took us down to Devon to visit a heritage railway because his other passion was steam trains. Unfortunately, there was something wrong with the engine that day and it wasn't running properly so what should have been a trip of about an hour, ended up as five or six. The train would chug along for a while, and then stop for ages while they tried to fix it. We had no food or drink with us so by mid-afternoon we were absolutely famished.

We pulled into a little village, and the conductor said we would be there for just five minutes if anyone needed to buy anything. John and I got off and ran up and down the street looking for a shop, desperate to find some food, but it was a half-day holiday and everything was closed. There was a pub at the corner of the street and even though we were only young lads we thought we might be able to buy some crisps and lemonade. We got the door open and called out:

'Anybody here?'

It was late afternoon, and the place was empty. Still calling out, we went past the bar and found our way into the kitchen, but there was no-one there either. However, on the table there was a massive chocolate cake.

It was obvious someone was in the midst of decorating the cake; there were bits of ribbon and candles lying about, but we couldn't hear anyone in the building. We just picked it up and ran back to the train which took off straight away, and we shared the cake with everyone there.

I've pictured the scene ever since. Whoever it was that was decorating that cake for someone's party, came out of the toilet or wherever they'd gone and found it had just vanished. They would have run out of the pub into the village, but found the street deserted. What happened to the cake will have been bewildering to them since that day, and they've probably told the story several times to anyone who will listen to them. So if you lost a cake in mysterious circumstances in a village near Buckfast Abbey in 1986, I'm really sorry. It was me. It's terrible isn't it?

Derek Jones was an amazing person and John and I really enjoyed being with him. He was an excellent ringer, quite famous in his day, and we became pretty good at it too. But then John joined a successful Midlands pop band called 'Nice 'n Easy' as a drummer and piano started to take over for me again, so we both gave up ringing after a while. I've taken it up again since movng to Edinburgh and I've made so many good friends all over the country doing it.

At the time I had no idea, but many years later I discovered through other ringing friends that Derek was a convicted paedophile. He'd been a Maths teacher in Hitchin and had been caught interfering with young boys. Even now when I mention his name in ringing circles, there are people who remember only that about him. But I have to say he never once tried anything on with either of us. The only time I might have got even a hint of his problem was when he was almost in tears because I had my long curly hair cut shorter. I couldn't understand why it bothered him so much. As appalled as I am about what he did to those innocent children, I can't help but feel sad for the Derek I knew. These days, he might have been able to get some help with his predilection, and that could have prevented damage to young lives.

John was my very best friend from quite a young age. He lived just around the corner from me and we did everything together. He had no idea that I was carrying the secret of being gay at the time. I pretended to fancy all the girls he fancied and behaved exactly how I was expected to. I don't really know why I never said anything to him because I'm sure it wouldn't have affected our good friendship even at that age. He was a very open-minded person and I never heard him use the word 'poof' or similar with anyone. Of course when I did tell him, after I'd gone to college, he was more upset that I'd not told him years before.

We both had paper rounds but he was quite conscientious about it and didn't just collect the money and throw the papers in the canal like I used to. He complained to me one day when we were about thirteen that the saddle on his bike was making his balls ache, so we went out and bought another one and fitted it. But he was still getting pain in his groin and eventually he went to the doctor.

He had testicular cancer.

He was given chemotherapy when he was not yet fifteen and went through a really hard time when all his hair fell out. He was ill for at least a year and I used to go up to The Queen Elizabeth hospital in Birmingham to visit him. Gradually he got better, and the doctors took the precaution of freezing some of his sperm.

But the cancer came back. In all, he had cancer five times.

He managed to survive long enough to get married to Becky and although his teenage sperm was long past its use-by date, doctors were eventually persuaded to let them try for a baby. There were people who called them selfish to do this, because he was so ill and the child might be born without its father. Somehow the tabloids got hold of the story of the out of date sperm, and it was awful the things that were said about them by ignorant people on newspaper websites.

John did live to meet his son but inevitably, despite his determination to fight it off, the cancer got him. I cried when I saw the picture of the two of them together, and now when Becky sends me photos of young Joe, he looks just like the boy I grew up with. The two of them speak of John as Joe's 'Daddy Heaven.'

He was my very best friend, and I miss him terribly.

Apart from the paper-round the first job I ever had was with an ex-teacher from our school who had gone into organ restoration. I used to help with his work tuning church organs on Saturdays. I would lie on the bench as he went inside the instrument, and I would play each note in turn as he tuned, cleaned and fixed the pipes. It was a filthy and awkward job crawling around inside the workings and I was being paid one pound per hour. This wasn't long after I had taken up bell ringing and I remember a strange conversation with him from inside the organ. He said:

'Aren't there a lot of queers in bellringing?'

I was so young and naïve that I didn't know what he meant by 'queers'. I hadn't really heard the word used that way before, so I said:

'Oh yes, there's lots of odd people, we're all very queer'.

A few years later I found out he'd been arrested for cottaging but he never tried anything on with me either. And for the record, there are just as many 'queers' in bellringing as there are anywhere else.

The second job I had was making Melba toast in a posh hotel and restaurant near my home, called The Dog & Partridge. I hated the work and burnt all the toast. But I noticed that they had a grand piano in the corner that never seemed to get used so I suggested I could play that instead and negotiated a fee with them. Later they used me at a sister venue called Mackworth House and so quite a lot of my adolescent years were taken up improvising around Cole Porter songs and such-like in restaurants.

At the age of fifteen I was getting fifty pounds a set and eventually I was playing seven sets a week, so I was relatively well off as a teenager. It was good fun, although sometimes I would feel a bit like a pot plant sitting in the corner being ignored by everyone. I remember once a famous businessman came in (his initials are JCB) and he had me play for him and his drunken friends as they sipped champagne from their shoes. He gave me a fifty-pound tip so I didn't mind a bit.

I had a brilliant music teacher at school called Philip Marshall, who was a very fine piano player and, as a conductor, quite famous in the Midlands back then. He conducted the school wind band which used to win national prizes. He gave me piano lessons at his house once a week and he was a superb teacher. He is the person responsible (apart from my parents of course) for getting me into the Royal College of Music. He convinced me that I could do it. He was a nice and inspiring man, and I'm still in touch with his wife, Margie who is a fine musician herself. She comes to our concerts when she can.

I entered all the local piano competitions. I liked the pressure of it even though it made me terribly anxious. I'm afraid I never relaxed into a performance and it's the most horrible feeling in the world being so nervous. But my fingers were always quite fast and I did win most of the competitions. I remember being horrified one time when I was beaten by a young local pianist by the name of Christopher Langdown. It was a shock to me that someone could play as fast as he did. We met again at the Royal College of Music years later.

Between the ages of thirteen and seventeen my parents and I travelled all over the country while I was competing at national competitions, sometimes winning, sometimes not. There was a big prize in 1988: the Yamaha National Piano Competition at The Crucible in Sheffield. That success made it pretty certain I would get a place at a music college. Unfortunately that day I had developed a wart on my eyelid. As they were announcing the prizes I was picking at it and made it bleed, at the very moment they called my name to go up onto the stage and receive the trophy. There's a photo of me with blood pouring down my face. It's like a scene from Steven King's *Carrie*!

I found out very late that, to get into a music college it wasn't enough just to be good on the piano. To ensure all-round musicianship the major music conservatoires all require pianists to be able to play a second instrument to at least grade six level. They don't even let you audition without that level of accomplishment. It works the other way round too; instrumentalists need a grade six pass on the piano.

I was horrified when I discovered this, and had to decide very quickly which other instrument I should learn and get on with it as fast as I could. I chose the flute for the simple reason it was small and portable. I managed to find a teacher in Burton whose name was Anne Aleksa, and she taught me very well. Philip Marshall let me join the school wind band which helped, and I enjoyed it thoroughly. I found playing the flute quite easy and I progressed to grade seven very quickly, but to be honest I didn't produce a very good tone. I simply hadn't had time to refine my embouchure and I made a rather breathy sound.

I applied for the Royal College of Music and the Royal Academy and I was accepted at both. I chose the College because it seemed to be in a nicer area of London. The audition panels were not very welcoming; they seemed to go out of their way to make you feel uncomfortable. One of the people examining me was John Barstow, who was head of keyboards at the College for years. He said to me:

'Who's your favourite pianist?'

I said: 'Vladimir Horowitz'.

And all three of them on the panel just burst out laughing. I suppose it was because he was a bit of a controversial player who would play in his own style whatever the composer. It would have been like saying that your favourite artists were Gilbert & George.

[K: I had the same questions. I really wish I had answered: 'Well of course there's no one better than Richard Claydermann. Or Mrs Mills! Name any pub song you like, and she can churn it out!]

After that they got me to improvise something based on just a few notes. I think that's what got me a place because I was always pretty good at improvisation, probably because I had learnt everything by ear when I was younger.

When the acceptance letter arrived, you could tell as soon as the postman dropped it through the door that it wasn't a rejection. It was just too thick an envelope. I remember it being delivered when I was alone in the house in Burton, as I was about to leave for school. I ran out into the rain crying and screaming, I was so happy to have been accepted. It was like a scene from *Billy Eliot*. And this was in the days before mobile phones so I couldn't let my parents know until later that day.

[K: Those thick envelopes! Wouldn't it be cruel if they sent a rejection letter together with a brochure for holidays that might help you get over the sense of failure?]

My friend David-Joseph Brown also got accepted to a music college, at the Royal Birmingham Conservatoire. It meant we were split up but we kept in touch for a while. He didn't go on to have the bright future as a concert pianist that we'd dreamed of. Instead he went into business and was even more brilliant at that, winning awards and becoming very rich and successful at a young age. We eventually lost touch with each other. I suspect he wasn't too happy when he heard the rumours about me coming out as gay while I was at college. Many of my school friends were the same but I don't hold a grudge about that. Times were different then.

KEVIN

Music was there in my genes too; the whole family love different styles of music. When she was young my Mum was accepted at the Royal Ballet School, but when she won a scholarship to go on to the full-time school Grandad (her Dad) said to her:

'There's a lot of funny people in that business, and to get on you've got to be bloody funny yourself. I don't want a daughter of mine cocking her legs up on the stage!'

So she never took up her place and she just went to the Saturday morning classes. Ironically, years later I ended up working as a repetiteur at the Royal Ballet School, joining all those funny people. I fitted in quite well.

We had a piano in the house because my older brother was supposed to be learning, but he wasn't interested in the slightest.

[S: Your family were posh. You even had a cleaner!]

My grandmother could play quite well, but she only seemed to know the one piece. Every time she came round, she would sit down and play the same thing: a Mazurka. Apparently when I was about three, I climbed up on the stool and just played it straight through. My parents phoned my grandmother and asked if she'd been teaching me secretly, and when she said 'No', they told her:

'You need to come round and listen to this!'

It was just a rather freaky thing; I'd obviously been sitting there letting it soak in. My parents tried to find a piano teacher for me even before I went to primary school but it was hard to get anyone to take me on at such a young age. Eventually I was sent to a lady called Mrs Davis who was a bit brutal. If I went wrong, she would tug my hair. To be fair, she would always give me an option as to whether she pulled it upwards or from side to side.

[S: You need therapy!]

I started with her at the age of four and, even though I passed several grade exams, she never discovered that she hadn't managed to teach me to read music at all. In fact, it only came out when I was eleven when I changed teachers and the new one - Bill Moss - found out I was pretending. The problem was the previous teacher would get frustrated when I didn't play a piece straight away, and so she would always play it to me. Having heard it, I could then just play it back to her. In some ways that may have hindered me but it does mean that I soak up music very easily and I only need to hear something a couple of times before I can reproduce it. It's been a very useful skill to have.

A few years ago, I spotted one of my Primary School teachers in the audience on a cruise ship. She watched one of our performances without realising it was me. I introduced myself afterwards and when she had got over the surprise she said:

'Kevin Farrell! You were an odd child!'

[S: Was that because you wrote SH*T on the vicar's wall?
K: I wrote it on his shed. And I've never been allowed to forget it!]

She told me that when I was nine I suddenly said to her, out of the blue:

'When I grow up, I want to be a Catholic priest!'

And when she asked why, I said:

'Because they can turn water into wine!'

From a very early age I've had a religious dedication to alcohol. My parents gave me just a thimble-full of Drambuie when I was very young, and the first taste of this golden liquid, this explosion of pleasure in my mouth, told me that I had discovered a substance with which I was going to be great friends. Later I developed something of an obsession with the Dudley Moore film *Arthur*, watching it several times a week, fantasising about the glamourous cocktail world of New York with all those gorgeous people dressing up in tuxedos, drinking from champagne fountains. I could really see the attraction of living a life with alcohol at its heart, making people laugh.

I had already worked out for myself that I was an odd child, that there were certain things about me that weren't normal and shouldn't be discussed. One of those was that I heard music in my head and, from what I gathered, no one else did. I wanted to play the pieces I imagined but I didn't think I could tell anyone they were mine. When I performed one of them to my Grandma and my Aunts and they liked it, I told them I had heard it on the radio and that it was called *'Angels in the Sky'*. That seemed acceptable, and they just started chatting about a picture they'd seen at the 'Good Shepherd' in Nottingham called the same thing.

The other thing I didn't dare to talk about was that I had a crush on Keith, my sixer at Cub Scouts. He was beautiful, and he was heroic. I didn't understand my feelings, but to me he was like a god. I was only eight, but my heart just melted thinking about him and I wanted to be as important to Keith as he was to me. No one had told me this innocent first love was wrong but something made me know that I must never tell a soul about how I felt.

My mother was a member of the local Roman Catholic Church, and I was encouraged to go there and to play for them when I was still a small lad. Because there were so few musicians in the area who could (or would) play, I also did the Church of England services and the Spiritualists in the evening, so I covered just about any branch of Christianity!

Mrs Davis's husband was a local vicar who didn't have a parish. He used to tour around the remote churches in the area conducting wedding ceremonies and for a fiver a week he would take me with him to play the organs. I turned up at one church and couldn't find the switch for the electric motor and realised in horror that I was going to have to pedal the blower myself. It was like riding an exercise bike. If I slowed down at all, the note would start drifting away as though the whole thing was dying on me, and by the end of the wedding I was absolutely exhausted.

I had had to learn to play church organs when one of my cousins asked me to provide the music for their wedding. They had no idea how the dynamics of the organ differed from the piano. The father of my friend Simon Bowler (a great conductor and musician now) was an organist and offered to give me a few lessons, especially in how to use the pedals.

[S: You're actually good at the organ pedals, aren't you? Despite me not trusting you to use the ones on the piano.]

Playing at the Catholic church, I used to improvise so much that I would get people coming in before the service asking me to slip in specific pieces of music. One Christmas morning I arrived a bit late and was told:

'Just get up there and play something Christmassy as the priest comes down the aisle.'

He came in, with all the incense, to *Rudolph the Red-nosed Reindeer*, and highly amused he announced it as the first hymn.

Later on, whenever I came home from college, I would still turn up to play for services, but the new priest was quite the opposite in terms of sense of humour. He interrupted me one day and asked for something more holy. After he'd asked three times for 'something more holy' I'm afraid I had to explain to him I had a lot of other requests to get through before I reached his. Surprisingly, he then banned me from playing there altogether.

A few years ago I went back and discovered that there was going to be no organist for the Christmas service, so I offered my services again. Steven and I were performing in a play at the time that involved us playing Bach's D Minor piano concerto and I was intrigued to find out how it would sound on a full organ. I went along to the local Methodist church to practise.

A woman challenged me: 'Excuse me. Are you supposed to be doing that?'

'No. You're right' I said. 'I am really a burglar, and like so many burglars do, I have decided to see what the D Minor piano concerto sounds like played on an organ!'

[S: You didn't tell her where to go, then?

K: Not quite.]

Like Steven, I was playing background music in restaurants and pubs from quite a young age. I started at The Reindeer in East Bridgford and also The Peacock restaurant, but they didn't pay me as much as he got. I had some gigs at the Masonic Lodges around Nottingham where all sorts of strange things went on.

As you would expect they had their own music and traditions; the naval branch of the Masons used to have someone ring a ship's bell every half an hour. I got used to expecting unusual behaviour in the Lodges. Thinking back, I'm pretty sure at least one of the routines I was expected to adhere to was because the person telling me what to do, suffered from OCD.

I was there to play the organ and the Worshipful Master explained very carefully what had to be done when I switched it on. I had to lift a lamp up using only three fingers and then put it down again. And I had to do that three times before I went near the instrument. It was also essential that I went around the back of the organ and reached around to use the switch which was on the front. I went along with it all because I was only young, but I'm sure now that was something in his head rather than any real Masonic ritual.

I was blessed with perfect pitch, although that led to a bit of bullying. My music teacher at school was a man called Colin Smith. One day he was explaining to some older pupils in a music class about my rare talent:

'When Kevin hears a note, he recognises what it is immediately. It's like you seeing something and knowing the colour.'

Afterwards a group of lads came out looking for me in the playground:

'Ah! Mr. Farrell. We want to see you...We gather that you're a bit of a talented chap. Pin him down!'

They proceeded, in turn, to fart in my face and ask me what note it was. Of course, I was able to tell them.

Colin Smith was probably the most important musical influence I ever experienced. He was extremely clever in encouraging and guiding me in the directions I chose, even supporting me when I wanted to do a solo comedy spot.

He also ran the Toot Hill School Dance Band, a Glen Miller style showband which played gigs mainly around Nottingham, but occasionally abroad too. Despite the name, almost all of the rest of the band had already left school, and I was by far the youngest when I joined at about the age of thirteen. The oldest was around thirty, but we loved playing together It took up most of Colin's free time and he was utterly dedicated to us. The band was paid, but we didn't do it for money: anything we got went into buying instruments. We were the first youth band to play in East Germany when the wall came down. We also played most years at the German beer festivals in Bavaria.

My Mum and Dad probably thought it would be a good idea for me to join the Toot Hill band because it would keep me out of trouble; I suppose I was a bit wayward. In particular they wanted me to keep out of pubs, but as the band played at private functions and weddings I regularly got into places where alcohol was flowing, and I started drinking a lot earlier than any of my school friends. I got myself a paper round so I could buy drinks for everyone during the breaks. Even though I was thirteen and looked about eight, I was served pints for me and the lads, Babychams with a maraschino cherry and cherry brandies for the girls.

In fact, I lost my virginity while the dance band were playing *The Woodchoppers' Ball* by Hoagy Carmichael. We were in the room next to the hall where they were playing for the teachers' Christmas party. It doesn't last very long, just a couple of minutes and no-one seemed to have missed us. I think she and I can claim that as a unique experience, how many people have done it *to The Woodchoppers' Ball?*

[S: I lost mine to two girls from Derby who came over to stay when my Mum and Dad were on holiday. They made me drink loads of Diamond White and then they both took their clothes off. I got through it but afterwards I was sat on the stairs with a bucket, vomiting. My sister couldn't stop laughing. The sex was alright but the cider got to me.]

Colin seemed to turn a blind eye to everything we got up to, but I think by letting us do these things right under his nose, he knew we weren't doing anything he didn't see and could step in and control if he needed to. I remember him telling us as we arrived for a gig at a Nottingham Hotel that we should avoid the cocktail bar as there were strange men that hung around in there. Of course as soon as we got out of the mini van, my friend Bev and I headed straight there. All I remember is a dark and glamorous bar with fluorescent red and purple lighting, adorned with red velvet seating with some exotically dressed young men who paid absolutely no attention to us.

Looking back it is amazing the freedom I had, in what was really my late childhood. Most of the other members of the band remain close friends today. If we got up to things our parents wouldn't have approved of, I'm sure the behaviour was important to our growth as individuals.

It has to be admitted social drinking has been quite an important part of my life. My entire family (well on my Dad's side anyway) are all basically two glasses of wine away from being reasonable. Steven and I once noticed that someone we worked with would drink wine all day, but very slowly. He only had four glasses of wine a day but he would take several hours over each. Perhaps if I had a drip that topped me up a glass of wine every two hours, I could be a really nice person all the time.

There was a period when I didn't drink at all for two years because I was living with a drug addict, and I thought one of us needed to be sober. I was playing in a restaurant one night and overheard someone asking the manager if they could buy me a drink.

'I'm afraid our pianist, Kevin, is teetotal.'

I was horrified: I couldn't believe they were talking about me!

I didn't compete in any competitions as a teenager until I went in for one where the prize was to get a masterclass with Peter Donohoe. I turned up with two of the hardest pieces in the repertoire. To finish I played Gershwin's *I got Rhythm,* but before that I tried to give them Balakirev's I*slamey.* The judges were flabbergasted that I was even attempting to do it, and it didn't go very well. Of course now I know it is regarded as a warhorse, and if you can play it well you're good enough to win the Leeds International Piano competition.

It was my piano teacher's idea:

'If anyone says you shouldn't be playing it, tell them to f*** off. Listen to them, and they'll have you playing some crap by Mozart!'

It was actually very good advice, but on the day I was so mortified about the whole thing that as soon as I'd finished, I got up and ran away and my parents couldn't find me for hours. It wasn't a strop; I was just so embarrassed that I didn't want to face anybody. My Mum was furious with me.

When I arrived at College two people recognised me. There was a lad called Christopher Langdown, a very good pianist and a very nice guy, and he was with a girl called Carol Barker. I didn't realise when I first met them there that they had been at that competition.

Christopher said: 'Oh yes! You're the Kevin Farrell that did the *Islamey*'.

I shrank back and said: 'Don't remind me of that day, I was awful.'

He said: 'No, I remember when you were playing, my Dad leaned across and said to me: "Son, you're not going to win this one. Just go up there and enjoy yourself!"'

It obviously hadn't gone nearly as badly as I thought when I was playing but it also hadn't gone as well as I wanted it to.

[S: Those were the two people I used to compete against at the music festivals as well. They were really good.}

When it came to the time for applying to music colleges, I became so nervous about the idea of having to perfom in front of audition panels that my doctor prescribed beta-blockers. It probably wasn't the best thing to do.

At The Royal Academy of Music I sat at the keyboard and was just completely overwhelmed: by the building, by its history and by the panel who looked so at home there. I felt as though I was intruding. When I finished my performance of Scriabin's *Sonata No. 4,* there was a pause and then someone asked me to give my own critique of how it had gone. I knew I hadn't done myself justice, but I felt I needed to remain positive so I said:

'Well it was a bit messy in parts, but apparently Scriabin was a messy performer himself, so perhaps he might have approved.'

'Yes, but Scriabin was also deeply pretentious. And we wouldn't want you to be like that, would we?'

The audition at the Royal Northern was probably the worst. Unfortunately that morning I had accidentally taken double the dosage of beta-blockers and I was so relaxed I couldn't care less. The audition room was particularly uninspiring: rather like a typical comprehensive maths class. Someone looked up from my application:

'You've put down that your father is a Tutor? A Tutor in what?'

I stupidly replied with: 'I didn't know my father's occupation was relevant to my audition'.

They asked me what I was going to play, and told me to hand over the scores as I was to play from memory. At that moment the drugs suddenly stopped working, and I froze in a panic.

'It says on the audition form that only one piece needs to be from memory.'

'We'd like it all from memory.'

I tried to pass the score sheets to them, but I was in such a state that everything dropped to the floor, and it must have looked like I had actually thrown the papers at them. Needless to say my playing was another disaster and at the end of an hour of hell one of them said:

'You'll be lucky to get in to Trinity!'

As it happened Trinity was a joy. The two guys on the panel spent most of the time telling me about the pubs the students liked to go to. My prepared pieces went well, and then they gave me a scenario of a cat sitting in the sun and asked me to make up a piece of music on the spot. I found this as easy as drinking water.

But then they gave me a sheet of music to sight read. I was terrible, picking my way through.

'Good God! Is your sight reading always that bad?'

I told them it was, but they were lovely to me, and said they knew so many musicians that could either improvise or sight read but never both.

The place I really wanted to go was the Royal College of Music. When I went for my audition I was very late arriving and just ran into the hall completely out of breath. The panel was Ruth Gerald, Philip Cannon and John Barstow.

One of John's pupils, Barry Douglas, had just won the Tchaikovsky Medal. Barry was considered to be one of the greatest living pianists at the time. I was so late I hadn't had time to get nervous and fortunately I'd also forgotten to take my beta-blocker.

They asked why I wanted to do the academic course instead of the performance course. I told them it was because I was lazy, but the truth was that performing scared me too much

I handed them a composition I had been working on. Phillip Cannon took one look at it, and started questioning the key that I'd written on the score. Admittedly, my handwriting was terrible and the whole sheet was nearly illegible, but I think it should have been clear that I meant it to be three sharps.

He said: 'Bartok used to put the sharps in different areas. Are you trying to copy him?'

I said I wasn't. I'd just put them where I thought they went.

'Can you actually play this piece?'

They were obviously interested in my composition so I played it to them the way I wanted it to sound, even though I apparently hadn't written the score that way.

At the end of it, Ruth Gerald (who later became my teacher) said:
'I might have expected Franz Liszt to have written that!'
And I thought: 'I'm in!'

Chapter 3

In which we tell you about our College teachers, Steven preserves Rachmaninov's dirt, and Kevin acts as a pillow for his comic hero.

We took up our places at the Royal College of Music exactly one year apart and we both remember the same overwhelming feeling of that first day. To a young teenage lad from the Midlands, the moment of arrival was simply awesome. We walked along Prince Consort Road, past the expensive parked cars: BMWs, Mercedes and Ferraris. Everything about that whole area of London told stories of success. If we had approached from a different direction we would have been passing the Natural History Museum, the Science Museum, the Royal College of Art, and the home of the English National Ballet. And when we reached the jewel in the crown, the College itself, it was a magnificent piece of architecture in the red-brick style of Amsterdam, set right in the heart of South Kensington with the Royal Albert Hall directly opposite. Beyond is the greenery of Hyde Park with the fabulous statue of Prince Albert swathed in gold leaf at the entrance.

Inside, the first thing that greeted us was the sight of the marble staircase and a massive bust of Johann Sebastian Bach. But then another sense took over and we became aware of the sound of dozens of students practicing: a magical cacophony. It was exactly the noise you hear as an orchestra is tuning up before the conductor walks on stage, and in the same way it felt like something new and exciting, something splendid, was about to commence.

Neither of us could believe we were now about to become a part of this place of amazing musical history. This was the equivalent of Oxford or Cambridge; we were in the building where the musical gods were forged. It seemed ridiculous to think that we were really meant to be there and that no-one was going to find us out and ask us to leave. We saw the older students walking in so confidently and wondered if one day we would also have the arrogance to assume that we belonged in such an auspicious place.

But then we were brutally brought back down to earth as we listened, with our fellow first-year students, to a quite shocking opening speech made by the Vice Director, Nicholas King.

"Welcome to the Royal College of Music. The one thing you all have to realise is that you are not going to make it.'

STEVEN

Everyone was dumbfounded, and we didn't really know what he meant by not 'making it'. It just felt like an extraordinary thing to do to us at the start of our college education, as a welcome. It was incredibly deflating but I think his idea by doing that was to make us all the more determined to succeed, just to prove him wrong, but everyone left the room completely demoralised.

KEVIN

When I was nine our teacher, Mrs. Price told us that none of us were going to be as well known as Lord Mountbatten who had just been given a big state funeral. Julie Stevenson called out:

'No Miss, you're wrong. Kevin Farrell's going to be just as famous!'

Every one of us in Nicholas King's audience knew that we were going to be the next great performer, and that we were each going to change the world of music. That was what being accepted into the Royal College was all about. But here we were now, listening to this man daring to contradict nine-year-old Julie Stevenson, and telling us that if we hadn't already become a success then we never would.

I turned to my friend Simon Bowler (the boy whose father had taught me to play the organ) and said:

'We might as well go home now, then!'

Years later, Steven and I went out for a meal with our friend and old lecturer, Roderick Swanston, one of the world's greatest academic musical minds, and told him about the effect that opening speech had on us. Roderick was concerned about the idea that it was only possible to 'make it' as a performer:

'Surely, if you leave college and make a career out of music in some way, then you've made it. If you go on to become a musical journalist, a teacher or a music therapist then you've succeeded.'

If the speech was intended to broaden our horizons, and plant the idea that there are other forms of success apart from being a famous performer, it could have been spelled out more clearly. All we heard was that we were never going to achieve our ambitions. In me, it just created a desire to take the piss out of the classical music world and the people involved with it.

I was voted in as the representative for the composition students. One of my first ideas was that it would be good to set up a twentieth century music festival at the College, and I went along to see Nicholas King about it. Talking to some of the staff later I realised he hadn't told them anything about the idea, and in fact he later went on to deny any such meeting had taken place. After that, every time I saw him about anything, I had to write to all the College staff, telling them exactly what he had agreed to. The festival was actually very successful.

I also had to intervene when a conducting exchange student called Lee Beberman came over from California for a term. As part of his studies he was supposed to get the chance to conduct a concert at the College, but as time went on it looked like that wasn't going to happen. He came to complain to me about it and we managed to get the students to rally round and make the College change their mind.

Behind his back, King was known as Satan to everyone because he walked around the College smoking an evil-smelling pipe. The advantage of that was that you usually got a whiff of the tobacco before he appeared and it gave you the chance to scarper, and not have to speak to him.

STEVEN

If anything that Nicholas King lecture put even more pressure on some people than was necessary. They reacted to it by working even harder to prove him wrong. We would see talented pianists having nervous breakdowns because their piano scales weren't going well. Several of them resorted to drugs: a doctor at the nearby Imperial College would prescribe beta-blockers to students to get them through concerts.

I never took them because I saw what happened if you did. They did help to calm the nerves down and you could play the pieces perfectly with no mistakes, but the performance was dull and completely lacking in energy and emotion. You could immediately tell if someone was on the blockers because what they played would be robotic and lifeless.

Maybe King's speech did help us eventually. In our act we have made a philosophy of rejecting convention, and it could just be one of the reasons for that is having been told at an early stage that we had no chance of success as professional musicians.

KEVIN

I would still hate to think he really was the inspiration I needed. When Ruth Gerald, my last piano teacher, came up to see us in Edinburgh a few years ago we took her out for a meal and I started slagging off Nicholas King, and then suddenly realised that he was a great friend of hers. She couldn't understand why we disliked him so much. If she liked him, perhaps he wasn't so bad. But at the time I was incensed by the man.

By contrast, the Director Michael Gough-Matthews (known as Miriam to the students), was a fun character, especially as he used to address everyone in innuendo. He was extremely camp, but people were never completely sure whether that was who he was, or whether he was putting on an act. He was like a cross between an older Julian Clary and a shrivelled-up Kenneth Williams. He could often be seen out on Queen's Gate, dressed up in full leather. Whenever Miriam made an address, the lecture hall was packed with students eager to hear what he would come out with next.

"We have had new lights installed into the Recital Hall, and I just hope they are bright enough to enhance the natural colours of my cheeks!'

And another time:

'Now, many of you students are leaving us this term. One would hate for any of you to get into financial difficulties. I have this horrendous mental image of one of our students down on his knees in front of his bank manager! It would be terrible. (Unless, of course, your bank manager has God-given qualities!)'

KEVIN

I helped look after some of the great and the good at some performances during an event that was a collaboration between the Royal College of Art, the English National Ballet School and the Royal College of Music. It was a big occasion at the Britten Theatre at the Royal College and all the dignitaries were there.

We were putting on several ballets and new pieces of music. Paul Max Edlin had been commissioned to do a big ballet. Paul is now Director of Music at the Queen Mary University of London and leads the Deal Festival of Music and Art. My fellow student, Ken Hesketh was asked to do a brand-new arrangement of some ballet exercises, and he turned it into a fantastic piece.

Michael Gough-Matthews was chatting to one of the journalists of the *Evening Standard* about ballet. This was when the *Standard* was the only paper for London, and it was one of the major reviewers as well. In an unguarded moment, not thinking he was speaking 'on the record', Michael said to the journalist:

'I can wrap my ankles around the back of my neck, but you'll never catch me in a pair of tights. They're far too revealing and it makes you want to blush!'

The next day a huge scandal erupted when an article appeared in the Standard detailing what he had said. The English National Ballet were fuming about it and it was a big embarrassment for the College. Some students pinned copies of the article to the College notice boards. I took one down and years later we wrote a song based on it called *Why Does the Male Ballerina Make You Blush?* set to the *Nutcracker*. It seems such a tame song now, but it was deemed rather outrageous back in 2004.

Strangely, but perhaps as a result of that scandal, Michael Gough-Matthews was the only Director of the Royal College of Music who was never given a knighthood.

STEVEN

When I arrived at the College, I realised that the gentle warnings I'd had from my teacher Philip Marshall were true: there were people there who were a lot better than me, and I was just a small fish in a very big pond. I'd been the best at school and at competitions around the Midlands, but suddenly I was there amongst Russians and Polish people who were way better and could already play anything. And of course, they were getting all the opportunities to play concerts and concertos with the College orchestras. It was really quite a big shock.

My second teacher there was Yonty Soloman, a brilliant South African concert pianist and originally an excellent jazz pianist. He'd studied with the great Myra Hess and Charles Rosen who were very big names in classical piano. The sounds he could get out of a piano were spellbinding and as Kevin and I work on arrangements these days, I try to think of the sound-colours that he would produce. He had such a reputation as a teacher that he was chosen to coach Shirley MacLaine in the 1988 John Schlesinger film *Madame Sousatzka*, which is wonderful. It is Yonty himself playing the Schumann piano concerto in the final scene, as the boy actor mimes.

Despite that, my own view is that he wasn't the greatest teacher. He was more of a performer. For example, we would play that Schumann Piano concerto together (with him playing the orchestral part) and as we finished

I would wait for his critique, thinking that I'd played it badly. But he would just smile at me and say:

'Very fine, Steven, very fine. Would you like a packet of crisps?'

He was a very kind, and deservedly popular man but he was too nice to me and I didn't learn an awful lot from him technically. Sometimes I would go to his beautiful house in Canonbury (part of Islington) which was filled with wonderful sculptures and other original art pieces. He was an excellent cook, and after eating we'd drink tea and make a fuss of his over-fed dog who was called Sotherby.

Before that my main teacher was the wonderful Phyllis Sellick. She was already well into her eighties when I knew her, but in her time she had been one of the very best pianists in the country. Ralph Vaughan-Williams and Malcolm Arnold wrote pieces specifically for her and she had also been a great friend of Rachmaninov.

During one holiday I moved into a flat in Earl's Court. It was a very nice apartment but there were neighbours left right and centre, and that meant I couldn't play the piano at all because they objected to the noise. You could only book a practice room for an hour at the College, so I was turning up for my lessons with Phyllis without having done enough work on the piece. I wish that the digital pianos that we have today were available then. It would have changed my world.

Phyllis was getting quite frustrated with me, so I looked around for somewhere private and finally I made arrangements through the College appointments office with a very well-to-do lady who lived in a huge house off Regents Park. She said I could use the piano in her house every morning between ten and midday to practise.

It didn't work out because she would just come and sit and watch me as I was working, wearing just a negligee and trying to get me to chat to her. I was far too self-conscious to get any decent work done. Every pianist will tell you that you can't practise properly when people are listening, and that is especially true if they are in a state of undress.

In the end, Phyllis came up with a solution. She lent me a dummy keyboard with which I could do some silent practice at home. It was a magnificent piece of furniture – made of oak - that had been constructed in about 1930 It turned out that Rachmaninov had left it to her. Rachmaninov used to take it everywhere with him, so that he could practise wherever he was travelling: on ships and trains even. Phyllis told me that he'd used it a lot whilst composing his third piano concerto.

It didn't produce any sound as there were no strings, but it did have a controller on the right so that you could alter the resistance and weight of the keys. You would play it just like a normal piano and there would just be a clattering sound (a bit like my gay uncle's fingernails!). My mind's ear could hear the music I was playing, just as you can almost hear what you're playing if you switch off an electric keyboard.

[K: There is a story of a pianist going for an audition with a famous conductor at a hotel. Finding that there was no piano in the room, he had to play the piece with his fingers on a desktop. And the conductor kept stopping him and telling him he wanted it played differently, until the pianist was so exasperated that he paused and said: 'I'm sorry, but it sounded perfectly all right on my kitchen table.']

I practised on Rachmaninov's dummy keyboard for years and it was so good for me to have it. I remember taking it home to Earl's Court for the first time and noticing that the white keys were absolutely filthy. I got some Jif and a sponge and started carefully cleaning all the grime from the ivory. I'd only got two keys completely clean when I suddenly thought:

'Oh no! This is Rachmaninov's dirt, and I'm getting rid of it!' So, I stopped.

Eventually I had to give it back to Phyllis and I've no idea where it is now. Whoever has it can probably verify it has two gleaming white keys in the bottom octave.

Phyllis and her husband Cyril Smith (the famous concert pianist, not the MP!) were very good friends with Rachmaninov. He had a reputation for being rather a gloomy and grumpy man, but Phyllis said he wasn't like that at all; he just had a really dry sense of humour. The three of them would go on holidays together when they had finished a tour, but they'd always choose a rural cottage with no piano, completely remote from everywhere, and just go for walks and relax.

Phyllis told me a story about one of those times. They arrived at a little house in the countryside and were horrified to find there was a decrepit old upright piano in the living room. They were all disappointed that it was there because the whole point of the holiday was for them all to get away from pianos, but when they tried it they couldn't get a nice sound out of it and it felt alright to ignore it. One afternoon they were all completely startled when a silk purse Phyllis had left on top, dropped down onto the keys and made a really good sound.

She told me that story to emphasise a technique she was trying to teach me. Producing good quality sound is not about just hitting the keys, it's about the way you depress them. The best quality note comes from using something soft - the pad of the fingers - under no more than the force of gravity.

I still had to continue with the flute, and I was allocated to Christopher Hyde-Smith for tuition. Christopher is one of the finest and most accomplished flautists in the country (he even has a flute made of gold!), and I often thought it must have been awful for him having to teach me.

But we got on quite well and I suppose he just accepted the situation. Some of the best piano professors at the College also had to teach piano to instrumentalists.

At the end of the second year, we were allowed to drop the second-study lessons and I did so immediately. I was so relieved that I'd never have to play the flute again that I took a tube to Hungerford Bridge alongside the Royal Festival Hall on the south bank of the Thames, stood there in the pouring rain, held the shining silver flute out in my hands and dropped it into the river. I was free of the bloody thing! I'm actually very ashamed of this now. My parents had paid a few hundred pounds for it, and I should have donated it to someone who would have appreciated it.

While I was at college my family left the country. My parents bought a bar on Crete, and I lived out there during the holidays. We had a piano in the corner of the bar on which I could tinkle away in the background so it was a bit like being back in the restaurants of Burton. The business (which my parents called 'The European') was a great success, so much so that they decided to buy a second bar for my sister to look after.

This meant that when I graduated from the College no-one could take any time off to get away to see me at the ceremony. All the other students had their parents and brothers and sisters there, and I was there alone with no-one to celebrate with me, apart from my boyfriend Scott and his parents.

Scott was also studying piano at the College and we hit it off very quickly. We were together as partners for sixteen years and after college we got together with a friend and bought a house in Kings Cross. It was a big swanky place but we soon found it wasn't easy living as a couple with another person so after a while we sold up. We made a good profit then but if we'd kept it, we could have been rich by now (it sold recently for about £3 million). After that Scott bought a flat in Manor Park and eventually Kevin joined us living there.

Scott and I don't share a room anymore but we are as close as anyone can be, and we have lived together ever since our college days. You could say that Scott, Kevin and I are a somewhat unconventional family, living side by side in our house in Edinburgh.

My parents became victims of their own success, and they lost everything. The locals on Crete rather took against them for making more money than the Greek bars and tried to jeopardise the business. And when the local police started to make life difficult for them Mum and Dad had to do a runner overnight to get out of the country.

KEVIN

At the College, my first piano teacher was Professor Peter Wallfisch. He had grown up in Poland but saved himself from the Nazis by emigrating to Palestine when he was only fourteen, and then studied at the Jerusalem Conservatoire. My lessons with him were quite difficult; music had saved his life, and his relationship with it came from pain.

It wasn't something I could relate to then, but as time goes on I think I understand him better and I'm gaining more now from Peter than when I studied with him.

I felt a bit overwhelmed the first time I went to meet him. We had a general discussion and he wanted to know which composers I liked.

I said: 'What do you think of Francis Poulenc?'

Peter replied: 'He was a charming man.'

And suddenly it came to me that now I was working at a different level. I had been asking what Peter thought of Poulenc's music and he was responding about Poulenc as a person. It hadn't occurred to me until that moment that here at the College I was mixing with people who had themselves mixed with famous composers and musicians, who knew them not just as names on a music score or the cover of a recording.

Peter went on to say:

'I was greatly embarrassed when I was studying with Jacques Fevrier at the Conservatoire de Paris when he asked me if I'd like to meet Poulenc. I couldn't believe he knew him, so I said "My word! You know Poulenc? How do you know him?" And then I was so embarrassed because he said that Poulenc was his boyfriend.'

Listening to this, I couldn't believe what Peter Wallfisch was telling me. He had been embarrassed because he hadn't realised that these men were lovers, not by the fact that they were openly homosexual in a time before it was legal. His discomfort had been that he felt he should have known and not put his foot in it like that. Clearly, he wasn't at all bothered that they were gay; that wasn't the issue at all. I think he was the first adult of that age that I had met who accepted the idea of being gay as completely natural.

Years later, when I was playing in the West Five piano bar, I was chatting to a young American lad who was studying at the College and who was just finishing a thesis about Poulenc, so I told him what Peter Walfisch had said about him. He was absolutely astonished. Although he had been researching Poulenc for a while, he had never seen anything written that revealed that he and Fevrier were together in a relationship, and he went away excited that a brand-new avenue had opened up for him. He could now see connections that hadn't been obvious before. It was like putting together bits of a jigsaw that hadn't previously seemed to fit.

Even though I'd played in bands at school, I really couldn't cope with playing seriously in public, not solo classical music. When I started at the College my performing nerves were shot and the longer I worked under Peter the worse they got, until I could no longer perform at all. Peter was desperate for me to do well and I would spend weekends having extra lessons with him, but the pressure got too much and I would just fall apart.

During the summer of 1991 Peter suffered a terrible stroke. He was so angry that he was no longer able to play, and he died a couple of years later. He had done so much for the music world, especially promoting young previously unknown British composers.

I was taken under the wing of another lecturer, Ruth Gerald, and discovering my fear of public performance she told the whole department I was no longer to be examined on that. She spent my final year building up my confidence, and she succeeded. I was asked to play outrageous and loud background music for the students' end of year ball on the main concert hall grand piano, and I had all my peers cheering along as I played well-known pieces in the style of Les Dawson. The atmosphere was electric and it was my first real taste of what I wanted to do.

Before college, whenever there was a school concert, I would choose to do a comic sketch instead of playing anything serious. I would copy something Victor Borge had done for instance, and hope to make people laugh. Although my talent was in music I felt more passionate about comedy. As I went through college and my problems with performing in public got worse, I moved into comedy on an even grander scale.

I spent most of my weekend evenings going to stand-up shows in London. We saw Eddie Izzard do one of his very first gigs: there were only ten of us in the audience. The year before he had started out doing an escapology act and then moved on to hosting his own show called *The Raging Bull* at the back of the Raymond Revue Bar. It was a very seedy area and to get in you had to make your way through the strip club and then pay two pounds at the door of the back room.

Eddie's big skill was in ad-libbing. At the show we saw almost all of the acts had been crap. One of the audience got up on stage, pissed out of his head, and shouted:

'I'm going to shove this microphone up my a**ehole'.

Two security guys grabbed him immediately and threw him out, but Eddie Izzard came back on and said:

'Ladies and Gentlemen, I'm so sorry that the contortionist that we had booked to perform his trick of inserting a microphone into his own a**ehole has had to cancel at the last minute,' and from there he developed an extended routine about what a shame it was we were not going to see this unique act.

If I was going to make anything of my love for musical comedy, I knew it was going to be difficult to do it on my own so I was on the look-out for someone to collaborate with. A counsellor at the College phoned me one day and said:

'I've got a young lad here who does arrangements. He's very talented but we don't really have space for him at the College. Could you come and meet him?'

I was introduced to a chap called John Wilson, and I invited him to orchestrate some cabaret shows with me. Together we came up with some really outlandish ideas. There was a performance of the 1812 Overture with popping condoms for cannon. We had Rebecca Jones, the harpist, sitting at the side of the stage with a colostomy bag impersonating the Queen Mother (patron of the College). We only gave her one line to say, which she kept repeating:

'I'm ninety-two!'

It was outrageous stuff but performed with a full orchestra. These days the John Wilson Orchestra is one of the leading orchestras in the country – they do the Proms every year – but they've never used us. Maybe John doesn't trust me not to try to relive some of the things we got up to in those days!

I studied keyboard harmony with an amazingly bohemian tutor called Tim Salter who is quite a progressive composer in his own right. With hindsight I think it would have been better for me if I had studied composition with him. I went in one morning just as he took a call from a friend of a friend looking for some help in recording some music they had written. It was a woman called Mary-Ann Ephrave, and Tim was asking what exactly it was that she needed.

'I'm a South African, living in London. I compose, but I can't actually play any of my music and I would like to employ someone, one of your students maybe, to record my music ideas for me. I'm happy to pay them.'

Tim replied: 'I think I've got the student you need right here, but I need to ask you one question. Have you got a sense of humour... because you're going to need one!'

I was sent along to Mary-Ann's house in Kilburn. It was a lovely basement apartment with loads of artwork around the walls and lots of books and a beautiful staircase that she had made out of a fallen tree that she found. There was a great feeling about the place as soon as I went in. She showed me that she had set up her own little recording studio and then we went over some of the music that she wanted me to play. When she asked me what I was going to charge her for doing it, even though I knew that she wanted to pay me, I told her:

'My gut instinct is to not charge a penny.'

I would spend most afternoons while I was at college in Mary-Ann's flat and some of my friends became her friends. Her husband Jim was tall and elegant and for many years he was also our accountant.

[S: He would scream at us when we gave him the scraps of paper that made up our accounting records and, once, he even chased us onto stage in a theatre demanding our receipts.]

Mary-Ann and Jim were much older than me, so as well as being close friends they became my substitute parents in London, always looking out for me. They were happy to come and fetch me home when bad things happened with partners, even at three in the morning. There was one partner who was quite violent towards me and hit me with a wok.

[S: So that's why we had a wok with a dent in it?]

And they were first on the scene when something really bad happened.

Some evenings Mary-Ann and I would just sit writing songs for musicals that we dreamed were going to make us famous. She came up with one song called 'The Fifty-two-year-old woman masquerading as a songwriter Blues.' Part of the fantasy was that the one song that would make it big would be the one we didn't really like ourselves and so we wrote a song about that. One line went 'It would be typical to be famous/ for a song that's just an anus'.

On top of this, while I would record Mary-Ann's music in the studio she had created I could also record my own music ideas there. A lot of compositions that we perform as Worbey and Farrell started life in the creative environment that Mary-Ann gave me access to.

One day at the College I was introduced to someone who was a friend of the Fire Safety Officer and had been doing some cleaning for the Principal. There were several people who were quite enthralled with him because although he seemed to have fallen on hard times, he had had an interesting musical career. His name was Johnny Binns, and I learnt that he'd written songs with Annie Lennox and Boy George.

His career had gone down the pan as a result of some sort of nervous breakdown but now he was looking for someone to work with, to record the new ideas for songs he had. I said to him that it would probably be OK to come along to Mary-Ann's flat to record what he had and rushed out to phone her from a callbox.

'I think we've finally made it! I've just met Jonathan Binns who has written songs with loads of famous people, and he needs someone to collaborate with and a place to record. Can I bring him round?'

We were tickled pink; we believed we were now going to be right at the centre of the song-writing business. I took him round to the flat, and Mary-

Ann and I sat and listened to his life story. His father was a saxophonist who used to play with Barbra Streisand, and Paul McCartney would come to the house when Johnny was a boy. He told us how one night he was with Annie Lennox just after she had split from Dave Stewart, and he commented that Dave must have been a bit of a thorn in her side, and from that they produced the well-known song. And then he was telling us that *Karma Chameleon* had originally been written as a Country and Western song.

We all went into the studio and he started to sing us the song that he was working on, that he was sure was going to be a big hit. It was a bit of a tuneless tirade of shouting the same two lines over and over:

'Don't give up, don't think it's the end/ Happiness comes when you need a friend.'

We worked out a melody, and Mary-Ann gave him some help with some more lyrics and then we recorded it. For the most part he sang in a completely different key to the accompaniment, but then miraculously finished on the right note. The next morning, having slept on it, I phoned Mary-Ann.

'What a load of old sh*t!'

She laughed.

And then she said that, until I confirmed it, she hadn't quite been able to admit to herself that we'd been sold a load of old nonsense. Not a word of what he had said was true, he was a complete fantasist.

Mary-Ann has continued to be a major part of my life and she introduced me to South African music. Steven and I have had some really good experiences in South Africa, and sometimes I think that a finger has been pointing me in the direction of that country ever since I met her.

I'm afraid I rather made a mess of my final exams at the College and ended up with a third-class degree. I was suffering terribly with stress at the time because of a court case I had become caught up in, and the hearings were at exactly the same time as I was taking my exams. I was a witness for the defence in a case involving a friend of mine from Bingham.

A girl I knew who was the daughter of one of my teachers, worked in a pub in the town. Late one night after work, she was walking home and was attacked in the churchyard. Some other people I knew who lived in the cottage overlooking the church heard something going on at about one in the morning. They opened their windows and called out and the attacker ran off. The story was in the local newspaper: for Bingham it was big news.

Ten days later I was home for a break from college and I went for a drink with a friend who is a manic depressive. He had been ill for months, and was in such a depressive state that he couldn't even get out of bed for days. This was the first time he had felt able to come out of his house for weeks. I went up to the bar and was served by the same girl who had been attacked. She asked:

'What was your friend doing last Thursday?'

I said: 'I don't know, but he's been ill for a long time.'

She said: 'I think it could have been him.'

Within minutes five police cars arrived and he was arrested. The next day he was in the Magistrates court and was put on remand for five months in Lincoln prison, sharing cells with sex offenders. I went to the police to tell them they had got the wrong person. I asked them if they understood what manic depression is.

One of them suggested: 'It's like schizophrenia, isn't it?'

I explained that it's quite different. There's a manic state and there's a depressive state where you can hardly move or do anything. People don't just go from mania to depressive and back in hours. My friend's parents knew he was ill in bed, and even if he had wanted to, he couldn't have just got up and gone to the other side of the town in the early hours of the morning. As his parents said, to drive to the churchyard he would have had to move two vans they use in their business to get out without them hearing, and then move everything back again when he returned. It was just impossible.

The policemen I was talking to seemed quite bothered by what I was telling them, and one of them conceded that it looked like the real culprit was still out there. But the prosecution was going ahead with it anyway, and the defence wanted to call me as a witness, and that was right at the time of my exams. The prosecution counsel obviously hadn't read what I had written in my statement, and just resorted to calling me a liar. When I started to say something like:

'In my opinion ...'

the Judge slammed me down and told me: 'Opinions are not worth anything in this case!'

Other than the poor girl saying it might have been him, there was no real evidence against my friend, and so he won the case. Our barrister was quite well-known as a supporter of the underdog and she looked and behaved a bit like Miss Marple. You could see that the jury were quite affected by what was going on and when they came back into court to give their verdict one of them was giving her the thumbs up.

My college career ended on an academic low because I was stressed about the experience of giving evidence, but in another way, it ended with one of the best weeks of my life. Just as I was about to leave I was lucky enough to meet one of my heroes.

The College had an appointments desk where students could apply for work. Even after three years I'd never really worked out the layout of the building so one day, intending to go for a coffee I wandered down a wrong corridor and found myself outside the appointments office and decided I might as well go in. The office was run by a nice lady called Barbara Nias. I told her that I was leaving in about a month's time and asked if there was any work available.

She said lots of people were asking the same thing but agreed to offer me the next job that came in regardless of what it was. No sooner had I found the canteen and ordered a coffee than she came running in and said:

'I think this one is ideal for you.'

Channel 4 were making a follow up to their series *Orchestra* to be called *Concerto,* with Michael Tilson Thomas conducting the London Symphony Orchestra, Alicia de Larrocha playing Beethoven's second piano concerto, and Dudley Moore presenting. The film company needed someone to help the camera crew by giving them cues for when the different instruments should be seen; I would be making sure the clarinet solo was on screen, that sort of thing.

I absolutely adored Dudley Moore and had I not gone the wrong way that day, I wouldn't have got that job! It was just three days work but I couldn't have had a better first job out of college than working with my idol!

[S: He slept with you, didn't he?

K: He fell asleep on me, yes.]

I don't know whether it was jet lag or something to do with his brain disease, but he came and sat beside me while I was working with the film crew and fell asleep on my shoulder. It's probably the only time I've ever been completely star-struck. I just couldn't move, overwhelmed by the thought: 'My God! Arthur is fast asleep on my shoulder!'

It's a sign of a great piece of music that even after three solid days of listening to that one Beethoven concerto I still wanted to listen to it again the next day.

Chapter 4

In which we talk about being gay in 1990s London living in the shadow of AIDS. Steven meets Princess Diana, and Kevin gets mugged wearing rainbow trousers

We were allocated the same room in the College residential halls in consecutive years, but we are pretty sure that we had met some years before that.

STEVEN

I had completely forgotten about this but one day Kevin said to me, quite casually:

'Did you ever go shopping for shoes in Nottingham?'

And immediately I remembered. I could picture myself back in a shoe shop and seeing a boy of similar age who I found completely fascinating, walking away from the store. And it wasn't a gay thing (we were only about fourteen), I was just watching him and wondering why this boy was so captivating. I had a hunch that I knew him, although I didn't. Very odd, but it stuck with me.

KEVIN

For me it certainly was a gay thing. I had never seen anyone as stunningly beautiful, and when four years later Steven arrived at the College, I just couldn't believe it. I immediately remembered him and thought: 'My God, there's that lad I saw in the shoe shop!'

A lot of people at the College fancied Steven, with his Shirley Temple looks and his girlish curls. I had a friend at College called Lee Ward, who is now Head of Music at Liverpool Cathedral, but back then was one of the most outrageously flamboyant characters in the place. Anyone who was still not 'out' didn't stand a chance of remaining in the closet because Lee would drag young boys out into the open, kicking and screaming. We were walking down a corridor one day when we spotted Steven. But even Lee was in awe of him, and he had just plucked up the courage to say hello when he was shoved out of the way by a fat percussionist shouting:

'Hands off! I saw him first!'

At the time it was said that about eighty per cent of the boys at the College were gay... and the rest were just lying. As a consequence there were several frustrated girls during our time there, although fortunately for them all the male brass players were straight.

That is just a strange fact of life. Pianists: all gay, flautists: gay, singers definitely gay, but all brass players: straight. Percussionists: bisexual, they take what they can get. Gay trombonists did start to emerge in the mid-90s though, which we put down to the closure of the coal mines and the disbanding of the pit brass bands. They probably needed somewhere to go to express themselves.

STEVEN

This is why the place was known as The Royal Cottage of Music!

Having spent my teenage years pretending not to be gay, it was both invigorating and liberating to be amongst so many young men who were quite open about who they were. It was also a bit shocking what some people got up to.

One of my pianist friends spent the majority of his time touring the London public toilets ('cottages') for encounters rather than devoting time to practising his instrument. He would sometimes take a small hand drill with him and make holes in the cubicle wall to spy on men. I told him he was wasting valuable work time but he wouldn't have it.

For quite a while I lost track of him. He was neither in the College nor at the hall of residence, and I assumed he was still at his old tricks. Some years later he admitted that he was actually in the College more than I knew. He had discovered that two adjacent cubicles in the ground floor toilets had windows that opened on to an unused enclosed well of the building. It was closed off on all sides and quite dark because the building was very high. He'd worked out that he could lock the door to the first cubicle, prise open the sealed window, climb outside into the well, and then spy through a kind of grill over the second cubicle window. Every day he would spend hours out there being a voyeur. He said that cubicle was very busy in all sorts of ways but he always got very annoyed if he was trying to eat his sandwiches and someone came in to use the toilet as it was meant to be used!

After a year in the halls of residence, we all moved out and lived in the area around Earl's Court. It was the gay part of London, though we didn't live there for that reason; it was just reasonably close to the College. The gay scene had rather taken over from the Australian backpackers who had made it their home in the decades before and there were lots of gay pubs there. We used to see Kenny Everett in the area, and Freddie Mercury once not long before he died. The Philbeach Gardens Hotel used to have a 'Tranny Night' catering for the transvestites and drag queens, and it also had a sauna that had a carpet. You can imagine that it smelled quite disgusting.

Lee Ward was one of a group of rather badly behaved but brilliantly flamboyant Liverpudlians that we knew who had all grown up together. Lee shared a flat with Jonathan Harvey, an exceptional cellist who went on to become a famous playwright. Usually with them were their friends Kenneth Hesketh, who is now one of the most talented composers in the world, and the Clarke family – Frank, Angela, and Margi. Frank Clarke wrote episodes of *Brookside* and then the film *Letter to Brezhnev*, which his sister Margi starred in. Margi was already established as an actress and presenter and her sister Angela became an actress too. The whole set of them came from very humble backgrounds and were all incredibly bright, and also highly competitive in being outrageous, always trying to out-do each other. They were tremendous fun to know, and we both frequented the gay clubs with Jonathan and Lee.

KEVIN

One of the first times I met Jonathan Harvey he was in the local greengrocer's shop asking the assistant, in a very camp voice:

'Can you show me your largest carrot? I want to buy the largest carrot you have!'

One evening, during my first year, Lee Ward phoned me in the halls of residence and asked me to come up:

'Jonathan wants to show you something!'

I had a friend staying with me, a shy quiet lad, and the two of us went up as requested to find Jonathan lying in bed. He peeled back the duvet to show that he had perfected the ability to cover his entire cock with his scrotum. My poor friend was terribly embarrassed.

I absolutely loved living in London. I was at Robert Mayer Hall in South Kensington to start off with, and then around the Kensington and Earl's Court area for a number of years after that. From the time I arrived at the College until I was in my thirties, I felt like a kiddy in a sweet shop. I was out partying every night, meeting some very strange and exotic people. I'd teamed up with a bassoon player called Jo Spinak, who was also from the Midlands. She was fun, hyperactive, deeply sensitive and my partner in partying.

South Kensington was a very posh area and quite often you would see people holding champagne parties up on their balconies. Jo and I, being nineteen, thought nothing of just turning up uninvited. We'd buzz the door and say:

'Hi! We are friends of Michael.'

and usually the door would open and we would just walk in, grab a drink and start talking to anyone. And then we would be introducing that person to other people at the party, and soon enough everyone would assume we were meant to be there. If we turned up late in the evening it was easy to gate-crash because by then most people didn't know their own names let alone who else was invited.

One night, I had just arrived at a party on the Old Brompton Road as a guy started falling down the stairs towards me. I caught him just in time, and propped him up in the doorway as a group of policemen pushed past me on their way up to raid the flat for drugs. They just went by as I stood there holding this lad up and didn't pay any attention to us, so I helped him slide down the wall and sit on the ground - and left.

At the start of my second year I moved into a place in Penywern Road in Earl's Court and held a party myself, and the Liverpool group all turned up. They brought along a girl they knew from home who was staying with them. A classical guitarist friend of mine called David, got off with her but didn't realise that to have sex they would have to go to the house where Jonathan Harvey and that lot were living.

[S: I was at that party - it was my Freshers' Week.]

After the party Jonathan and the rest of them returned to their house just as David and the girl were getting into full swing. They overheard David promising:

'I'm going to split you in two!'

And for the rest of his time at the College David couldn't go anywhere without hearing a queenie scouse voice shouting out:

'Oh please! Split me in two!'

My house was owned by two old ladies who used to let rooms to students through their company called Cowan & Kumar. The places they rented were filthy, damp and dilapidated, and the chances were that when you arrived there would be no light bulbs. They were notorious for taking a big deposit at the start of the lease but never returning it at the end.

Across the road Lindi St Clair, a high-profile madam and dominatrix ran a brothel. She was also known as Miss Whiplash and had caused Norman Lamont (who was the Chancellor of the Exchequer at the time) some embarrassment when the papers found out she was renting his flat in Notting Hill. When I lived near her, she was getting involved in politics and setting up the Corrective Party in protest at the Inland Revenue wanting to tax her on her earnings, even though prostitution was illegal. She had a placard outside her house that said: 'Be effective, vote corrective!'

My flatmates and I were well aware of the reputation these two old ladies had for not returning deposits and we really couldn't afford to lose that money. One day, towards the end of our lease, my friend Carolyn who I was living with, noticed there was some mould on a wall. She was about to get the bleach out to clean it off but I thought we should encourage it to grow, and we sprayed it with salt water. After a few weeks it became a huge black mess growing right across the wall. Next, just before we were due to leave, we invited the local council health inspector round to have a look and they immediately condemned the place as unfit for human habitation. By law that meant that Cowan & Kumar were obliged to give us back our deposits in full. They were livid and they had to get the whole house gutted and redecorated before they could let it again.

For a while Steven and I lived in the same building, Finborough House. It was close to Chelsea football ground, and also the Brompton Cemetery, an established gay cruising venue.

[S: It was a really beautiful place. I used to go over there in the morning with my flatmate Sandie – a violinist - and we would sit and have a coffee and just watch the cruising going on around us. It was very theatrical, almost like being at a gay ballet.]

The wealthy gays of the area all used to go to a tiny pub called the Queen's Head in Chelsea, which amusingly was on Tryon Street just off the King's Road. It had two bars, one for local straights who used to ignore what was happening in the other bar. If you wanted to make some money as a student and were willing to rent yourself out, you could meet someone there. Not that either Steven or I ever did that!

The photographer Alan Warren lived a few doors down the street, famous for his pictures of Salvador Dali, and society figures. He was a very interesting man whom I got to know quite well. He had been an actor originally and started taking pictures of his fellow performers when he was in Alan Bennett's play *Forty Years On* as a teenager. He got offered the chance to take photos at Judy Garland's wedding to his friend Mickey Deans. From stars like Noel Coward and Britt Ekland he went on to do portraits of the Royal family and every Duke in the country. It seemed he had a great ability to capture people just at the right millisecond. He has written several books including a wonderful gossipy work called Dukes,

Queens and Other Stories, and for a while he was also Marc Bolan's manager.

His parties were wild but, according to him, Lionel Bart's were the most outrageous. I didn't go to any of those but Alan used to talk about them, and the stories all ended up in his book. There were lots of people on the fringes of the aristocracy involved in that scene, all of them black sheep of their families.

It was an area of colourful characters and at times quite sordid too. One of Alan's closest friends was a Portuguese aristocrat called Count de Paulo who seemed to have no other purpose in life but to tour around the cemeteries and toilets, picking up boys and men for sex. As far as I could see he did this all day every day, apart from when he was at the same parties as I went to. The story was that he was from a very wealthy high society family in Portugal but had been disowned by them. His father was mortified that he had a son who was incredibly effeminate, so he gave him enough money to live on for the rest of his life, on the condition that he promised to get married, father some children and never step foot in Portugal again.

Apparently he fulfilled all of those conditions and then took up his life as a professional cottager. I was at a party one evening when he told me that he had picked up a boy that afternoon and taken him back to Alan Warren's house because they couldn't get anywhere else. He was complaining about the boy's morals:

'I took him into the hallway, and he was kneeling in front of me, and then I felt his hands looking for my wallet in my back pocket. I mean! Can one not get anything for free these days?'

STEVEN

I think I might have worked even harder at the Royal College and immersed myself more in my musical studies if I hadn't also been overcome by that 'kiddy in the sweetshop' feeling. Whoever said: 'Education is wasted on the young', had a point. There were just too many other excitements and experiences to consume my energies.

I didn't get into drinking alcohol until I was in my mid-twenties. All the other college students used to go out and get pissed because that's what students do, and most people went to a place called the Queens Head near the College. Everyone referred to it as 'The Nines' because when they built the College they missed out room 99 by accident, so the pub became known as 'all the nines' – in the same way as golfers talk about the clubhouse as 'the nineteenth hole'.

I rarely went to The Nines because I wanted to be in the gay bars. The first one I tried was the Coleherne Arms and that was a baptism of fire because it was full of mature gays. I went in there, a really scared fresh-faced eighteen-year-old, but these old queens, dressed in full leather, were the friendliest of people and I would spend my evenings talking about classical music and exchanging recipes with them.

Easily the best place in Earl's Court for gays to go to was Manhattan's, the bar of the Redcliffe Hotel on the Fulham Road. Going into a place like that was a final and public admission of your sexuality, and I remember being so nervous and my heart pounding on my first visit. Everyone in there was supportive and friendly so it quickly became my favourite.

Going to Manhattan's seemed so sophisticated, being a part of the scene at this glamorous gay night club. The entrance was on the corner of Redcliffe Gardens and the Fulham Road, right on the edge of The Boltons, home to the great and the good of Kensington.

As you walked in, you were greeted by a big domineering doorman called Larry who always asked:

'How d'ya fancy getting off with an old Irish queen?'

Sadly, Larry was one of the first people we knew of who fell victim to Aids.

The bar was a very long one that took up most of the back of the venue. It was decorated with mirrors all the way round and there were high stools for people who liked to pose. There were very comfortable sofas to sit on, and in the corner to the left was a white piano. Further back was a dance area and at the end of the bar was the DJ's booth.

The music was mostly Hi NRG: typical 80s type disco but they also played Pet Shop Boys, Madonna and Liza Minnelli. It was one of the few bars we knew that was both very smart and also had a loyal group of regulars. The only downside was that Bill Tindall who ran the bar, wouldn't leave it alone and kept changing the theme, so that you never knew what the place was going to be. One week it might be a piano bar, the next a strip-club, and at one point he decided to turn it into a sleazier outfit and changed the name to Exit. And everyone did.

Another time he decided he loved Christmas so much that, in the middle of June, he recreated something like Harrods' Santa's Grotto with a massive Christmas tree and all the tinselly decorations. By the time it got to December the punters were so fed up with the décor, the place was empty. If you are going to run a club venue the one thing it needs is an identity, but Manhattan's always had a self-imposed identity crisis.

KEVIN

I fell in love with Manhattan's and it became my second home. There was a whole set of us who used to sit in one corner every night but it wasn't only gays that used to meet there. A lot of the girls at the College loved going there as they could flirt with all the boys without the worry of being harassed. I think it must also have been frustrating for them too, as there were a lot of very good-looking guys in the club every night.

Steven would often arrive with his flatmate, a girl called Sandie who was studying violin. I dated Sandie for a while but I knew she wasn't what I wanted. It turned out she hadn't settled on where she was sexually and just kept changing her mind about it. There came the point where we had to have a chat about who we were:

'I've got something to tell you, which I think you should know.'

'So have I.' (I'm not even sure who said which line!)

A straight friend of ours called Jeremy Ward often came in with us too. He was a bass player, very good-looking and quite astute. He would let all the guys chat him up and buy him drinks, and then would then leave with a girl who thought she was 'converting' him. His view was that if girls could exploit men to buy drinks for them without intending to put out, then he couldn't see why he shouldn't do the same.

I ended up going to Manhattan's almost every night for years. I think Bill Tindall always breathed a sigh of relief when I walked in because he was not the most sociable of people and I was like the young cute (unpaid) social host. There was one night when we had to repel a large group of middle-aged women who were trying to get in and who were behaving rather badly. It turned out that they were trying to get at the male-strippers troupe, The Chippendales who were staying in the hotel. Of course, they were all gay.

All the old queens liked me, and the nice thing was we younger gays really looked after the old men in there. It was a privileged position to be in. We knew that we had youth on our side, and they loved it if young boys started chatting to them. They were interesting; they all had stories to tell. It seems very different these days; the young gays can be very dismissive of the older ones (I know that sounds very fuddy-duddy!).

I developed a friendship with a retired barrister called Brian. Despite having had a successful legal career, Brian didn't have much confidence in himself, but he came alive in an alter-ego called 'Fergie' that he had developed. There was a deep-seated sadness in Brian's life which you could never approach. He'd had a wife and two daughters who shut their dad out of their lives when they found out about his cross-dressing.

But Fergie - or to give her the full name, Gillian Mahler Ferguson - was vivacious and glamourous and bought expensive ball gowns from Harrods, and frequented every gay bar in town. Everyone wanted her at their party; everyone apart from some of the drag queens, because Fergie had a habit of turning up at their gigs and upstaging them by making an appalling attempt to perform the last movement of Karl Weber's *Clarinet Concerto No.2.* I will confess that I was often the accompanist for these impromptu clarinet concerts. Sometimes she would explain her connection to Karl Weber:

'Karl's second name was Maria! I think his parents couldn't quite decide what he was when they named him and looking at me, I'm sure you will appreciate that my parents felt the same!'

Fergie did a lot for an HIV charity based in Earl's Court, called Body Positive. I spent a lot of time with her in those days and so ended up working with the charity too. We would drive around the night clubs, distributing box-loads of condoms and lube to anyone who needed them. Fergie was always dressed in some breathtakingly sumptious dress, and usually I would be dressed in some outrageous costume too. One night we were driving through Piccadilly Circus in a Vauxhall Estate, when the police stopped us to do a routine check. Heaven knows what they thought when they saw us: Fergie a seventy-year-old transvestite in thick bright red lipstick and a bad Marilyn Monroe style wig, and me dressed head to toe in a zebra skin outfit. And there were three thousand condoms on the back seat.

I had a lot of fun with Fergie; we did a lot of things together. But there was always the underlying problem of Brian, who was very much a sad man. I liked Brian very much but I could always tell if I was talking to Brian on the phone, or if it was Fergie. When people invited Fergie to parties, sometimes they would add:

'Don't bring Brian.'

As Brian got older, he decided he had to gradually retire Fergie. Eventually he went into a retirement home in Bayswater and sent all Fergie's clothes to a charity shop. He said it was like losing a limb. When I started working away from home with Steven the contact between us got less and less. A friend who did stay in touch with him for a bit told me she'd heard that he'd passed on, but I'm sure I spotted him in the audience of an episode of Judge Rinder a year or two ago.

STEVEN

Another gay pub we went to was called Harpo's. Not having much money as a student I used to go there because they had a promotion between five and eight. They had a machine with a spinning dial with a couple of offers on it: 'Half Price', or 'Free'. You pressed a button and stopped the dial, and they charged you whatever the dial said. It was set up so that most people landed on 'Full price', but because I had such a good sense of rhythm, I could always stop it in the right place. Every time I went in there they would groan:

'Oh no, here he comes again!'

For a while people would encourage me to go in there with them to get free drinks, but I had to stop doing it because Harpo's would have closed down. In the end they got rid of the machine - probably because of me.

The Coleherne Arms was Freddie Mercury's favourite and Princess Diana lived across the road from there. I met her, twice. One night I was working late at the College practising something on the piano on one of the top floors. I had a recital coming up and it wasn't going well. It was dark outside and starting to rain and not being able to play the piece was making me miserable, so I just decided to call it a day. I didn't think there was anyone else left in the building apart from the caretaker waiting to lock up.

I went downstairs and was making my way out along a corridor when two big burly men suddenly pushed by and pinned me up against the wall, demanding to know what I was doing there. I thought I was being attacked, but then Princess Diana came round the corner in a yellow polka-dot dress. She introduced herself and apologised for her security men, told them to leave me alone. She was very nice and made sure I was all right before she went on her way. It was such a brief moment but she really was lovely, and I went home much happier. She was President of the College so she must have been at a meeting with the Director or something.

The second time we didn't actually meet properly. Kevin and I and some friends were in the Royal Vauxhall Tavern; it's a former Music Hall that has turned into a gay club with drag acts. We used to see Kenny Everett in there quite often, sometimes with Cleo Rocos. This particular night Cleo was there with a couple of other people, one of whom was dressed in a sailor suit: white trousers, a striped blue and white top, a sailor's hat and wearing dark glasses.

I don't think I knew who it was straight away, but it was obviously a woman dressed as a man. I realised it was Princess Diana because her hair was quite distinctive even under the sailor's cap, and being there with Cleo Rocos fitted because they were known to be friends. When you spotted it, it was quite obvious who she was, but no-one could care less really. She was clearly having a good time, smiling away, thinking she was incognito, and everyone left her alone.

There's a coincidence about her sailor suit though. A few years later Scott and I inadvertently found ourselves in a rather dodgy club run by Suzie Kruger. Suzie is quite extreme, famous for hosting alternative party nights in London. On this particular night she let us into her club for free as we had a mutual friend with us. We had gone along for a bit of fancy-dress fun, but what we found there was quite an eye-opener, but there was a wonderful atmosphere. Very freeing.

I was wearing a sailor suit although this one was an all-in-one jump-suit, not trousers and top like Diana's had been, but when I saw it in the shop I thought of her immediately. But it wasn't the best of parties so after a while Scott and I decided to just go home. We came out, got into the back of a taxi, and as we drove along the news came over the radio that Diana had been injured in a car crash. Everyone remembers where they were when they heard about her accident. That's where I was: on the back seat of a taxi, wearing a sailor suit just like hers.

KEVIN

The evening we saw Diana in the Royal Vauxhall was the night I got mugged. I left the Tavern a bit earlier than my friends. Everyone else had been sniffing poppers in the club and being young and naïve I didn't know what that was so I hadn't had anything, although I had had rather a lot to drink. I do remember thinking that it might not be safe for anyone to come to the bus stop with me, because they weren't in any state to get back in, so I decided I would just get a taxi home.

[S: I was not sniffing poppers!]

I was wearing a rather extravagant lacy shirt and some rainbow trousers. Oh, and the zebra skin shoes, so I may have been a bit conspicuous. I had just moved to Streatham and I asked a mini-cab driver outside how much that would cost. He said it would be six pounds, which was fine because that was exactly how much money I had.

He drove me only a short distance around the corner, and then stopped and several lads got into the car with me and pinned me down. I was drunk enough to not panic but I was very confused about what was happening. The car stopped again, and they dragged me out of the car and marched me to a cash machine. Somehow, even though I didn't give them my number they managed to get sixty pounds out; it's still a mystery how they managed that. And then they pushed me back into the car again and held me down.

It's all a bit of a blur what happened after that until we got to a housing estate where there was another car full of youths waiting for us. I've chosen not to think about this since, but I have a memory that one of them said:

'That's for the body.'

That may be a dream that has replayed the incident in my mind since then, but that's the phrase that comes back to me. I do know there was a bigger gang of youths waiting there and there definitely seemed to be a purpose for taking me to this particular place. If there hadn't been, they could have just thrown me out after they got the money from the machine.

It was obvious I was in big danger, but I kept calm. One of them went to do something at the back of the car and for a split second they let go of me. I took my chance and ran. I got to a big fence and threw myself over, and then there was another fence, and another and I felt I was going to be OK if I could just keep one fence ahead of them. Then there was a brick wall, and though I had no idea what was on the other side and how far the drop was, I just went over it as fast as I could.

Luckily, the ground was soft on the other side and I landed in a bush. I just rolled over and lay still and stayed there for ages until I could no longer hear them running around looking for me. Goodness knows how long I was there, but eventually I crawled out and found a phone box. I didn't want to phone anyone in my family and frighten them, so I called a friend even though he was miles away in the Midlands. I had no idea where I was, so he asked what I could see. The only thing I could read was a shop front for a taxi company so I gave him the number, and he said he would find out where it was and call the police.

I couldn't stay in the phone box so I ran across to the mini-cab office, got inside and banged the door shut behind me. An elderly Jamaican gentleman was sitting behind the counter. I explained what had happened and that the police were coming to rescue me because I had no money for another cab. The first thing he said was:

'Were they black?'

His sad eyes showed the disappointment behind his question, so despite everything I'd been through I told him that perhaps just one of them might have been – even though I knew they all were.

When the police arrived, they were just irritated that I couldn't really remember much about what had happened. They told me to get another taxi home.

'I've already tried that,' I said. 'It didn't work out, and now I've got no money.'

Reluctantly they put me in the back of the car and drove me home to Streatham.

Anyone could have been the victim of a mugging like that, but there was definitely an additional vulnerability about being young and gay in London in those days. I used to have a taxi driver bothering me around South Kensington just before this happened. The same man used to pull up beside me and ask if I wanted to get in the back when I hadn't been hailing him. I refused every time, and in the end I managed to get his number and reported him to the police. Some weeks later they wrote to me saying they'd taken away his licence.

STEVEN

I was very aware of those kinds of dangers and could easily have come to a very sticky end. There was a man on Gaydar, the dating website, who used to message me quite a lot when I was in South London, and ask me to go and meet him. It's fortunate that I never did because he turned out to be Stephen Port, the serial killer who used to lure men to his flat, give them GHB and then kill them.

He wasn't the only unpleasant character who tried to get me. Years later, after we'd moved to Edinburgh, I used to get messages on the Grindr app from Darryl Rowe – he was the one who was convicted of deliberately infecting people with HIV. I was never tempted to meet him though because he came across as being odd and very rude.

One thing I never did was drugs. I purposely didn't stay around anyone that did them. I treasured life and music too much to waste my time with people who put everything at risk. I was on a high already with my work and excited about the future.

Looking back I feel a little embarrassed about the importance we put on gay bars, festivals and Gay Pride and how we made such a fuss about our sexuality. I suppose it was a reaction to what we had been through as teenagers, hiding everything and being made to feel out of place. It was already a quarter of a century since laws against homosexuality had been repealed but there was still so much prejudice around that we felt we had to make ourselves seen and acknowledged. Perhaps we did need to do that: without our attitude, life for young gay men might not be as it is today.

Obviously the gay scene was a very big part of our lives in Earl's Court during our college years and after. And the background to that, of course, was that this was right at the height of the Aids epidemic. For us and our gay friends that period was all about avoiding that dreadful disease. In some ways we were probably quite lucky – not just with avoiding serial killers. I often wonder whether, if I had been a few years older, I'd still be here or whether I would have succumbed to the disease myself. Just a short time before I became active no-one was aware that they had to be so careful about it, but fortunately by the time I went to college everyone knew how important it was to be safe. I was just too young in the mid to late 1980s to be at serious risk at the most dangerous time. I wasn't up to much then - just fumbling with friends, thankfully.

We both knew a lot of people who contracted HIV – not all of them through sex. We had a friend called Andrew who was a fine composer at the College and was a haemophiliac. He was given the virus in a blood transfusion. And of course, not everyone died: we know a few people who were diagnosed more than twenty years ago and have come through it. One friend is in the fortunate position of having the genetic mutation known as Delta 32, which somehow prevents HIV getting in and destroying the immune system.

A few months ago, we were reminded of how hard those times were when a young lad of twenty-five died of Aids in Edinburgh. He hadn't been tested for HIV to start with because people thought he had contracted MRSA, but eventually he was diagnosed as being positive. Even then it didn't seem likely that it was going to be a problem because the treatment is so good these days and someone with HIV dying is now quite rare in this country. But the disease is still there: Aids could rear its head again.

The very fact that it is now a huge shock if someone dies of Aids, brings back how normal it seemed then. Death was something that had lost its power to shock in those days; it was something we were aware of all the time. We were continuously living with the fear of catching the death sentence. Even in the gay community where you might expect sympathy and understanding, we were all wary around anyone who had caught it. You instinctively knew when you met someone who had contracted Aids, because there was a look about them. Even though you had been told repeatedly that the virus wasn't airborne it did feel as though there was a 'dirtiness' about the people who had caught the disease. It wasn't just sex that had to be safe, Aids affected all of our everyday lives. In bars, you wouldn't put your drink down on a table because you wouldn't want it to be picked up by someone who was infected.

And then if a friend tested positive, you just felt quite hopeless about it as though they had transformed into a different person, someone who had crossed to the other side. What could you say?

STEVEN

From the early 1990s onwards, much of the gay scene in London started shifting from Earl's Court to Soho; a lot of gay pubs and clubs opened there around that time. We went to the opening nights of the famous Village Bar, the Rupert Street Bar, Halfway to Heaven, Kudos and The Admiral Duncan. And there were others. The Soho scene was busy every night of the week and it was tremendous fun. We would also go to the Black Cap in Camden Town on Tuesdays quite regularly to see the legendary Reg Bundy doing his drag act show "Her Imperial Highness Regina Fong".

The idea behind the Fong character was that she was a Russian princess, the last of the Romanovs who escaped during the Russian Revolution. She had an enormous following and the pub would be packed for her madcap show where she lip-synced to famous movie clips and involved the audience in the songs and sound effects. We were part of the huge crowd of 'Fongettes', clog-dancing to A Windmill in Old Amsterdam. Reg took the show to Edinburgh and also had a long run at the Bloomsbury Theatre, but he died in 2003. The legend lives on though and people still post videos and stories about Regina Fong in a Fongettes' Facebook group.

KEVIN

One of the people we knew from Manhattan's was Michael Topping. He was a big part of the cabaret circuit in London and had many guises. When I first met him he called his act Dream Topping and later he invented a lesbian character called the Countess Malitza Von Hove. Some of his costume choices were rather dubious; he'd wear see-through dresses, leaving nothing to the imagination. For some time he worked with another chap called Patrick Fyffe who had a successful drag act as Perri St Clair. Perri featured in the film version of Steptoe and Son as a misguided love interest for Albert Steptoe.

Patrick was keen for them to take their act on tour, but Michael was unwilling to commit because he was also involved in another double act with a rather camp lady called Doreen, and this was where most of his work was coming from. Instead, he put Patrick in touch with a Scot called George Logan, and those two became 'Hinge and Bracket', and became hugely popular in the 1970s and 1980s.

Years later I asked George what made them choose Hinge and Bracket as a name. He said he didn't really know, and that he'd really have preferred for them to be called 'Benson and Hedges'. Looking back, I remember Michael Topping suggesting 'Mary Hinge' would be a good stage name, and I suspect this spoonerism was probably the origin of Dr Evadne Hinge's name.

It was Michael Topping who told me that Regina Fong had died. He called me and said:

'I'm in trouble.'

'Why?'

'I've had a phone call to say Regina has died, and that Titti and Sandra were with her as she passed, and all I said was: "This is three grown men."'

Regina Fong Sandra and Titti le Camp were such close friends that they had bought houses next door to each other. Although the drag queens were always in competition and used to bitch about one another, they were also a close-knit community and mutually supportive. They were always at the forefront of raising money for any Aids charity; many of them did at least one charity gig a week. There was no financial support coming from the Conservative Government, so we in the gay community just had to get our act together and raise the money needed to get the care our friends needed.

The drag circuit was a big part of the London scene - it still is. I used to like going to pub called The Sebright Arms in Bethnal Green where they would have a variety night on Thursday which attracted a lot of the main acts on the circuit, but also include other singers, comedians and what was known as "spesh acts". What we do now would have qualified as a "spesh act" back then.

There was no entrance charge for these events, so there was always a big crowd in. The pub was run by a very big guy called Colin Devereaux who doubled as Dockyard Doris, one of London's most famous drag queens. Doris was very much a throwback to the Music Hall years and wore big wigs and gowns with feather boas; she was an absolute tribute to Marie Lloyd at the height of her fame.

Colin/Doris drank a lot and didn't really look after himself and he died at the age of fifty. The funeral service was at St Peter's church and was like an East End gangster occasion, with a horse-drawn carriage and flowers all over the coffin. Amongst the mourners were a host of celebrities including Danny La Rue and also several officers from the Inland Revenue, who were big fans even though he hadn't paid his taxes. The eulogy was given by one of his star performers, Phil Starr, who had to keep apologising to the vicar for saying 'F***!'

Another drag queen we first saw at Manhattan's was Lily Savage (Paul O'Grady), who was the only one that really made the leap to wider fame. I did wonder if this was going to be possible because there was a lot of swearing in the act. His partner Murphy managed him and together they persuaded some unlikely venues like the London Palladium to take a risk on Lily, but it really paid off. Soon places were anxious to book Lily; having him on the bill almost guaranteed the place would be packed out. And as a bonus Lily would only do about fifteen minutes so the punters would be back spending money at the bar as soon as the act was finished.

I worked for a whole year with Maisie Trollette. David Raven is still performing as 'Maisie' well into his eighties, and he's probably now the world's oldest drag queen. He has the same genius capacity for telling gags that Bob Monkhouse used to have and he's also a very generous performer. As a second business he ran a guest house in Brighton that he used to promote during the show:

'The other day, when I was leaving Rowland House – very good rates - if you're outside Brighton the dialling code is 01273...'

There was one big gig that Maisie and I did in a boys' public school. It was a lunch time function to raise funds for Brighton Cares with Peter James the crime writer as guest of honour, and as well as Maisie and me the other acts were Christopher Biggins and Simon Fanshawe. I was doing a Victor Borge style routine where I played Happy Birthday in any style audience members chose.

Maisie started off:

'Welcome to this all-boys' school! Kevin and I have already been around the dormitory, sniffing all the sheets!'

Simon announced that he'd been educated at a single sex boys' public school.

'On my first day, Dad told me to watch the older boys. So, I did exactly that for the next seven years!'

STEVEN

In 1991 I met a man called Rob Cooper at a party; we chatted and got on very well. He was a well-paid computer programmer at the time and had a lovely house in Ealing and a sports car. There was no physical attraction between us, but we became very good friends and often went out to concerts together;- he was very much into classical music. I was having difficulty finding somewhere to live that could not only house my grand piano but would be a place where I could practise for eight hours a day without annoying people.

Rob introduced me to a friend of his called Alan who had a very large house near Lammas Park in Ealing. Rob lived there for a while when he worked with Alan. The house was lovely but rather run-down, and it was obvious that Alan was a bit of a hoarder. He happily offered to let me move in with my piano and practise to my heart's content and suggested a rent of £200 a month, which was very cheap. The only problem was the house was absolutely infested with fleas as Alan had five cats. Scott moved in shortly after and it was the perfect place to live. Buut, much as we tried to get the flea infestation under control, we just couldn't.

Alan was very supportive and enjoyed the fact that the house was full of music again. This was the place which had previously been home to Jimmy Somerville, the singer with Bronski Beat and The Communards. Alan used to tell us that Jimmy couldn't sing, and that he was always asking him to shut up! Many musicians had come and gone through that front door before I arrived and it was there that I found the large pink object that I mutilated in our kitchen. Chris Lowe was still working in the Ealing pet shop while my friend Rob was in the house with them.

Scott and I lived in that house for many years, and we kept it clean and redecorated it for Alan. Somehow, we stopped paying rent, but Alan didn't seem to mind as long as we kept the place nice, and we often cooked for him. We lived in Ealing for around nine years and during that time many of my friends stayed at Alan's house with us, including my sister Dawn who moved in for a year whilst getting her London career off the ground. Alan was really very generous to everyone, and I'm still in touch with him to this day.

We had a lovely friend called Neil who was a gardener and he helped us with the garden at Alan's house. We would go out with him lots of times to the West Five piano bar when Kevin was playing there, and then stay on to dance to Steps at the disco. Towards the end of our time living in that area we noticed that he started to look quite ill. We took him aside to discuss it, and he said he had already decided to go and have an HIV test. I was quite anxious about him and I called to find out if he had got the result.

He said: 'Oh, I'm fine. It was negative.'

I felt so relieved for him. He was such a lovely friend.

Scott, Rob and I decided to club together to buy somewhere of our own. It was a little tricky getting a mortgage at first; life insurance companies were still asking about sexuality on their forms because of the threat of Aids. Most gay men were just lying about it, but we found out that the Nationwide Building Society had dropped the question from their forms, so we opted for them. We bought a large, rather swanky penthouse apartment in an old converted Victorian school in Kings Cross.

Neil came to our flat-warming party, but because we had moved away, we rather lost touch with him after that. The next I heard of him, a year later, was that he had died. His test had been positive, but he couldn't admit to anyone, even himself, that he had the virus. He was so ashamed of his result that he lied to me and tried to ignore the illness, until it was too late to be able to get any treatment. It was as though he felt he had let us all down by catching it. I hate to think that he thought I wouldn't have been supportive. I was devastated when I heard about his death, and now feel I should have noticed that he wasn't telling the complete truth.

Too many people just disappeared like that. Remember, this was a time before mobile phones and social media and it wasn't so easy to keep in contact with friends. But when anyone stopped being seen regularly, it became normal to assume that they were gone.

KEVIN

I remember a friend who tested positive. He worked behind a bar in a pub we went to. People would go up to him and say:

'Sorry mate', in the same way you'd say, 'I'm sorry for your loss.' when someone is grieving.

In reality they were saying: "I'm sorry that you're going to die soon.'

And then, as there was really nothing more to be said, they would follow up with:

'Pint of Stella and a packet of scampi fries, please.'

Fortunately, that particular friend has never had a day's sickness from it and is still very healthy thirty years later. But there was another barman I knew in Manhattan's who found he had contracted HIV and went home and killed himself.

Like Steven, I'm sure if we had been there a few years earlier we both would be dead by now, although I was almost celibate in those days. I never went in for casual sex because I wanted to find romance. Although most of my friends didn't expect me to reach thirty for another reason - I drank so much.

I met a Texan called Art at the Body Positive self-help group in Earl's Court. He was the chaplain at Windsor Castle but was also heavily involved with counselling people living with HIV and Aids and he needed help with fund raising. I would organise my friends – including Steven – to perform at concerts for him.

I especially remember a concert we did at a vigil held in Windsor for the Thames Valley Aids support group. On this occasion candles were lit for everybody who had died in their small community: hundreds upon hundreds of tiny flickering flames. There were so many people being affected by this awful illness, yet it seemed that the government weren't bothered. They thought it was only killing off the one part of the population they didn't approve of anyway: Section 28 had told us that.

But that wasn't even true; one of the most shocking things about going to these benefit events was seeing ill young women, with their children. The newspapers and television had made everyone believe that it was only a male illness, but as a nineteen-year-old I was meeting young mothers who were infected and who probably only had months to live.

A friend of mine, Angela, was volunteering at the Royal Free Hospital, where most of the victims in London were transferred to die. She took me with her a few times and it was almost too much to comprehend. I was in a hospital where the wards were filled with young men of our own age. But these were young men with dementia, young men with diseases that were only usually only found in the elderly, and in animals. It was as if we were in some apocalyptic movie.

Angela was as gorgeous and glamourous as Princess Diana and the eyes of these living corpses would light up whenever she walked in. She made them feel human. Her role was to act as a surrogate mother to the many patients whose own mothers had cut them off and disowned them. It was quite common for these victims to be ostracised by their families while they were dying, but in a way, it was just the sad continuance of everything they had been used to. Because homosexuality had been illegal for so much of their lives, the community had shut them out when they were growing up, and as they lay dying even their families would have nothing to do with them.

On one visit a young lad came over to speak to us. He looked like a skeleton with a thin veil of skin, but he told us that he was beating this disease, he was sure he was winning. The next time we went we heard he had died days after. Another time we found an Italian friend called Leno, who begged us to find some strong drugs for him so that he could kill himself. Leno had been such a vibrant human being, really naughty and full of life, and the last time I had seen him before this was also with Angela. He was telling us about picking men up on Hampstead Heath, even though Angela was shouting at him:

'Stop this! Now!'

He would just dismiss this with a flick of his arm: his usual Italian diva gesture of defiance. Back then he had been a good-looking guy who was always the heart and soul of every party and now here he was, wanting so much to die.

We would witness the fatal decline so many times. We knew a dancer called Christopher who had been very successful on Broadway. He turned up on Angela's doorstep in Finchley Road one day, sobbing because he just wanted to know what was wrong with him and the doctors weren't being helpful. She took him to The Royal Free and had him tested, and we soon got the news everyone dreaded. In hospital he wanted us to keep visiting right to the end, to keep his connection to the world of the performing arts and so we would go day after day, hoping this wouldn't be the last time.

Living with the fear of death had a definite effect on the culture we were a part of, and the way we felt about the lives we led. We didn't really react with surprise that we were the potential victims of this horrible new plague. It had become so ingrained all through our childhood and our teenage years, that we were the ones who were 'wrong'. We were the ones who were hiding who and what we were, and everything around us spelled out that the Aids epidemic was a backlash and proof that everyone else was 'right'.

But for many of us the disease intensified the need to be seen and acknowledged. If being 'different' was the reason we could die young then that difference was something to be displayed, not hidden. The reason there was so much flamboyance in the gay world was that we simply didn't know whether we were going to be alive in three years' time, so it really didn't matter who was shocked by our behaviour. If there was anger, it was expressed in an attitude of: 'Leave me alone to be as outrageous as I want, while I'm still here!'

We were like hunchbacks who were so sick of people trying to ignore our malformed bodies that we put glitter over our humps, and loudly celebrated them! And if people didn't acknowledge our presence - then we added another hump, and decorated that, and forced everyone to see us as we were.

All of that genuinely angry posturing has gone now; we are not in such danger anymore. We see younger drag queens playing the same stereotype sometimes and it just comes across as bitchiness. It's quite obvious that they can't really have the same feeling about the gay community's position in society that we did back then. Happily, for them, they haven't had to live with the constant threat of catching an incurable disease the way we did, and it is a good thing that they don't have an understanding of where that sincere 'F*** YOU!' anger came from.

Being gay is still seen by even some of those who are not homophobic as something that is a bit amusing, light hearted, harmless fun. But homophobia is still there, alongside all the other forms of bigotry and hatred and nothing will change until we get an administration that applies zero tolerance to all forms of hate.

KEVIN

Some years ago we were rehearsing at the Hotel Mimosa in Magaluf when a man came over and chatted to us about his love of music, in particular the band Queen. It was a pleasant conversation, but I had a feeling that at any moment he was going to say something hateful. He didn't disappoint:

'It's a shame what happened to Freddie Mercury, but I suppose it served him right for being a poof'.

Chapter 5

In which Kevin hides from a conductor and sets fire to his employer's eyebrows, and Steven nearly makes it into the Big Brother house.

KEVIN

It's not every day you find yourself in a bush hiding from one of the most famous musicians this country has to offer!

One of the first jobs I got when I left the Royal College was through David, Steven's boyfriend before Scott. David is a great viola player and at that time he was in charge of the viola section of the Young Musicians' Symphony Orchestra. Through him I got a chance to meet James Blair, their Principal Conductor and I ended up working for him as the manager responsible for booking musicians to play in the orchestra's concerts. James is an entertaining character, but he is also quite difficult to work for. He was well known for calling or sending faxes at all hours, demanding attention as soon as something came into his head.

Frequently he would phone me in the middle of the night, wanting to talk about who we were booking. There was one night when he kept calling and I'd had enough.

'Kevin, it's James. Have we sorted out the horn section yet?'

'James, it's three in the morning. Leave me alone!'

I slammed the phone down. He called straight back.

'You know what, James? You can take your orchestra and shove it up your arsehole!'

He didn't care: he kept on calling back, and I kept on hanging up on him. When I stopped answering I heard him leaving a message on the answerphone in a squeaky voice:

'Oooh Kevin, sweet Kevin, how could you be so nasty to James?'

It was so funny that I actually warmed to him, and he soon became one of my dearest friends.

We had a number of famous musicians appearing as soloists at our concerts and I had to book the musicians to play alongside them. One night I had organised a concert at the Barbican for the YMSO to perform with Julian Lloyd Webber on the cello with James conducting. My transvestite friend Brian/Fergie let me know that he/she had booked seats right in the middle of the dress circle, the seats that are usually reserved for the Royal Family or other people of any importance.

So as not to cause embarrassment or confusion to anyone she might encounter doing a last-minute adjustment, Fergie would always leave it to the final moment to go to the Ladies' loo before a concert started. But this time she left it a little too late.

Just as James led Julian Lloyd Webber on to the stage, the audience started clapping and in the same moment, Fergie emerged from the toilet at the back of the dress circle wearing a huge bright white ball gown. She made her way down to her prominent and very visible seat, her progress precisely matching the soloist and conductor taking up their positions on the stage. Julian sat down to start performing Elgar's Cello Concerto, and James Blair raised his baton to the air.

But now the audience's attention had been diverted to Fergie and, presumably under the impression that this aging transvestite was someone of the status of Princess Michael of Kent, they carried on clapping. Julian and James couldn't understand why they hadn't stopped. Fergie, realising that nearly two thousand people were applauding her, gave a regal wave, curtsied and then took her seat.

One of the last jobs I had to deal with in my time at the YMSO, was finding players for an orchestra to support soloists in the Yehudi Menuhin violin competition. Menuhin was the patron of the orchestra and came along every year to conduct and judge the competition. Given his position in the musical world it should have been a great experience, but the truth was that every concert that Menuhin conducted with the orchestra almost turned into a disaster. When he conducted *Belshazzar's Feast* there was the longest rendition of the word 'Slain' in history because he made the chorus hold the note for so long before he finally brought his baton down, and let them draw breath.

On the morning of a concert at the Barbican in front of Princess Alexandra, Menuhin sent a message to say that he wanted to play the full national anthem with all the verses as a piece of music. James Blair told him:

'You can't, the protocol says she's only allowed a certain number of bars because she's not the Queen.'

But Menuhin started sending James faxes with drawings of his hand holding the baton, asking which he should use for the upbeat and which for the downbeat. James said to me:

'Have you seen these diagrams!? He's supposed to be concentrating on the Bartok for tonight and he's fussing about how he should conduct the national anthem!'

[S: Orchestral students in the College used to say that if Menuhin was conducting, the best thing to do was not look at him. They just kept their heads down and ignored all his waving-the-baton antics. If you tried to follow him, everyone would go out of time. There was more chance of finishing the piece if everyone just winged it.]

When Menuhin got to the rehearsal hall, he wasted lots of precious time regaling the orchestra with anecdotes about his personal friendship with Bartok. He really was appalling as a conductor, but he got away with it when he was working with good musicians. That bubble was about to burst.

The Yehudi Menuhin violin competition was being held in Southend and I was supposed to be finding a backing orchestra for the competitors. But try as I might I couldn't get anyone good to commit to doing it. For one thing no-one was going to get paid (they were supposed to do it for the honour of working with Yehudi Menuhin), and everyone who had played for him before knew what it would be like so they really didn't want to do it.

Also that week my old friend John Wilson was hiring for his orchestra and anyone with any talent was holding off from committing to me because they were hoping to get a chance there. No sooner had I got a flautist to say they could come, than they were calling me back to say:

'I'm terribly sorry to do this to you, but I've now got a paid gig that night with John Wilson'.

I compiled the longest list of harp players ever. I went through absolutely everyone who had ever played a harp on stage anywhere in the country, and finally got one to turn up on the night. Every other instrument was almost as bad, and in the end, I just took anyone with a pulse who could hold an instrument the right way up. No-one had played together before, and luckily not many of them had previously had the pleasure of being conducted by Menuhin.

We arrived at the rehearsal, and I was just relieved to have bums on seats. Menuhin was there with his friends from the Moscow Conservatoire who were going to be his fellow judges, some seriously important people in the music world. The orchestra started up and much as I would like to be proud of what I had managed to assemble, it sounded simply appalling. It was much worse than the very worst kind of school orchestra.

James caught my eye and started mouthing:

'This sounds awful...'

I whispered back: 'I know...'

I looked across at the VIPs who were all wearing open-mouthed expressions of astonishment. James paused a second or two and then came back with:

'Shall we leave..?'

We slipped down out of view and started to crawl on hands and knees behind the chairs of the adjudicators. We didn't dare stand up until we got to the door, and then we escaped outside. A moment of 'what do we do now?' passed between us and then James said:

'It wouldn't be wrong if we had gone for a coffee during the rehearsal.'

We went out into Southend, and up the road and found a café. We had only just sat down at a table near the window when we saw Menuhin hurrying out of the concert hall, quite obviously looking for me to give me a bollocking. We jumped up, left the coffees on the table, ran outside, and managed to get ourselves hidden in the shrubbery before Menuhin got there. He was running up and down the street trying to find us, and I suddenly got a fit of the giggles. It just seemed so absurd to be crouched in a bush, hiding from the most famous musician in the world! I had probably spent a lot of my youth dreaming of the time when such a famous conductor would be that desperate to talk with me, but it hadn't quite worked out the way I'd imagined it.

James got out a packet of cigarettes and offered me one, maybe to settle our nerves. I got out a lighter and flicked it a little too close to his face, and his eyebrows caught fire. He got the giggles too; so, the pair of us were squatting in a flower bed, stifling laughter, amidst a dreadful smell of singed hair.

Fortunately, we weren't spotted, but we didn't dare show our faces at the concert that evening. James probably knew the aftermath was going to be bad so we decided the best way of coping with the situation was to go back to the hotel and start drinking. We were still sat at the bar when ashen-faced adjudicators started filing in later in the evening.

After the weekend I went into the office and heard James on the phone apologising to the backers for what they had witnessed. Yehudi had just cancelled a big tour of France that was supposed to follow the competition, even though it would have been the regular orchestra, not my army of bit-part players. I could only hear one side of the conversation but there is one line that sticks in my memory: James telling someone:

'Well. The trouble with Menuhin is he thinks he is God. And unfortunately, a lot of people still believe in God!'

STEVEN

When I left college, I actually went along with the traditional style of performing that we have rejected now. I genuinely thought I would spend my life walking onto the platform looking miserable, and I would have been quite happy to do it because I loved the music, and I liked the idea of being up there on the stage playing the piano. I certainly didn't have any intention of putting any humour into concerts.

I was lucky enough to be invited to do some piano duet recitals at the Fairfield Hall in Croydon with Peter Katin, a very famous British pianist. Looking back, I didn't enjoy those evenings at all because I was too nervous. It was entirely my fault because I was never properly prepared. I had always been the kid who did his homework on the bus on the way to school, and all my rehearsals for those concerts were very last-minute. I've learnt the lesson since and I can't bear to work that way now. I used to have a recurring nightmare of sitting on the stage with the orchestra playing the opening bars, and then realising I'd forgotten to learn the piece.

Working with Peter was a fantastic start for a classical musician's performance career. To this day he is probably the most recorded British pianist in history. He had been my teacher for a year, and he was a really lovely man. He was also quite brave in that he was campaigning for legalising homosexuality back in the sixties when it was still illegal. He was even banned by Tunbridge Wells's council from performing there because of his position on gay rights.

Even though he was really well-off he lived in a tiny house in Croydon into which he had managed to cram two Steinway D grand pianos. You had to be something of a contortionist – and thin – to squeeze past them to get to the kitchen. His neighbours must have been very tolerant to put up with the noise when those two instruments were going together.

He only had one leg, so there were times when I would have to go out to Croydon for my lesson or to practise with him, but the College were happy to pay for a taxi to take him all the way into South Kensington so mostly we worked together there. I'm afraid things went a bit sour towards the end; he seemed to have fallen for me a bit. He kept sending me faxes which I gradually began to ignore, and he didn't like that. We didn't work together again.

We found out several years later that Peter had been coming to some of our concerts. He sent me a very nice message to say that he admired what we did and had really enjoyed our show, particularly our version of *Carnival of the Animals.* It brought back happy memories of performing the piece himself in the 1960s, with Dame Flora Robson doing the narrative. I'm so glad he got in touch. It made me feel much better about how things had been left between us. This was a nice happy resolution before he died.

I quickly realised that the air is a bit thin 'up there' at the higher levels of concert piano performance; there just isn't enough work to go around for everyone who wants to make a living out of it. And apart from anything else I had discovered that it is rather lonely performing on your own on stage. There was a definite feeling of wanting to be a part of something, rather than being a solo performer. I did carry on playing professionally, I didn't give up completely, but there is no money in playing regular concerts. All those Russian and Polish highflyers we used to know at the College, the ones who were going to be the stand-out concert pianists, even they were just chasing the chance to play for fifty quid at St Mary's Abbott Kensington every now and again.

The obvious alternative to performance was teaching people to play, which I did for a while and had many young local students. Word spread quickly in Ealing that I was a fun teacher and I really enjoyed inspiring young musicians. I had too many to cope with at one point and had to have a cull of the ones that didn't practise enough.

The thing about teaching was having to go into people's homes and be polite about whatever you found there. I was asked to teach a little girl in a nice house in Ealing, very middle class. The first time I went there, I knocked at the door and the mother answered it, obviously having made a big effort – she was looking gorgeous, all nicely dressed. The little girl who I was going to teach came running through the hallway excitedly, and said to me:

'My Mummy's just had a big poo, and it smells awful!'

I'd never met them before, and the mother's face went puce. I bet the little girl was in trouble when I left.

Then there was a little boy called Christopher who kept trying to kiss me. He was about ten and the son of a TV producer who lived in a very nice penthouse flat. In every other way he was quite charming, but he would keep grabbing hold of me and trying to kiss me whenever his mother was out of the room. In the end it became so much of a problem that I had to write her a letter and say that I was giving up teaching; I just had to lie. I had a distinct feeling that he had been doing the same thing with someone else before me. I do know she had just been through a difficult divorce, so there were probably attachment problems for him. He was actually a really talented young lad, and perhaps he went on to be a very good pianist.

Don't get me wrong, I really enjoyed teaching, but I knew I couldn't do that and nothing else, so I started to look for something I enjoyed more and decided to have a go at being an actor.

KEVIN

I never really took up piano teaching. In fact I think I only ever had one pupil, a lad called Harry. He was very nice but his family were quite crazy. They owned a very famous dance group called the Jiving Lindy Hoppers, and through teaching Harry I ended up working for them.

The family dynamics were a bit bizarre. Harry's mum was Monica, but his dad Terry was with Monica's sister, Eileen. Eileen's daughter Jenny was not only Harry's cousin but also his half-sister. It was a rather bohemian arrangement and, before I went there to teach Harry, they all used to live with a chap called John Bird and his family in something like a commune. John Bird went on to set up *The Big Issue*. When I was with them it was all very happy, but I gather it turned sour later. The Lindy Hoppers troupe was run from within the house.

I got involved with them when they were converting Berthold Brecht's *In the Jungle of Cities* into a jazz ballet, and they asked me to write the music for it. As a ballet it was ahead of its time, and we were criticised for things that are now quite commonplace in the dance world. The story is essentially a war between city types and country folk and the climax was a scene where the two male protagonists danced a tango together before a lynch mob came. The audiences sometimes felt a bit uncomfortable at these two very masculine straight guys dancing together – not realising that the tango was originally written as a form of competitive dance for two men. We set it in a boxing ring.

The Brecht Society wanted us to give them a copy of the score. They said we couldn't tour the show unless they had copyright over the music. I sent them a message saying that unfortunately I couldn't supply the score, because I'd never written it down. I'd dictated it to all the musicians, and they'd learnt it off by heart. The Brecht Society couldn't work out a way of copyrighting something that only existed in my head and the others' memories, so we didn't hear any more about it.

This was no accident. It meant that the company could only employ me and our group of musicians, because without us nobody could reproduce the music. It was a year's worth of work and doing that meant that none of us could be sacked. Working that way is not uncommon; it has the benefit that no-one can get their hands on your work very easily. The downside is that, if nothing is written down, the composer doesn't have the copyright either. If someone wants to come along and steal what you've done, there is nothing you can do to prove it was originally yours. For my own protection I took a recording of one of the performances of the show and mailed it registered post to myself, and it remains unopened.

After that and after a terrible episode in my life, I spent some time as a film composer; I wrote music for some of the worst films ever made. We found one of them in a bargain bin in a shop in Guatemala recently, a film called *Never Play with the Dead* which is, of course, some great advice. I did try to treat all the films with the respect they deserved, which, in retrospect, wasn't very much. There was another film called *Slayers* which was so badly acted that I had to turn the volume down while I watched it.

Throughout this time, I was also playing background music in bars, restaurants and hotels. One of those was Tom Kenwright's Italian-style restaurant Azzurro which he opened in the heart of Soho in the mid 1990s. Tom's brother is Bill Kenwright who, apart from being the Chairman of Everton football club, is one of the most important theatre producers in the country. He's also well known for paying the least amount possible to anyone involved with any of his productions. The joke in the West End was that if you managed to get a part in one of Bill Kenwright's shows you needed another job to fund it. And when there is a change in the cast of *Blood Brothers,* Bill saves money by not getting new posters printed. He just has the old head chopped off and pasted over with the new face.

Tom became a great friend when I played for him, and his restaurant was frequented by the stars of his brother's productions and other well known legends. I spent many nights drinking there with likes of Victor Spinetti, Jenny Seagrove and Marty Feldman's widow, Loretta.

One night playing in the restaurant I thought my big break had arrived at last. Larry Adler used to eat there, and quite often he would get his harmonica out and we would play duets together in the restaurant. After one of those times, he said to me:

'How would you like to play on my next album?'

I was thrilled, and said that if we were going to be playing together, I would really like to compose a piece of music for it.

'Absolutely!' he said.

He went on to tell me stories about knowing Rachmaninov, and Gershwin, of course, because he played *Rhapsody in Blue* on his harmonica. Gershwin told him that he played it as though it had been written for the instrument. But, he said, although he had known all these important people, he was always too nervous around them. He had wanted them to write pieces of music for him, but never had the courage to ask them, and no-one had ever offered. It seemed to please him that I wanted to compose something, so I went home that night and started to get something together for him.

And then before it was finished, he bloody died! Just as I was thinking I was going to be on Larry Adler's new album, and writing for it, he snatched it away from me by having cancer!

Another job I had was playing with a function band in the Green Room at the Cafe Royale in Piccadilly. It was the top cabaret venue in those days, and we were there to play after the star for the night had finished. We were following people like Eartha Kitt, Harold Melvin and the Blue Notes and Alan Price onto the stage. The place was frequented by some very colourful people from the London criminal gangs, and I met people who went by names like 'Brown-bread Fred' and 'You're Dead Foreman'. It turned out Larry Adler knew them all too! One of the people I drank with there most regularly was Gillian Burns, who was then the longest running Nancy in *Oliver!*, taking on the role originally created by her cousin Georgia Brown. It was a family of singing stars: her Dad was Raymond Burns who had a hit in the 1950s with a song called *Mobile*. I heard that the Richardson gangster family once kidnapped him – as a joke.

One evening David Soul, the actor and singer famous for *Starsky and Hutch* came in with Gillian. She got up to sing and asked me if I would accompany her on the grand piano. Later David, whom I'd never met before, came over and said he liked my playing, and explained that the reason he was in the Green Room that evening was because he was booked to perform there himself a few weeks later. He had just come in to check out the quality of the band. He apologised that he wouldn't need me because his Musical Director would be doing the piano accompaniment.

The band leader got very excited, and told us that the famous David Soul was going to hire us all and then, with a certain amount of pleasure born out of years of rivalry, added:

'Everyone except Kevin, that is.'

In fact, the precise opposite happened. David's Musical Director - Roger Webb - called in another evening and said David had changed his mind about having a band, and wanted a simpler accompaniment with me on keyboards.

On the night there was an absolute buzz about the place, because David hadn't performed in public as a singer for about a decade. Bill Kenwright got up and gave a speech describing David as a genius, something he never said lightly. The show was such a success that we went on to do a run of two weeks.

I stayed out of David's way that evening as I felt people were fawning over him, and I guessed he didn't really like that. It turned out to be the right move because when he wanted some down time, he came over to join me and a long and brilliant friendship was struck up which eventually led to me arranging the music for his production of Nick Darke's *The Dead Monkey*.

I was really excited that my first professional engagement as a composer and arranger was in a major West End theatre, with a big star. The opening night was amazing, and sitting near the front I saw people I knew from the past really surprised to see my name in the programme as being in charge of the music.

After that first performance of course, there was a champagne party and I found myself drinking with Mary-Ann and Jim (they'd invested in the production), Charles Aznavour and David Hemmings, really adding to my stock of names to drop! David taught me so much about the business - even how to sack someone kindly. He could be hard on me, but I took it. He knew what he wanted, and I respected him as a professional and enjoyed our friendship. David regarded Charles Aznavour as his surrogate father, having known him for many years and he has taken on Aznavour's passion and can be quite intensely serious about his performances.

But sadly, the production didn't last. *The Daily Mirror* critic, Matthew Wright, wrote a scathing review calling it the worst production he had ever seen and said that there were only forty-five people in the audience and some of them were laughing with derision at David.

It wasn't true, and Matthew Wright hadn't even been to see the show, but things like that are hard to get past in the London theatre, and the production ended, and that was the first and last time I wrote music for the West End. David successfully sued *The Daily Mirror* for libel, and they ended up paying out £170,000 but by then Matthew Wright had left to host his television show on Channel 5.

STEVEN

I had already dabbled in acting before I went into it seriously. Having completed a degree at the Royal College, there was no way I could get funding to do another few years studying acting so I took some training at the Bridewell Youth Theatre. This was where I first met my now good friend Shazia Mirza, while we were queuing up to audition. She has become a famous stand-up comic, one of the few Muslim comedians in the country, and back then she was eccentric, hilarious and never fully learnt her lines. In the actual performances when she didn't know the script, she would start making things up, and going into little comedy routines – even when they weren't appropriate.

I remember her suddenly throwing oranges and bananas around in the middle of a Schnitzler play. The audience loved it, although it was nothing to do with the work, which was not a comedy. Some of my acting teachers were there for that performance, and one of them came up to me afterwards and said:

'I've had a marvellous evening!'

I probably looked pleased, but he followed up with:

'But this wasn't it!'

He'd hated it, but at least he was honest.

This was in the late 1990s, way before Shazia got into proper comedy. I always thought she could have made it as a great actor, but she prefers to do her own thing rather than keeping to a script, and she is naturally a very funny comic.

I tried a couple of theatrical agencies without much success, but eventually I signed up with a cooperative agency where a group of actors looked after themselves. We knew each other's strengths, and we used to answer the phones and make the calls with the casting directors ourselves. We didn't take on too many actors: there were only fourteen of us. My boyfriend Scott and I created the website in the early days of the internet, and it is still being used after all these years. As an agency it worked extremely well and between us we were cast in some good plays touring all over the country.

One of them was Kevin Elyot's *My Night with Reg,* about a group of gay friends in which I had a ten-minute nude scene. One night at the Playhouse in Harlow, it was absolutely freezing. I was standing in the wings taking my clothes off for that scene and looked down and realised that my bits were so shrivelled with the cold that there wasn't much to see! I was desperately trying to get it all going - building up my part, as it were.

I was muttering:

'C'mon you b*st*rd!'

but nothing was working: I still looked like Barbie's boyfriend, Ken. We walked on, and the guy I was doing the scene with came on from the other side, and I was reassured because he was a worse sight than I was. One woman in the audience immediately went into fits of hilarity, and wouldn't stop screaming with laughter for the whole ten minutes! We were both desperately trying to take it seriously and probably should have just stopped and waited until they had her removed.

I like to think she was laughing at him. She probably was.

I had some other good little acting jobs. I was in a couple of episodes of Kathy Burke's *Gimme Gimme Gimme,* written by our old friend Jonathan Harvey and I worked with Ronnie Corbett in some adverts for Pizza Hut, and some other commercials for Fujitsu that were filmed at Silverstone race circuit. Those ones were nicely paid and, even better, I got to drive a Formula One race car which was great fun. They had to tailor the pod that you sit in specially to fit me.

Early in 2001 I saw an article about the second series of *Big Brother* and put myself up for it. They invited me and several others to a big house in

Russell Square in London for an audition. They got us to play games together to see how we coped being with lots of different types of people, especially how we worked in teams. At one point there was a huge ball of wool which we had to untangle together which led to big arguments, which I think is what they were looking for. They phoned me after that first audition and called me back for another session. In all I had to go back two or three times, progressing through the audition process.

It was evident that Endemol were looking for a gay boy character for the series, and in the end, it seemed the choice was between me and a lad called Brian Dowling. One of the questions they asked towards the end was 'Who do you fancy?' Brian said he fancied Kylie Minogue, and I said 'David Beckham' and the room seemed to go quiet. Looking back, I think they didn't want someone who was too confident as a gay. They wanted someone who was going to come out during the series.

In the end of course they went with Brian. At the time I was really disappointed, but in hindsight it wouldn't have been good for me. I think I would have hated being locked up in the house and I'm sure they made the right decision with Brian as he was more confident, charismatic and camp than me, and he managed to be everybody's friend. Also, he went on to win the series!

Around that time, I was picking up some voice work too. I was the voice of the cartoon character Pod in two series of *Pod's Mission* for the BBC. It was one of the most enjoyable jobs you could imagine, fantastic fun and something I found really easy to do. I have what is known in the business as 'a spotty voice', and even now I still sound like a teenage lad with acne.

One Christmas I was in a pantomime in Brighton with Dora Bryan. She was hilarious, and a fantastic actress and she had been quite a looker in her day, but this was towards the end of her life. I loved her performance in the film *A Taste of Honey,* so it was wonderful to be able to meet her and be on the same stage together.

While we were rehearsing, she spent all her time chatting to friends on her mobile phone. The rest of the cast were getting a bit fed up with it ringing so often, interrupting the scenes we are working on. It especially annoyed the Director, so he took her aside at the end of one day and said:

'Dora, you've got to stop bringing your phone into rehearsals with you.'

'Have I? Alright I won't bring it with me tomorrow!'

Next day we got through a full rehearsal with no phone ringing. At the end the director called us all together and thanked Dora, on behalf of us all, for leaving her phone at home.'

'Ooh no, I forgot about that! I've got it with me'.

She opened up her handbag and pulled out the TV remote control from home. When she got home her husband said he had been looking for it all day, because he had wanted to watch the cricket.

Chapter 6

In which Kevin establishes a Bohemian commune, falls in love and turns down an offer from Sidney Poitier

KEVIN

The morning after the mugging in the taxi, I woke up in the flat in Streatham feeling bruised and very scared. Being attacked was horrifying but, as I couldn't work out exactly where it had happened, what was most disturbing was that nowhere around there felt like a safe place to be.

Perhaps hoping to clear my head, I decided to take a walk around the one part of London where I always felt comfortable and free from danger. I went back to South Kensington, the area around the Royal College of Music. I was just walking around the streets trying to bring a little calmness into my mind, when I found myself in Cranley Gardens and realised that Anne Ballard, the Reverend Chaplain for the College, lived nearby. At that moment I was in need of a sympathetic ear.

Her house was known as 'St Peter's Parsonage' even though the church which stood next door was now no longer connected. St Peter's church had been declared redundant about twenty years previously and sold off and was now in use as an Armenian Orthodox church, called St Yeghiche. The parsonage was still owned by the local Diocese though. I knocked, and Anne came to the door.

'Oh my God, Kevin! You're an answer to my prayers! Here it is, the summer, the College is closed, and I've just been thinking that I don't know anybody in London. I was feeling really lonely, and now here you are! Come on in!'

I followed her in and started to explain about the attack the night before, how I was feeling rather vulnerable, and that I didn't know if I could ever feel safe where I was living any more.

'Well. I'm going to be away for six weeks, so would you like to come and live here and look after my cat Winston for me?'

And so that is what happened. While she was away I moved in, and when she came back from her travels, I asked:

'How long can I stay here? Because I need to be honest with you, I really am frightened to go back to Streatham.'

'Well, it is a very big house for just me, and I do get lonely here, so let's come to an agreement.' And my life was changed as easily as that.

It was indeed a very big house. Spread over two floors it had loads of rooms including what seemed like a ballroom and there were two massive kitchens. On one side stood the Armenian church, and on the other side, our neighbour was Nanette Newman. Bill Wyman lived across the road. I had moved into a nearly empty house in a very classy area, and I paid her about forty pounds a week to stay there.

I hadn't been there very long when Anne applied for another job and was appointed Precentor at the Cathedral Church of Christ in Oxford. This was at the time that I was working with James Blair and the Young Musicians' Symphony Orchestra and when she moved out I quite expected to have to find somewhere else to live, but it seemed reasonable to wait and see what the next College Chaplain thought about me being there.

It was decided that the West London Diocese could manage without a College chaplain, and she was never replaced. From time to time young curates would be given a temporary home in the parsonage but otherwise they seemed to have forgotten about the building and that I was there, so I just stayed. In all it was more than three years that I was there, and I lived completely rent free. It was far too big a house to be empty, so I started to invite people to come and stay with me.

It became something of a bohemian commune. Over the three years I think I allowed more than thirty people to join me. Some of them were friends, but most of them were just people we encountered who needed a place to stay for a while - just as I had done. There was a couple called Shauna and Peter who were there much of the time, and they once described their life in the house as like living in the *Rocky Horror Show*. It really was quite an outrageous time, and I was drinking a lot.

[S: You asked me if I wanted to move in, but I can't remember why I never did.]

I was in my early twenties and living what seemed the most charmed life ever, despite the drink. Everybody thought I was destined for fame, including me, because it felt like I could do no wrong. I'd gone from the commissioning job with the Young Musician's Symphony Orchestra to composing the jazz ballet for the Jiving Lindy Hoppers and English National Ballet. There was a string of part-time jobs too, which included playing for the Royal Ballet, with all those 'funny people' my grandfather had warned my mother about. I was really doing quite well.

My friend Jonathan Harvey wrote a play called *Beautiful Thing* and it was put on in a small theatre above a pub in Shepherds Bush and then adapted as a film by Channel 4. We used to joke that we were in competition with each other for success because everything seemed to be going well for both of us. We started to write a musical together but it didn't come to anything because neither of us had the time to devote to it. The one thing that was missing from my life was romance; I really felt a need to meet someone I could share my life with.

The parsonage was a very happy community, a lovely house full of fun people. I can barely remember all the people that lived with me over those three years. I would regularly walk past people in that house that I didn't know - but I also didn't care. As well as Shauna and Peter the person who was there longest was a pianist friend and fellow composer called Therese Miller. I would come home and hear wonderful music being played, Chopin Nocturnes, and then I would open the door to the ballroom and there she would be, sitting at the piano with a massive joint in the corner of her mouth.

Among the people who came to stay when they needed to sort their lives out was an actress who wasn't doing too well. She brought her eighteen-year-old daughter, Hannah, with her. I walked into the house one day, and young Hannah casually remarked:

'Oh, a friend of yours came today. I told him you weren't here.'

'Who was it?'

She said she didn't know and started to describe him; I really couldn't think who she was talking about.

'Well? What happened?'

'I was walking up the stairs and this guy was climbing up the drainpipe and then came in through the bathroom window,'

'Yes. And what did you say'?

'I said: "If you've come for Kevin, he's not here." He seemed a bit startled so I just showed him the way back down to the front door.'

'Hannah. I don't really think any of my friends would climb up the drainpipe. I think the person who you met was actually a burglar.'

And she said: 'Ooh. I feel really stupid now.'

One night a group of us were chatting in Manhattan's when a big American guy walked through the door. For some reason, even though we had never met, I went over to him and gave him a big hug. He looked surprised, but then embraced me back and said:

'That's really weird!'

He explained that he'd been touring Europe with his partner, who was now very ill.

'I've just had to go and see him in the Chelsea and Westminster Hospital, and he's reached the last stages of Aids. I came out of there and felt that I really needed a drink, but I didn't know where to go. Someone at the hospital told me about this place, and as I was walking along the street, I realised it wasn't a drink I needed so much as a cuddle. And you just did that as soon as I came in!'

His name was David Lipsom. We invited him to join our group, and we all got on very well. He told us that when his partner became ill they had decided to have a final big holiday touring around Europe whilst he was well enough to do it, but obviously things hadn't turned out as they'd planned. We looked after him for a few weeks; every day would start with breakfast at the parsonage, then he would go in and out of the Thomas Macaulay ward, and then we would go sightseeing around London.

The Chelsea and Westminster hospital had some unfortunate names for their wards. As far as we were concerned, Thomas McCawley was the gym instructor on the *Titanic!* The ward opposite was called Marie Celeste! Although it turns out both the ship and the ward were named after some eighteenth-century lady, it didn't inspire anyone to think their stay in hospital was going to have a good outcome. In time David's partner was nursed back to health, at least to the point where he was well enough to go home. And then they left without giving any details of where they lived or even any indication that they wanted to stay in touch.

Eventually the Diocese cottoned on to the fact that they had a valuable empty building and started to think about selling the parsonage. It turned out that I had been living there for so long that I had a right to buy the place. I did look into it and I could have had it for £110,000 if I'd been able to raise the money. Since then it's been converted into flats and one of those sold for more than £10 million in 2015, so I guess the whole house is worth at least twice that now. If only I'd known!

One evening, Therese brought round a very shy lad called Neil Vint. He was an excellent pianist who had studied at Chetham's School of Music and then gone on to Oxford. He was the same age as me, charming, well-educated and utterly beautiful. Everyone adored him and it was quite clear Therese was in love with him. As soon as I saw him, I fell for him too: it was really the first time I had fallen in love. But as far as I knew, he wasn't gay: he had just broken up with a girlfriend called Victoria who he had been with for four years.

It was coming up to Christmas, and I had just got a job for a few weeks as Musical Director at the Shaw Theatre pantomime. One evening I went out to see Kit and the Widow at the Lyric Hammersmith, and when I got back I found Neil had stayed up waiting for me in the kitchen. We sat and chatted and he was asking all sorts of questions about how it was for me, being gay. We carried on talking well into the early hours and eventually I plucked up the courage to ask if I could kiss him. I so feared the rejection as this was someone who made my heart pound.

'That would be nice.'

The whole scene was quite sweet really; we were just entwined. He said it was quite strange to be embracing another man, but he liked kissing me. I couldn't believe that someone I really wanted also fancied me. We eventually fell asleep together, both of us in a sleeping bag for one person.

We woke the next morning when Therese came looking for us. I remember as the door opened, I hid under the sleeping bag, and for a moment no-one spoke. Eventually Neil said:

'If you're looking for Kevin, he's here', so I had to show my face. She just left. I knew she would be upset, but she never said anything about it.

And so the relationship developed. We were just so happy together, laughing all the time. In love, it's always the simple things that are the most magical. He wanted to introduce me to his favourite film *Cinema Paradiso,* and so everyone living in the parsonage sat down to watch it together. No one was at all bothered that Neil and I lay spooned on the carpet as we watched this beautiful film.

I particularly remember one of our many walks around Chelsea Harbour. It was a lovely evening; the moon was shining, and the Albert Bridge was lit up and sparkling. The narrow boats were all lined up, looking like secret gin palaces. We strolled along Cheyne Walk, holding hands and occasionally kissing when we knew no one was around, not wanting to cause offence. As we got to the foot of the harbour Neil put his arms around me, and I said to him:

'I think I must be the most content, and the luckiest person on the planet.'

We were together for about eight months, and that is an eternity when you're twenty-three. He didn't come out as gay to his family at all, and he kept all his other friends apart from us too. I never met any of them.

[S: I remember you did that thing that so many people do when they start a relationship: you cut friends off a little while you were with him. Although, that was also around the time you were touring with the jazz ballet.]

Neil was working at Tower Records. While my working life appeared to be going well, his seemed to be more and more of a disappointment to him. He had been such a success as a child, an academic high-flyer and a brilliant pianist, first at Chetham's and then at Oxford. He used to say that he was no good as an adult, and that he didn't see a position for himself in the world. It was as though he believed he had peaked too soon, and the future would all be downhill.

He desperately wanted to make it as a pianist, but he told me one day that he had decided that it was pointless learning the great pieces of music as he could never play them well enough. When he listened to something like the Horowitz recording of the Rachmaninov Sonata he knew that no-one need ever record it again. As far as he was concerned that recording could never be surpassed, so why would he even try to play it?

I was so in love with him that I didn't see how he was becoming more and more fatalistic. Almost since the night I told him how content and lucky I felt, I have regretted using those words because I can see now that those weren't the emotions he was feeling, despite the fact that we were so happy together.

One weekend, his parents asked him to go home to play the piano at a Soirée that some of their friends were holding. He really didn't want to do it, but I looked out a book of music from the twenties for him, because that was the style of music they wanted to hear. As it happened, I was going to be away from home as well; I had just got the job working in Brighton with Maisie Trollette. I was quite excited by the prospect because it looked like it could lead to something that would be quite lucrative. I was always short of cash.

We were both leaving the parsonage at lunchtime, going our separate ways. During the morning we had been listening to an old cassette recording of me with my Grandma from when I was about eight, and Neil was laughing at how northern I sounded as a little boy. As we were about to set off, I reminded him that he had borrowed some money, and I asked if he had it because I might need cash over the weekend.

He gave me a look of almost disgust, and threw twenty pounds onto the floor.

This was so out of character that I was shocked and confused, and I had a moment of panic.

'Neil? Are you about to leave me?'

But then he came over with a sudden grin on his face, grabbed my cheeks and kissed me full on the lips.

'Absolutely not. How could I ever do that? Just get that accent back. I love it!'

I went off to Brighton and did the gig and then went back to Maisie Trollette's guest house, where I was staying. It was quite late, and I thought

Neil would have got home by then, so I called the parsonage. Peter answered, and I asked him to put Neil on.

'No, sorry. He's not back'.

I thought that was a bit strange, but I supposed his parents might have got him to stay the night. I just asked Peter to pin a message where Neil would see it: 'Kevin phoned to say he loves you very much.'

Peter did put that up - it was still there the following day when I got back. Neil didn't come back on the Monday and I had no way of contacting him other than to phone his parents. I was really getting very worried, so in the evening that is what I did. I'd never spoken to them before, and of course they didn't know who I was. I asked if Neil was with them.

'No, he isn't, and we are furious with him. He should have come to the party yesterday. We were mortified when he didn't appear, so upset! We are very angry.'

I just said: 'I'm sorry: I thought he was there.'

They put the phone down on me, but about twenty minutes later Neil's Dad phoned back, much calmer this time, but saying:

'I don't know who you are'.

'I'm a very close friend of Neil's. He stays with us here in St Peter's Parsonage. I'm rather concerned that he hasn't been seen for a couple of days.'

He started to say that this was typical of Neil, but I said:

'Obviously, you're his parents and I don't know the relationship you have with him, but I am certain he wouldn't have done that to me. This feels very wrong.'

A little while later, Neil's brother Colin called. I think he knew about me because Neil had told him at Christmas that he had started going out with a man.

He said: 'What's been going on? Have you two had a falling out?'

'No. We really haven't. I'm absolutely beside myself with worry - this is so not right.'

The Tuesday went by, and there was still no sign of him. In the evening I called the police and reported Neil as a missing person. I got through the embarrassment of asking them not to tell his family that I was in a relationship with Neil, that he was my boyfriend, because he hadn't come out to them. I didn't want that known; it had to be his decision to tell them. I needn't have worried; the policeman was very kind and reassuring about that and seemed to understand why I needed to keep it from them.

On the Wednesday evening, with still no news, I went into work at Manhattan's. It was perhaps slightly self- indulgent, but I sang a song at the piano that night. I am probably one of the world's worst singers, and I never usually sang there but Noel Coward's song *If Love Were All* came into my mind as I played. It was a song that I had always liked, but the lyrics seemed so poignant that night. And the whole place went silent because I think people there knew what it meant.

And as I sang, I realised that I knew where he was. It was a special place where he loved to go - somewhere where he used to entertain his family with piano concerts as a child. I asked a friend to come with me to Kensington High Street Police Station. I knew that the worst was about to happen.

' I've reported somebody missing, and this is the address where I think he is. It's his grandparents' house, and I believe they are on holiday. If there is no answer, then you're to smash the door down and if he's not there, I will pay for the damage.'

I went home and waited, but nothing happened that night. On the Thursday morning, in desperation, I phoned his parents' house. A police sergeant answered, and I could hear screaming in the background. I said to the policeman:

'I'm phoning about Neil.'

'Yes. He has been found.'

A heartbeat of hope.

'Oh, really? How is he?'

'He's not.'

I put the phone down and looked out of the window, and there on the step the police procedural cliché was waiting for me: two policemen with long faces, one with his hat under his arm. Even before they told me Neil had hung himself, I already knew.

Of course I did.

After that, my life went into slow motion. There was an overwhelming sense of loneliness and a loss of my own identity, as though I was being forced to live in a bizarre new world. Just before this all happened, I had been asked about becoming Ealing Film Studio's in-house composer –a dream job - but now I had no sense of a future, no feeling that anything was possible. My life just seemed to have stopped moving forward.

I called Peter at his work and told him. All the phone calls that day followed the same pattern.

'He's been found...'

'Oh? Great!' Everyone grasping at hope as I had, followed by:

'No. It's not good...'

Dreadful as it always is to have to tell people that someone has died, normally there is some explanation that you can give – an illness, a terrible accident, something. But when there is nothing to say, it never really leaves you that you should be able to explain what has happened, and why. Even now, I live with that feeling at some point each day.

The first to call round was Bill Tindall from Manhattan's piano bar. He hugged me and said:

'I'm not here for tears, I'm here to cheer you up.'

Next came Angela, my friend with whom I visited the motherless men dying in the wards of the Royal Free Hospital. We had had a brief fling in the past, but now she was acting as my manager. And then Mary-Ann appeared with cress soup and lots of simple good things she had bought from Marks & Spencer. She said it was 'soul-food'. She is a spiritual person, and one of the best friends anyone could ask for.

Later my parents turned up. That added to the ordeal because we hadn't properly addressed the gay thing before that, and the moment of your partner's death is really not a good time to come out to your parents. They knew that I had been helping to raise money for HIV charities, and they had surely worked out now that there was a reason for me being so involved with that kind of volunteering. If they had any doubts at all about the kind of company I was keeping, they arrived at the same time as another friend, Paulo Rae, a rather vivacious Frenchman who turned up wearing dark sunglasses, bright white trousers and speaking in a Hollywood movie accent.

All I could say was:

'Mum. Neil and I were together...'

She said: 'We understand that Kevin... but did Neil have Aids?'

I realised they must have endured one of the most nightmarish of journeys getting down to London to be with me. They had probably been worried sick that they were facing the prospect of me dying too. I told them he wasn't ill at all, and neither was I, and they were obviously so relieved that I knew that they could deal with anything after that. To my surprise, my Dad really got on with Paulo that day, and years later he hinted that he wished that he had been my partner.

I went to stay at Angela's place that night and managed to sleep a little, on her sofa. The next morning was the first of endless days of waking up to a realisation that the fantasy of having a whole life with Neil was now only ever going to be a dream. I was devastated. I was inconsolable.

All of us living at the Parsonage suffered and grieved together – especially Peter, Shauna, and Therese. Away from home though it was difficult; my friends couldn't empathise with what I was going through. No one I knew had lost a partner; it was too much of an adult thing to have happened. There were times when I wanted to talk about Neil to someone because for a short period of time a part of him would come back to life, as though the curtain he was hiding behind had been drawn aside. But no-one else wanted to have those conversations, and that created a feeling of awkwardness between me and friends.

At the funeral I couldn't say goodbye to Neil properly and acknowledge him as my partner because hardly anyone from his family, his school and University friends, knew that was who he was. I actually felt disgusted by the occasion, especially by the vicar who really hadn't wanted it to happen in his church because Neil had taken his own life. There was no real celebration of Neil's life in the service: it was all conducted on the level of 'What a friend we have in Jesus'.

His family established a bursary in Neil's name for graduates of Chetham's to help them establish themselves as musicians. They have never acknowledged our relationship, and the only contact I have had with them has been from his young sister who was only seven when he died. She reached out to me a couple of years ago, needing her own understanding of what had happened.

I went through day after day feeling that I couldn't cope any more. For a long time I promised myself that if it all got too much then it would be OK to follow Neil and kill myself.

One evening a friend took me to Manhattan's and bought me a pint but I found I couldn't drink it. I have always associated alcohol with good times and I couldn't see that there would ever be any of those again, so I left the bar and went home to the parsonage. Peter's note telling Neil that I loved him was still there, pinned where it had been since the day he died. I realised I needed to talk to someone who wasn't involved so I looked out the number of Lee Beberman, the American exchange student I had helped at the College and called him.

'Hi Kevin! How are you?'

'I'm not very good,' and I explained it all.

'So... when are you going to come and see me in Hollywood, then?'

It had been over a month since Neil died but this was the first time that I had any feeling that everything could be OK. I said I would be there as soon as I could get a ticket.

A large Bahamian guy picked me up at the airport. He introduced himself as Cedric Scott, Lee's brother-in-law, and it turned out he was a film producer.

I was in America for a month or so with Lee and his friends and family in West Hollywood and they all really looked after me. I was invited to play the piano at a party Cedric was throwing for his daughter's graduation and a very nice man called Sidney came along. He and I, and Cedric, sat chatting for a while about my music and how I had a chance to compose for films back in England, and they suggested that perhaps I might like to stay in Hollywood and create the music for a film they were going to make about Nelson Mandela and President de Klerk. Of course, Sidney was Sidney Poitier, but it wasn't until I came back that I found out how famous this man actually was.

I was enjoying being in America and it looked like exciting things could happen for me in Hollywood, but it was still only a couple of months after Neil's death, and I was very confused. I had a definite sense that he was still with me somehow. Lee suggested we make a trip down to Mexico and said he would come by to pick me up the next morning after conducting a choir in church. I went into a bar and sat alone for a while and then went into the toilet. Standing there I spoke to Neil in my head.

'If you are still around, please just give me some proof?'

I thought I heard a voice saying: 'Don't go to Mexico, stay around this area tomorrow. You'll bump into a friend.'

As it happened Gay Pride was happening in West Hollywood the following day, and as I hadn't been to a Pride before, I'd offered to help sell tickets whilst Lee was conducting. It wasn't particularly busy in the morning, but guys started turning up in all sorts of outfits. They seemed to love my English accent, so I turned it on even more. I wandered around the park looking at all sorts of stalls; there was even a fortune teller's tent. It was all rather fun: the garish costumes gave it the atmosphere of a pantomime.

But just as more people started arriving, the Sunday services at the churches were coming to an end, and I couldn't believe what I was seeing. Large groups of people, seemingly families with grandparents, Mums and Dads and little children were setting up a protest, shouting and waving placards. I saw one small child, probably no more than five years old, holding a sign that said:

'AIDS CURES HOMOSEXUALITY'

That was the one that stood out, but there were many more. Looking back, I feel more shocked now about these people who claimed to be Christians than I did then; I was so used to that kind of behaviour that I had become desensitised.

Lee turned up in the car later in the morning, and I told him that I wasn't going with him, although I offered no explanation as I didn't want to jinx anything that might be about to happen. I knew it was highly unlikely that I was going to bump into anyone I knew, but I felt really uneasy. By mid-afternoon, this joyous colourful event had swelled to around half a million people. The voice came back into my head:

'Walk into the meadow.'

I did and made my way towards the little stage that had been built in the meadow for the event, when suddenly standing in front of me I found David Lipsom – the American I had spent weeks entertaining in London. I couldn't believe that the voice in my head had been right.

David's jaw dropped. He screamed and threw his arms around me. We chatted for a while and then parted, and we never saw each other again.

I wandered on, taking in the sights, thinking about the amazing thing that had just happened to me. I must have passed the fortune teller's tent so many times, that she eventually called out:

'Well, are you coming in or not? You've been walking past all day wanting to come in.'

I went in to listen to what she had to say. Her advice was:

'You can't stay here, you know. Something really bad has happened to you, but you can't stay. You need to go back there, before you can come back here.'

Although I don't think anyone was expecting to see me in London again, I went back and faced up to it all. But the feeling that part of me was missing stayed with me for years, and I went through several bouts of depression. It was something that I just couldn't lay to rest.

Ten years later I was talking to our friend Michael Topping about it one night. Michael had been one of the first people whom I told about Neil's death. His response stays with me, because it was completely at odds with what everyone else said when they heard the news:

'Oh well. Neil's probably getting his own back at you for doing it to him in a previous life!'

As crazy and flippant as that sounds, it was perhaps the best thing anyone said to me that week because it opened up the possibility that we had always been together and that, after this blip, perhaps we would be together again in another life.

All those years later he had another helpful insight. He suggested that there was more to my problems than just having lost Neil. Perhaps I had never been able to let go because of the way the funeral had been conducted, and maybe if I could find a way of saying goodbye properly then I might escape the anguish. He got together with some other friends, and between them they found a wonderfully sympathetic priest for me. I went to see him, and he asked me what I wanted to do, what could bring me closure.

'I want a ceremony. I want the church to recognise me as Neil's partner, and I also want the church to respect his decision to take his own life.'

He did all that for me. And it was wonderful.

Then we listened to a tape of Neil playing the piano, and as we sat together in silence, the sun shone through the stained glass of the window above us and we were lit up in beautiful colours.

And at last, I felt at peace.

Chapter 7

In which a night of drinking leads to us forming our double act. We launch in a fabulous venue, go on our first cruise, and run the gauntlet of American immigration

STEVEN

We had been friends for years before we started to work together. We had gone our separate ways after college and for years we met only occasionally. We both had a bit of a reputation for missing appointments with friends, but we never cancelled a chance to meet one another even if it was only once or twice a year. The idea of collaborating or appearing together never came up though.

I would have happily carried on acting, and I was actually poised for a big break into the West End. I was cast in a play by a brilliant writer called Patrick Wilde, who had written a ground-breaking gay piece called *What's Wrong with Angry?* in the early 1990s. Around the same time our old friend Jonathan Harvey had written *Beautiful Thing* and Patrick's play was slightly overshadowed by it.

Sometime later Patrick took a couple of the characters from the earlier play and wrote a sequel called *You Couldn't Make It Up*. I got a part in that one when it went up to the Edinburgh fringe to be staged at the Gilded Balloon. It came to me through the co-operative agency: I was the 'young pretty thing' amongst us so I was always put forward for the gay bits and pieces. It was a great chance, though I didn't get paid for the Fringe Festival run but we were all set for a transfer to the West End. Patrick remains a good friend, and we're working with him again at the moment.

Just before that there was another voice acting job that I very nearly got, and which would definitely have stopped us working together. It was another children's TV show called *The Fimbles*, and I was up to do the voice of one of the three main puppet characters called Fimbo. I honestly thought I had it in the bag. They had even told me what I was going to get paid, and it was an absolute fortune. It really would have been too much money to turn down. In my mind I was already choosing what colour my Audi TT was going to be. At the last minute they decided that the voice I was doing for Fimbo was too close to the one I used for Pod, so they went and got somebody else – a lad with a northern accent. They made 200 episodes of it between 2002 and 2009 and it's been sold to over 100 countries. Had I done that show, I wouldn't be writing this book now – but I would be a lot richer!

[K: But would you be happy? What would have happened is that because you had lots of money, you would have gone to lots of sex parties, and then developed a drugs habit, and then because you were exposed by the *News of the World*, the BBC sacked you. And then ... it all got worse.
S: You've got that all worked out, haven't you?]

KEVIN

As we tell our audiences, Worbey and Farrell came into existence through the pure accident of getting drunk one evening.

Ever since I can remember I had been fascinated by the possibility of being a part of a double act. I tried out various ideas with different people over the years after I left college and in 2002 I started rehearsing with a lad called Lee. Just after that partnership began, I went round to see Steven one evening and we started improvising on his pianos. We were getting on really well and Steven said:

'If it doesn't work out for you with Lee, why don't we do something?'

I went home and sat up late, drinking with my friend John Dobson. I said to him:

'I'm in a bit of a dilemma. I went round to see Steven this evening, and what we made up, improvising on the piano, I would never in a million years be able to rehearse with this other lad. It was like a telepathic connection.'

The 'other lad' used to come and stay with me, but one night we were out in town and a massive row developed partly because I was planning to go up to Edinburgh to visit Steven who was going to be performing in You Couldn't Make It Up on the Fringe. I had even phoned Steven to say that I wasn't going to be able to get away because of the jealousy, but soon after that the arguing with Lee came to a head and he left me.

I vividly remember making an excited call to Michael Topping, about two in the morning and saying:

'He's gone! I'm so relieved! I'm going to call Steven, because I want us to do the double act together.'

I did make the trip to Edinburgh after all, in a bit of a panic and very nervous about having the discussion. I knew Steven had been offered a chance to continue in Patrick's play when it transferred to the West End the next year, and he had also been making plans to do some writing with a friend. Selfishly, I suddenly knew that a double act was the right thing to do for me: I just had to convince him it would be right for him too.

STEVEN

It may seem like nonsense but I think the shoe-shop incident, when we registered each other even though we had never met, was just the first example of what we have come to think of as a subconscious connection between us. We found we could make things up at the piano without talking to each other, somehow always knowing what the other was going to do next. Playing together, it was almost like one person with four hands sat at the piano.

I remember that night we had really intended to go out and get drunk; I was living in Kings Cross in London with Scott at the time. Unfortunately, our other flatmate locked us in and went away with the key, so we were stuck there all evening. I had two grand pianos, so we sat down at those with lots and lots of wine and just started playing together. It was like a magic moment; we improvised in the same way, we had the same sense of humour and we spent the whole evening laughing. It was completely spontaneous and an act was born out of alcohol.

There was a germ of an idea but it wasn't enough yet to give up all of our other work. We started working on a novelty piano act with lots of comic sketches and silly little musical pieces, running around each other to play different parts as we do now. Each piece we performed was technically quite difficult, but the physical fun was a part of everything we did.

One decision we made right at the start was that there would be only one piano. Most theatres only have one piano, so insisting on having another one hired for the show would just make things difficult. And we knew that sitting looking at each other across two keyboards made it harder to make the arrangements work.

We decided to call ourselves 'Katzenjammer'. We wanted something that was really catchy, one word that looked good on a flyer. With 'Katzenjammer' you can emphasise a big, tall 'K' and the 'j' hanging down in the middle, and then balance the 'K' with the 'R" at the end. The name came from The Katzenjammer Kids which was the first ever newspaper comic-strip cartoon, in the New York Journal. It started in 1897 and was based on a German children's story called Max and Moritz and it inspired many double acts, and later cartoons like Tom and Jerry. Compare pictures of the Katzenjammer Kids with photographs of us in 2003 and you'll see we actually looked like them back then.

What we didn't know when we chose the name is that 'Katzenjammer' means two things in German. Strictly it translates as 'the wailing of cats', but apparently it is also an expression that is used to describe a feeling which has no single-word equivalent in English: 'misery and contrition during a hangover'. Which may, or may not, be appropriate for us.

We made our first appearance with a fifteen-minute spot at a charity concert in support of HIV education.

KEVIN

I was on Gaydar one evening chatting to someone who called himself Tom the Cat; his real name was Larry. Larry had been travelling in Africa, and after seeing the effect Aids was having on children's lives, had decided to set up a charity whereby schools in the UK and in Africa could be matched to promote awareness of the HIV virus. One of his best ideas was to get pupils at a British school to paint pictures of how they saw their lives, and for pupils at an African school to do the same so that they could compare and understand through art the impact of the illness.

Larry took the African artwork into a British school and discussed it with a group of nine-year-old children. He got them to think about what it would be like to have a friend who was HIV positive. Then at the end of the day he said:

'Tomorrow, I'm going to introduce you to someone who is HIV positive, how do you feel about that?'

They seemed to be OK with it and their parents were as well, so the next morning in Assembly he checked again that the children were happy to meet someone who was positive. When they said they were, he left the room, as though going to collect this person, but all he did was take off his jumper and walk back in. It was such a clever idea; having got to know him, the children thought of him as their friend already, and now they understood what it was like to have a friend with the condition.

I was so enthused by the project that I volunteered to help set up the fundraising launch event. I got Mary-Ann's husband Jim involved as an accountant and found some acts. Larry wanted a big star to attract attention and I immediately thought of David Soul. I knew he would be up for it.

At one time David Soul was so famous that he was treated almost as some kind of heroic mystical figure. Quite regularly he would spend a morning in a hospital with some young person who was terminally ill, because their wish was that they could meet him before they died. Once, when he was on the set of *Starsky and Hutch,* someone was threatening to commit suicide, and they would only agree to talk to David.

It is an awful lot to deal with if you do your best to respond to all these demands, but in this case I had no hesitation in asking him to get involved because the cause was actually quite poignant. David's best friend (and *Starsky and Hutch* partner) Paul Michael Glazer had recently lost both his wife and his young daughter to Aids, contracted during a blood transfusion given in childbirth, and so the need for HIV awareness education was close to David's heart. Larry had actually tried to make contact with the Elizabeth Glaser foundation just before this, and he couldn't believe his luck when I said we could bring David on board.

Members of the cast of *The Lion King* were recruited and Hugh Durrant gave us the original design for Cher's costume for the video for her song *Believe* to be sold at the auction. Hugh first designed costumes for Cher's 'farewell tour' and then went on to design more costumes for all of her farewell tours since then: she does have a lot of people to say goodbye to. The auction alone raised around £16,000.

David Soul wanted a chance to rehearse his performance with me as his accompanist. We agreed to meet up to go through David's famous hit *Don't Give Up on Us Baby* (or 'Don't throw up on me baby', as he calls it).

One hot afternoon we arrived at Steinway Hall to rehearse. David brought his guitar, and I brought a mini disc recorder because he had asked me to record the rehearsal, to be sure I would understand what he wanted from me. Unfortunately, there was some building work going on that day. As there was no other time we could meet before the concert, there was nothing for it but to set up the microphones and get on with it. I still have the recording.

Although it wasn't continuous, every so often the sound of drilling or hammering interrupted us, and every time it seemed as though the noises had been inserted into the song for comedy effect, answering the lines he was singing. 'I lost my head last night', was followed by a particularly loud crash.

David, professional as ever, ploughed on as though nothing was happening and never acknowledged the interruptions. When I played the recording back to my mother, she practically wet herself laughing. Years later, Steven and I put together a sketch based on that day, with Steven trying to perform a piece to the accompaniment of my feeble DIY efforts hammering and drilling backstage.

The compere for the auction was Sadie Nine, a radio presenter on BBC London. I had worked with her on Liberty Radio. Sadie used to have me in with her on a Friday to tell Londoners about the upcoming shows to see in the week ahead. I would usually tell them that the best entertainment to be had in London at the weekend was Speakers' Corner on a Sunday morning.

Sadie had become famous in Russia by accident when she performed to a few hundred people in Moscow without realising that she was being broadcast on television to over four hundred million. As a result, she became a big star across Russia, but the mafia tried to take over her career. She had to escape overnight and arrived at Heathrow with her entourage. She was under the impression that she was famous everywhere by now, but the border guards had no idea who she was.

'I'm Sadie Nine, the Russian Madonna', she said.

The guard replied: 'Yes, and I'm the Bulgarian Boy George. Take her in!'

For a while the two of us had a regular spot for an hour on Sadie's Wednesday evening show on BBC London, doing "piano bar radio". People would phone in and ask to sing a song of their choice, and we would attempt to accompany them. We had no idea in advance of what they were going to request. This was long before Pop Idol, X factor and Britain's Got Talent and there were, surprisingly, a lot of good singers out there, mixed in with the occasional eccentric. The show was very entertaining and along with the piano bar circus Sadie would always have a special guest.

We love doing live radio: we always feel quite high after doing a radio interview. The studios are always very cosy and inviting, and for some reason it really sharpens your brain, as you need to be so focused.

KEVIN

The BBC London building was on Marylebone Road, right in the centre of London, and quite near to Steinway Hall. They had a strict policy that no-one who had been drinking could be let in through the doors but our usual Wednesday routine was to come out of Steinway Hall, go for a drink at Carluccio's and then buy chewing gum to mask the smell of alcohol before making our way along to the BBC. Sometimes it was a bit of a battle having to blag our way past security if they got a whiff of Pinot Grigio or limoncello on our breath.

On a couple of occasions Sadie was short of a famous guest, and I called David Soul to help out and come to the rescue. We walked in with him one evening, Steven and I chewing fresh gum as usual, and the security man refused to let David in because he had been drinking.

The lovely thing about having a regular spot at the BBC was there would be a courtesy car to pick us up after the show to take us on to anywhere we wanted to go. Quite often that would be the Shadow lounge club, or as we called it the Shallow lounge, a rather glamorous Soho club that was high camp with pink glittered walls and a dark interior. Symeon Cosburn would be there, singing with his band.

So we had managed to assemble a cast of glitterati for Larry's concert, and that was the opportunity for our new double-act Katzenjammer to make its first fifteen-minute public appearance, immediately before David Soul on the bill. We got a better response than we could possibly have hoped for and realised that we had stumbled across something that went down so well that we needed to take it further. In truth, most of the time spent in the entertainment business is all about being involved with 'turkeys'. So, for both of us, after years of working in some really dreadful productions discovering that we were a part of something really good, was a revelation!

If we were going to put ourselves out there as available for bookings, we needed to put together a showreel; a professional recording and a film of what we could do. It had to be in front of a live audience; no-one would be interested if we just put something together in the living room. For that we were going to need a proper venue, but although we searched all over London, through all the seedy places we might be able to afford we just weren't finding anywhere. Scott was getting exasperated at our lack of progress and told us one morning:

'Just go out and get a venue! Don't come back to the house until you've got somewhere!'

[S: To which I replied: 'Oh you know us; we'll find somewhere absolutely fabulous!']

KEVIN

That morning I had the idea that we should try the Concert Artistes' Association (it is now called the Club for Acts and Actors), a magnificent building in Covent Garden. There's a show every Monday evening and a bar serving lager at £1.50 a pint. To be a member you have to have been some kind of 'theatrical turn' in the past. It is full of people who have had their career, but still believe they are major stars, people who used to appear in *Allo Allo*, *Hi-de-Hi* and shows like that. It's the only place in town where you can find a hundred sopranos singing *Old Man River*.

We called in to see Barbara, the Secretary at the CAA, and explained that we were putting a show together and we would quite like to perform it there. I tried some flattery, saying the CAA is known as a centre of cabaret, and that so many acts like ours had started out from there.

'Well, there is one problem, Kevin,' she said. 'You haven't paid this year's subs.'

'Well, all right, how much is that?'

'It's sixty pounds'.

I wrote out a cheque for sixty pounds.

'There. Can we have a look at some dates?'

'You haven't paid last year's either.'

So, I had to hand over another sixty pounds. Barbara then went through the booking diary page by page finding a problem with every free date.

'Well, that date's maybe taken by someone... and so is that one... And you might have had that one except there'll be nobody here... oh, and this one I'd quite like my staff to have a day off because they work so hard.'

She went through the entire diary, and then closed it and said:

'I'm sorry, it seems we don't have any free dates for you.'

I'd paid her £120, and we didn't get a booking. It seemed that even though they needed young people to join, they didn't actually want anyone young to be seen there and at just over thirty we were way too young for the club.

STEVEN

A regular at the CAA then was Barrie Stacey, who has only recently passed away. He was one of the most famous and legendary of London's agents. Most of Barrie's clients seemed to be teenage boys who had just left drama school.

I auditioned for Barrie when I was starting out as an actor. I was sitting in front of him in his office near Leicester Square, performing a monologue, and all the way through he was looking at what I have between my legs. The phone kept ringing and ringing, and I thought: 'Is he not going to answer this?', but he kept saying:

'Carry on daughter, carry on!'

Eventually he picked up the phone and yelled 'F*** off!' and slammed it back down.

'I'll take you on, dear. Send me some ten by eights.'

And I was left wondering: do I really want him as my agent? He gave me some stickers to put on my publicity photos, but I never got any work through him.

We were pretty despondent not to get a booking at the CAA. As we were just across the road from the Royal Opera House, Kevin phoned his friend Emily who worked in the publicity department for advice.

'Come over for a coffee and let's talk about it'.

Her first suggestion was a surprise:

'Why don't you do it here?'

We laughed, but she was absolutely serious. Then we were given a tour round the Opera House, the huge stage and the costume department. It was hard to believe that the humble place across the road had been so pompous, and yet the 'real deal' venue was filled with really nice people. We find this repeatedly – the more professional the venue, the more welcoming they can be.

A date was settled, a fee of £1,500 was agreed and the Opera House offered to print tickets for our inaugural concert.

We got home that evening and were greeted by Scott, who honestly believed we would never get around to finding a venue.

'We've got somewhere for the show.'

'Really? Where?'

'The Royal Opera House.'

Scott laughed.

'No, seriously. We're doing it at the Opera House'.

The Royal Opera House Covent Garden is about as grand as it gets for the debut performance of a new act. It really is a magnificent building, home of the Royal Opera and the Royal Ballet, and Scott wasn't the only person who couldn't quite believe we'd pulled this one off. There has been a theatre on the site since 1732 and Handel had his first season of operas performed there. There was a major reconstruction in the 1980s and 1990s but the main auditorium dates from the middle of the nineteenth century. It seats more than two thousand people, so that was a little beyond our budget.

As a part of the reconstruction, additional rehearsal and performance spaces were created and it was one of these, The Clore Studio that we booked. It is situated upstairs, right beside the champagne bar, which just added to the grandeur of the occasion. The acoustics were fantastic, and the Yamaha Grand was a model C7 in exceptional condition. As a venue it was just perfect.

Everyone we knew wanted a ticket, so there was no problem in getting a full house. We were a bit concerned that we were taking on too much in going for such a prestigious venue after so little experience, but friends persuaded us it was absolutely the right thing to do, and even helped us with the cost of the hire. As the date got closer, we both got very nervous.

KEVIN

Looking back that first show was quite muddled. The premise of the opening of the concert was that Steven had turned up at the Opera House to give a recital, and I had arrived unexpectedly (and unwanted). We had a big on-stage row, and then I set out to ruin Steven's performance by playing something different over him.

The Rachmaninov C# prelude was covered over with *Summertime*. Rachmaninov's 18th variation was spoiled with *Love Changes Everything*, and then after a few minutes of competing the two tunes would come together. It was a trick of making two different melodies work together as a medley, with some slapstick thrown in.

Steven pretended to get stuck like a broken record in Bach's *Toccata*, and I would give him a shove to the bottom of the keyboard and convert it into *Robin's Return* – a camp old Music Hall song.

STEVEN

We also did our *Fur Elise* sketch which we still dust off and use sometimes, all these years later. It involves us playing Beethoven's piece with each of us using the wrong hand. Kevin is on the left playing the base part with his right hand, and I'm on the right playing with my left. That leaves both of us with a free hand on the outside which we use to pour two gin and tonics, complete with ice and lemon and cocktail umbrellas. The music is completely uninterrupted, and we fetch glasses and bottles from inside the piano as we play. Sometimes we pull some pork scratchings out from down below the base strings as well.

It was put together especially for that evening and took weeks of rehearsal. A lot of gin was spilled on our piano, and lemon pips got stuck between the keys. Scott came to hate the sketch just because of the tension involved in putting it together. The final rehearsals were at Steinway Hall where their pianos are worth £150,000 each, so we blocked out the windows in the doors, so no-one could see what we were up to.

We were petrified doing it live for the first time because so much could go wrong, coordinating the actions with playing the music and not slopping the liquids around too much. For instance, we found that the tonic bottle had to be filled just to the right level – enough in it for it to make a fizzing noise when it was opened, but not too much that it frothed up and poured out over everything on stage.

It was introduced with a long shaggy-dog story about Beethoven making a Thai green curry for Schubert, forgetting about it and letting it turn into a 'furry sleaze'. Our scripts have got better since then, but the physical comedy went down a storm on the night, and still does.

At the end of the concert, we felt like kings. The following morning, lots of people were calling to say that they'd never experienced a show like it. Everyone seemed to have enjoyed it so much that we knew we were on to something. Then a few days later we saw the film of the concert that Screen Partners had put together, and it was as good as a Hollywood film, really glossy, and just fabulously produced. And there was also a superb sound recording made by our friend Spencer Cousins, a brilliant musician who had worked with Joan Armatrading, and who later married Emily (the same friend who got us the booking).

It would take a little while to get the film out to the people that mattered, the ones who make the bookings for venues and tours, but we knew we had the best possible chance with such a high-quality film to showcase what we were capable of. It was surely only a matter of time before our career took off.

KEVIN

I had been doing a bit of work composing music for films, but my main income at that time still came from playing at the Lanesborough Hotel at Hyde Park Corner in the heart of Knightsbridge. It has two beacons of fire outside the front entrance and boasts of having London's most expensive hotel room. The price is absolutely eye-watering, but to be fair they do throw in breakfast. The main restaurant was modelled on the Brighton Pavilion and it is famous for its afternoon tea.

The champagne bar was run by one of the most celebrated bar tenders in the world, Salvatore Calabrese; he was known as the King of Cognac. Americans would fly over just to smoke a vintage Cuban cigar with the Castro stamp on it at £500 each. I once saw Bill Gates buying a round of drinks there for a few friends that came to £60,000.

In fact I saw a lot there. People always make the mistake of thinking that waiters are concentrating on what they're doing and pay no attention to what the diners are up to. They couldn't be more wrong, and the same is true of the pianist playing in the background. I'd played in restaurants for four hours virtually every day of my life since I was fifteen, so there were times when I would fall asleep and then wake up to find my hands were playing some Gershwin.

[S: You can sit there playing for hours and no-one pays any attention to you at all. It's just like being a pot plant in the corner of the room. But the minute you decide it's safe to let out a fart, you can guarantee there will be someone at your elbow wanting to talk to you.]

Sometimes I would sit down and let my hands do the job and just listen to everyone's conversations. If I saw or heard something interesting going on, I had a code to alert the waiters. When I played *Over the Rainbow*, it meant there was someone obviously gay at a table, but if I struck up the theme to *The Godfather,* they would know something dodgy was happening. Someone would then hover around the table, and quietly pour water for each guest and listen to the conversation. On at least one occasion an arms deal was going on.

Working at the Lanesborough sometimes led to me playing for major celebrities at functions in the private rooms. On different occasions I entertained Prince Charles, Stevie Wonder, Joan Collins, Lionel Richie, Will Smith, Wayne Sleep, Mariah Carey, Bon Jovi, Cher, and Honor Blackman. Courtney Love caused a scene in the reception area, arguing with someone while stark naked. Robbie Williams was an absolutely beautiful presence with his deep blue eyes.

Perhaps the most boring evening of my life was playing in the corner of a private dinner for John Major and President George HW Bush. Every background pianist in London was phoning me wanting that gig when they heard I'd got it, and I rather wish I'd let someone else do it.

One night when I arrived at the hotel the manager greeted me saying:

'You've got an interesting night ahead. You are the private pianist for the Osmond family.'

I was really pleased because Donny and Marie and little Jimmy and all the others have such a wonderful reputation for being very pleasant. I couldn't wait to meet them.

Either the manager misspoke, or I misheard him. It wasn't the Osmond family; it was the Osbourne family. There amongst the towering palm trees and chinois details of the restaurant was Ozzy Osbourne in his tracksuit, and with him were the rest of his band who had followed his lead in not dressing for the occasion. Sharron however looked absolutely gorgeous, very glamourous.

Their TV reality series had started a few months before, and they were in London because Ozzy was performing at the Queen's Golden Jubilee. When I sat down at the piano, Ozzy came lunging towards me with all the charm of King Edward (the potato, not the monarch) and let me know all the pieces he wanted to hear: mainly Beatles songs.

After an hour and a half, I took a break, and when I went back I found the band's keyboard player had taken over at the piano and was belting out songs they all knew at the volume of a rock concert at the o2. It was very good, and it had turned the group into a rather more raucous rabble. It was also very difficult to follow, and I wished at the time that I knew more of their material.

On a separate table from the rest of the group sat a couple of very beautiful girls. One of them turned out to be Aimee, the daughter who didn't want to be a part of the rest of her family's TV circus. Ozzy kept shouting across to her and blowing her a kiss, and she would just giggle shyly. The difference between her and everyone else in the room was striking; it made me wonder how she had managed to turn out normal. But it was clear that Ozzy and Sharron were very loving parents, and it doesn't matter how eccentric your upbringing is, if it's done with love you should be fine.

The Lanesborough is part of an American hotel chain with mostly American guests and when the Iraqi war broke out, guests just stopped coming to Europe and the hotel started cutting back on costs. They had no idea how long the war was going to last, and entertainment was the first saving they made.

Just as that line of work stopped for me, our first opportunity to perform as a double act came up. I got a call about performing on a cruise ship. It was starting from Bermuda and they were interested in booking us for a couple of concerts on board. I knew it was a potentially life-changing step but I was unsure about accepting as it meant Steven would have to give up his other projects. I phoned him.

STEVEN

I remember that day well. I was teaching a very small girl called Amy. She was just daft and driving me nuts! I was on the verge of losing it with her, which I never did as a teacher. I was pointing at D on the keyboard:

'This key is a D. D is for donkey so it's between the two long black donkey ears, the C Sharp and the E flat.'

And she kept just saying 'Amy! Amy!'

So, when Kevin phoned and said we were off to Bermuda, all of a sudden I was really nice to her:

'You're such a sweet little girl!'

She probably couldn't understand how we had so quickly turned a corner in our relationship.

My fellow actors were disappointed I wasn't going to carry on with the play, but they understood my reasons; they knew we were going to be making some good money as well as flying to Bermuda. To be honest I think they wanted to be pleased for me, but at the same time they were more than a bit pissed off about it. They would have to find a replacement actor and that meant extra rehearsals for them all.

Of course, there was no way of knowing how well the play would do or how long it would last in the West End. I had once been Musical Director for a musical called *When Pigs Fly, a show* which had previously done very well in America. A friend of mine was producer and we put together a superb cast. We had quite a long run at the Arts Theatre in London, but it wasn't the great success we had all hoped for and we had to close a week or so early.

The memory of that experience helped me with my decision. My instinct was that working with Kevin had more potential than the play. The double act idea was definitely going to be more fun, and probably more lucrative. If I ever had any doubts about what we were doing I just had to think back to our first gig at the charity concert, when everyone went crazy for us.

KEVIN

As well as the Lanesborough, I was also still playing in Bill Tindall's piano bar, so I had to get some time off for the cruise. I already knew I didn't want to be sitting in the background playing music in restaurants and bars or playing for ballet classes for the rest of my life. I had been starting to cut down on that kind of work, and I was trying to work out how little I could live on.

[S: We know people who have been background pianists for decades, and they are still sitting there, living a dream, waiting to be discovered.]

A few weeks before the Bermuda job turned up, I was out one afternoon with Chris Jarvis (a friend of Steven's), who was presenting on CBBC at the time. We called in at Selfridge's for a coffee, and saw an old man playing background music there, just as I would be later that evening. When I went in to work at the piano bar, I remarked on this to Bill.

'I really don't want to be doing that at his age.'

To which he responded: 'Why? What else can you do?'

And when I told him about the plans Steven and I had been discussing, he said:

'I can't imagine anyone wanting to watch that!'

He really was quite difficult about it, and when a few weeks later I told him I was taking a week off because we were going to Bermuda, he announced:

'I don't like playing second fiddle to anyone, make tomorrow night your last night.'

That left me with no work apart from the cruise: after that there would be nothing. I'd worked for Bill on and off for ten years and it made me feel very vulnerable if there was going to be no work with him when I got back. He sent me an email to the effect that my future career was doomed:

'The smell of burning bridges is on the wind, and tears will surely follow'.

[S: Very poetic.]

Looking back, I can completely understand that Bill felt more than a bit betrayed by my leaving. He was probably looking forward to many more years of me running piano bars for him, and he was just as anxious about the change that was coming as I was. But I was very surprised by his reaction at the time, especially as he had been so good to me over the years and looked after me through some very difficult times. He was particularly kind and understanding when Neil died, and I had to escape to America.

I suppose it was like the change in a parental relationship when a son or daughter wants to leave home and do their own thing. I see now that he was quite hurt that I wanted to move on. Even though the bar was hugely profitable, he actually closed it down after asking me to go.

We met Bill five or so years later when we were asked to play at West Five piano bar to celebrate their ten-year anniversary. He was very nice, and he seemed to have completely erased the memory of what had been said between us. He even seemed to take some pride in our success.

[S: It was very odd. He was acting as though he'd discovered us.]

Free of our respective commitments, we set off for our first real professional engagement together. We were flown out to St Thomas to join the Royal Caribbean ship "The Brilliance of the Seas". Funnily enough, considering all the cruises we have done since, it is the only time we've ever sailed with that line.

That first cruise was an amazing experience. The ship was a really posh, state-of-the art vessel, and it was brand new. We were blown away with how luxurious it all was and how much money had been spent on every detail. For instance, they had pool tables that were able to compensate for the movement of the waves, each costing a vast amount of money.

[S: We heard they were a million dollars each. I sat on one once and I was completely still while the ship was moving around me.]

The theatre we were to perform in seated fifteen hundred people. We were both extremely nervous, but fortunately we were adopted on board by an angel. Her name is Mary Lee LaBay, and she is still working as a hypnotherapist and life coach, based in Seattle. That week she was on board giving lectures on life enrichment.

On the first morning we were practising our routines in a room that was about to be used for one of her lectures. We admitted we were very nervous as we had never done anything like this before, so she invited us to stay to hear her speak each day, and then play a short piece at the end of her talk, just as a way of preparing us for performing.

Looking at the photographs from that trip now it's obvious that we must have seemed very young and inexperienced, especially compared to the other guest entertainers there. On the American ships back then, the entertainers were mainly retired Las Vegas stars: all very much older than us. We were just in our early thirties and, we like to think, we passed for much younger than that! It was quite a novelty for the guests to have such a young act on the ship..

Mary and her husband Scott really looked after us that week. It turned out that Mary is a big believer in reincarnation, and she specialises in telling people about their past lives. We told her where we came from and she said that she knew Nottinghamshire very well, because she had had four past lives in the area. In fact, she had been the original Maid Marian.

[S: That was a surprise to us as we always thought it was all a legend.

K: She gave us rather too much detail about what went on between her and Mr Hood.]

She seemed to be aware that she was a bit eccentric and living in a fantasy world, but there was also something very normal and lovely about her. During the week she would come to our cabins every day and hypnotise us, and with our eyes closed make us envisage, over and over again, walking out onto the stage and greeting our audience and then walking back to applause. She would say:

'Imagine looking out at all those people: some of them might be ill, some of them have other sorts of problems. All of them, though, just want to be entertained by you! Reach out and mentally embrace them. Go through the show in your head, and then reverse it all and walk back off the stage,'

It really helped, as when we came to make our entrance on the day of the show, it was as though we'd already done it so many times before and, although we were still nervous, it felt like familiar territory.

Even with all this preparation the first show didn't go down as well as we had hoped. One lesson we learnt very quickly was that some parts of the act just didn't work for that audience. Americans have rather different tastes and reference points compared to European audiences. Performing the Spice Girls in the style of Rachmaninov went over some people's heads, and a Les Dawson-style badly played piano rendition of the Blue Danube, with off-key notes at the top of the scale, bombed because these people had never seen anything like it. They didn't understand that the wrong notes were deliberate. Our second set that same night was very different, and we got a partial standing ovation.

Our shows were on our last day aboard, and of course we didn't drink anything that day. Being new to cruises we didn't understand the protocols around life on the waves. For instance, we had been told that it is important to tip the staff, but no one told us that you did this at the end of the cruise. Every night we tipped our waiter rather generously, and this probably explains the exceptional service we seemed to get every time we went to the restaurant. Because we weren't performing until the last night, we decided to try every bar.

We managed to build up a bill of $750 over five days, even though, as entertainers, we were getting everything at half price.

We tried justifying it to ourselves by working out how much it was each in pounds per night and telling ourselves we could easily spend that much on a normal night out in London.

[S: That was the ship where there was all that mess with the chocolates on the pillow, wasn't it?]

We're not really sure why we have never performed on a Royal Caribbean ship since that first cruise. Perhaps we shouldn't have been quite so honest with everybody and admitted that we were just starting out and weren't the established act they all thought we were. Or maybe we shouldn't have experimented with putting chocolate treats where they shouldn't go.

We soon got other cruise bookings. The next engagement was for the Constellation and by the time we did that one we had absolutely worked out what was needed, so they invited us back. Unlike our first cruise, this time our show was during the week and that introduced us to a new phenomenon: fame.

We had a baptism of fire trying to get to breakfast the morning after the show. It took us ninety minutes to get from our stateroom to the lido for just a cup of coffee. We were stopped by everyone we met wanting to congratulate us for the show and asking questions. It was deeply flattering, but completely unexpected. We had performed two shows to maybe three thousand people, and overnight we had gone from complete anonymity to everyone knowing who we were and wanting to greet us.

Three thousand people might not seem like a lot, but as that was just about everyone on the ship, it is the equivalent of the whole world knowing you. And then when the ship came into port people were coming up to us wanting to have photos taken of us with them: it was really quite bizarre. The locals were looking at us, curious to know who the hell we were. Quite often people want to say something other than 'Hello!' or 'I enjoyed the show', but they seem to ask the same questions or say the same things, so we found ourselves building up a database of replies. It is all very charming, but when you're not used to fame, it does seem a little daft too.

[K: Magicians always get asked: "Can you make my wife disappear?"]

Next, the Saga Line and Holland America took us on. At the time Saga had a policy of buying older ships and refurbishing them rather nicely. Their guests were mostly elderly Brits who knew all about Les Dawson and appreciated what we were doing. The clients weren't quite as well to do, and one of the ships even had a 'bag lady' who would wander around the ship stinking of chicken stock, with a sack full of plastic bags.

[S: She burst in on us during a rehearsal and said: 'Well! O<u>ne</u> of you can play!']

It turned out her family had sent her away on a world cruise without consulting her. It's not uncommon, especially at Christmas, for wealthy families to get rid of their elderly relatives for a while by putting them on board a ship and have the crew look after them instead. Apparently, this old lady had no idea she was going on a cruise until the special limousine service came out to her house to pick her up, and they had to wait while she packed her bags. Presumably, her children hadn't wanted to spoil the nice surprise of her 'present' by warning her.

Holland America was a good source of income for our first few years together. We were a bit of an unusual choice for them: not because of the content of our act but because we were so much younger than everyone else that they were using. When we first joined one of their ships in Canada, the Cruise Director, a man called Tom Lee, was waiting in the reception area for the entertainers to come on board. As we walked up the gangway he called out:

'My God! There are two children coming aboard. What are these kids going to do?'

We liked Tom because he kept saying all the wrong things on stage.

'Hello, Ladies and Gentlemen. My name is Tom Cruise... Not really, I'm Tom the Cruise Director... Tonight after the show, there's country dancing taking place near the lido, and tonight's country is Hungary! So, get your best Hungarian dances out of your system. God gave you those hip replacements for a reason!'

We knew that the main booking team weren't that keen on taking a double act regularly. Two people means two cabins (or it should!) and the cost of two flights in and out. Tom was good to us though:

as soon as he saw the reaction that we were getting from the audiences he sent a message back to the Seattle head office:

'Katzenjammer. Keep them!'

And so started a long and very fruitful relationship.

We had the feeling that a lot of the older entertainers didn't particularly like us. It may be they were a bit scared of the new kids on the block, but it was probably because they thought we were deeply unprofessional with all the partying that went on and couldn't relate to us. We were just getting used to life on the seas and it was natural that we would want to enjoy ourselves with people of our own age. As the old Vegas stars and the passengers weren't that, we took to holding parties in our rooms and invited the young people from the show casts, the dancers and the backing singers, and also the office staff and shopkeepers.

KEVIN

There was one night we were having a party in our cabin when the phone rang. It was the front desk receptionist saying:

'Could you turn the music down, please? There's been a complaint from next door."

I apologised, but then she said:

'And, as you're a guest entertainer I'm afraid we are going to have to inform the Cruise Director about this incident.'

I said that I totally understood and apologised again. I put the phone down and said:

'Liz, you're going to get a phone call about us tomorrow!'

She was there with us.

STEVEN

The next night someone from Security knocked on the door and the Cruise Director jumped into Kevin's wardrobe to hide!

We had these parties for some of the lower ranking officers and the shop workers, because these people didn't get treated very well. The food they were given was nowhere as good as what was served to the guests. Because we weren't crew, we had passenger status, so we got them to come to our cabin and we would order room service for them. One night we arranged to have a wine and cheese party in our cabin. We had loads of cheese, but everyone turned up with more, and there were about thirty plates of the stuff left over at the end of the night. The place stank of ripe gorgonzola for the whole cruise.

Another time we were having a drink with a hairdresser called Keith and his partner in their room when there came a loud banging on the wall and a woman shouted out:

'If you don't shut up, I'm going to send my grandson round! He's eighteen!'

Keith shouted back, 'Please do! 'Cause we're going to s**g him!'

Being nice to people has its rewards. There was a man on board who ran the shop dealing in amber objects who was known as "Yang Yang, the amber man". When we went to St Petersburg in Russia, he invited us to join him at an amazing restaurant as a thank you.

Cruise passengers can't just get off the ship and wander around in Russia. You either have to obtain a special visa, which is really hard to get, or go on the conducted tours accompanied by the police. The great thing for the crew is that they aren't restricted in the same way. We went to get off with all the shop assistants, but when we got to security a woman stopped us because we were on the passenger manifest.

'But we work on the ship!'

'You can't go, you're not crew.'

'Technically yes, but we do work on the ship. Look - do we seem like people who can afford to pay for a cruise?!'

'No.'

She stamped the entry permit and we got through and went with everyone to a lovely restaurant, Putin's favourite apparently, where they served amazing fish dishes and caviar and the most incredible vodka. From there we went on to a ballet at the Comedy Theatre, with a full orchestra playing The Nutcracker. The musicians were just fantastic. Before the performance we were treated to champagne and some more caviar in a VIP suite, and then again at the interval.

The theatre was packed, but some of the audience had sneaked in without paying. Whoever was running the concert seemed to turn a blind eye, and allowed poorer people to stand at the back and watch for free. It was wonderful to see them taking it all in, inhaling the culture. It was a really special day out.

Apart from partying and eating and drinking we soon realised that you have to find ways of whiling away the time between shows when you're at sea for long periods. We took to binge-watching TV series long before doing that had a name. We were so hooked on the Kiefer Sutherland series *24* that we were shortening our performances in order to fit in another episode between the two shows.

We stopped doing encores to have time to watch some more, and we got so concerned about what was happening to Jack Bauer that we wouldn't sell our merchandise, nor meet the audience. We just ran back to our cabins to watch some more *24*.

One of the entertainers on Holland America that we got on really well with was Jeff Trachta, despite him being ten years older than us. He had been a major star in America, playing one of the main characters in CBS's soap opera *The Bold and the Beautiful* for several years, so at the time there were about 400 million people in the world who would recognise him.

From that he went on to appear in *Grease* and, like so many others we met on those ships, he had had his own show in Vegas. Celine Dion used to appear as his guest.

He arranged for us to go to Vegas to see him and organised suites for us at the Rio Grande Hotel. He showed us all round the city, and it was interesting being there with him because there is quite a community amongst all the different acts doing shows. Toni Braxton was appearing across the road from Jeff, and he was sharing his showroom with The Chippendales.

[K: In the middle of the show, he got the spotlights turned onto us. 'Ladies and Gentlemen, I've got two talented friends from the UK here tonight!' and explained our act. No-one had the faintest idea who we were, but I stood up and milked a standing ovation. Steven and Scott were mortified by it all, and just wanted the earth to open and swallow them up, but I loved it!]

In the last few years Jeff has relaunched his career. He is a brilliant impressionist as well as an actor and a singer, and he's now known as The Singing Trump. He makes a great Donald Trump and did quite well on *America's Got Talent*.

It was good to be getting regular work, but the downside was we were running a risk with the American immigration service. We only had normal tourist visas and you're not supposed to do any work in the country with one of those. Of course we weren't performing anywhere on land, but we had to pick up the ships from there and when we were in American waters they counted it as working in the country.

Typically, we would be engaged for a voyage from Barbados into Miami, and then from Canada back into Miami. In a couple of weeks, we could be in and out of the country four or five times each time picking up another stamp in our passports. Eventually we were stopped and questioned as we arrived in Houston.

STEVEN

I was detained and put into a dormitory with a load of Mexicans. After a few hours I was taken up for questioning by a female immigration officer.

'Why do you keeping coming into America? In and out, in and out.'

We couldn't tell them exactly what we were doing there so I said:

'Because I love it. You have such a wonderful country!'

Clearly, she didn't swallow that line and it was down to her whether I was deported or locked up, but it was the last thing she was dealing with that day and she wanted to go home.

So she gave me the benefit of the doubt and a warning and stamped my passport.

We got on a plane, flew to Boston and did another trip up to Canada.

But we were petrified because we knew that at the end of the voyage we were going back into America yet again. We were shaking as we went through the immigration process on the ship and we fully expected questions about what we were doing, but this time we passed with no problem.

And then just as we were relaxing again, over the tannoy came an announcement:

'Kevin Farrell and Steven Worbey. Return to immigration control immediately!'

This was going to be it: there would be a $20,000 fine each, and we would be banned from entering America for ten years.

Our hearts were in our throats because we had lied so many times at immigration during those few weeks, saying that we weren't working. Before going back we asked the Cruise Director what we should do but he just shrugged: there wasn't any help to be had.

We were taken back into the immigration office and greeted by an angry Chinese-American man.

'You took my pen!'

For a moment we couldn't take in what was being said.

'You took my pen! It has special memory for me. Give it back!'

We gave him his old biro and scarpered. We had got away with it again!

Chapter 8

In which we thoroughly enjoy ourselves on Cunard's Queens. We are surprised by armed police in a public toilet and Kevin has a strange encounter with a chocolate cake in Kenya.

The glossy DVD production of *Katzenjammer Live at the Royal Opera House* had worked wonders. As soon as it went out, offers started coming in. It so impressed one American booker that he gave us a string of jobs, including the maiden voyage of the Queen Mary 2, the largest ocean liner ever built. It felt as though we were cheating our way to success because he just assumed that we were already famous in the UK because of the quality of the film and the fact that we were performing at the Royal Opera House.

The first part of the Queen Mary 2's maiden voyage had been across the Atlantic from Southampton, and we were booked to join the ship in Fort Lauderdale. We flew in before the ship arrived and spent a day or two ashore, living like celebrities. As soon as we mentioned in bars and restaurants that we were going to be performing on the QM2, our meals and drinks were 'on the house', and there would be a request that we tell the guests about the establishment. By the end of our stay, we had boasted our way up to being the headline act and no-one had the faintest idea who we were.

In fact Shirley Bassey was top of the bill that week. Shirley had only two conditions on her contract. She wanted an excellent suite with a high-quality exercise bike, and there had to be unlimited caviar and champagne available. Unfortunately, she had to miss her first performance because the sea was rough, and she was throwing up in her cabin.

We found there was a huge amount of interest in this brand-new ship coming into port for the first time, and the security measures in place in the town made it almost impossible to get within five miles of the dock.

Unsure as to how we were supposed to get to the ship through the security cordon, we managed to secure a lift on a bus that was taking the Filipino crew members out to the ship. When we got there, everyone had to prove that they were staff, so we confessed to the police that we were passengers rather than crew and that we had just hitched a lift. All they had was a list of the crew members, and that confirmed what we were telling them: we weren't supposed to be there. They had no idea what to do with us. Indeed no-one seemed to know what they were doing: the whole scene was chaotic. We hung around for a while, but then just sneaked on board without being checked by anyone.

In the last few years, we have found security around actually boarding and leaving ships has got much tighter than was the case then. Everyone is checked thouroughly before going up the gangway. It's not just terrorists they are concerned about; the authorities are getting wise to the fact that elderly passengers on cruise ships have been recruited to be drugs couriers for criminals. After all, who would think a couple of old crinklies would have a few kilos of cocaine in their hand luggage? We had dinner with an old couple a few years ago who, although they were perfectly pleasant, just didn't seem to fit in with everyone else. They were last seen being taken off the ship in handcuffs having been arrested for smuggling cannabis into Japan.

The QM2 maiden voyage was the first time that Cunard had launched a ship of this importance for about forty years, and it must have been very difficult to prepare properly for such a rare event. Having docked in Fort Lauderdale they had about two thousand passengers to disembark, and then the same number of new passengers to get on board for the next part of the voyage. Normally these things work like clockwork in a very short time: the passengers get off, their luggage is delivered to them and then the same happens in reverse. On this occasion the shoreside team seemed to be a bit out of their depth. The sheer size of the ship put all of the logistics on a far bigger scale than they were used to.

It took until five in the afternoon to get everyone off, usually that is finished soon after breakfast. People were delayed by several hours and they were missing their flights home. There was a massive queue of people at reception trying to claim compensation for the extra costs they were incurring. There was screaming, shouting, violence threatened. Total chaos.

The ship employed a brilliant four-part acapella group called Royal Flush, to sing songs to the guests in bars and restaurants during the evening. During the afternoon of what should have been their day off, they received a call to go along to the reception area to 'lighten the atmosphere' of what was fast turning into a full-scale riot. Amongst the angry shouting of hundreds of people foaming at the mouth, a little reedy harmonica sounded a note, and they started up a rendition of *Ain't She Sweet?* It made people even angrier.

Eventually they got everyone off and started to load the new guests. The start of the cruise had been a little spoiled. The new passengers had been kept hanging around for several hours, and many of them were journalists there to write travel stories for television, newspapers and magazines about the wonderful new Cunard ship. For their benefit, the first couple of days were to be spent on a 'cruise to nowhere'. The ship would leave Fort Lauderdale, sail around while everyone experienced the food, entertainment and luxury, and then go back to the same port to let the journalists off again.

Fortunately, the new guests were in a better mood than those who had just got off. As soon as they were on board it was obvious to everyone that this was the most fantastic ocean liner that had ever been launched. We were bowled over by it and ever since that first voyage it's been our favourite ship. We absolutely adore the QM2.

The first evening started well: it was just one big, relaxed party. The booze was free for everybody, except for the most expensive spirits. The only person we found that evening who had actually bought any alcohol was an American who had spent a couple of hundred dollars on a Louis XIII brandy. He was passing through the crowd, inviting everyone to smell the aroma of his expensive drink, and then telling them how much he had paid for it. Most people seemed to be finding this display of wealth pretty obnoxious.

[K: Steven asked him if he could have a sniff of the brandy, so he handed it over and then watched, aghast, as Steven drank the whole glass down in one. It didn't even touch the sides! The American was shell-shocked, but everyone around him just howled with laughter.

S: It was very naughty of me, but I think everyone else had wanted to do the same thing. To be honest it wasn't a very clever thing to do. I sat there with my oesophagus burning, expecting a fist in the face, but he just disappeared!]

It wasn't only the guests that were having a good time. The girl running the Veuve Clicquot champagne bar was leading the way in sampling her wines. She suddenly burst through the kitchen doors carrying a tray of champagne flutes, fell across a table and then slid along it, trying to keep the tray upright. Everyone was very concerned for her welfare, but she happily announced:

'I'm trashed!'

We were quite surprised she kept her job after that. We struck up a good rapport with "The Veuve Clicquot girl'; she was funny and quite lovely, but she was frequently to be seen bending down behind the counter swigging back the dregs of empty glasses and necking from bottles she had cleared from the tables. We benefited several times when she brought us glasses of champagne (a whole bottle of Grande Dame once) and let us have them, signed off to the captain's bill: 'courtesy of Commodore Warwick'.

We thoroughly enjoyed the party, but then we noticed that we weren't down to perform until after the ship came back from the short tour, so we didn't really have to do the 'cruise to nowhere' at all. And so, having sneaked on at lunchtime, and having had our fill of free alcohol, we went back to our cabin and gathered a few essential things together in a couple of minutes –toothbrushes, hair gel, clean underwear - and sneaked off again.

Back in Fort Lauderdale we went to a shopping mall and found a toilet to get changed in, ready for a night out. We were standing at the sinks, when suddenly the door flew open and there was a shout of 'Armed Police!' Several policemen burst in and surrounded us. Apparently, someone on the staff of the mall had seen us go into the toilet together and as we'd spent a quite a long time in there without coming out, they assumed we were in there having sex.

We just stood there aghast: one dripping toothpaste from an open mouth, the other razor in hand, covered in shaving foam. It was our George Michael moment.

Despite the shaky start, that first voyage of the QM2 was a massive success, and wherever she went in the world for the next year or so, she was the biggest star in town. When the ship arrived in port, everyone that was travelling on her was treated like royalty or rock stars – people were even trying to touch our hair as we came off the gangplank.

As relative novices it was a fantastic experience for us to be amongst such A-list stars on board. Apart from Shirley Bassey, there was also the comedian John Martin, who used to provide material for Ken Dodd and Jimmy Tarbuck, and who also holds a record for telling jokes continuously for over one hundred hours. Of course, he did a much shorter set that week. He is a very funny man, and it turns out he is also quite a military historian: he wrote the book *The Mirror Caught the Sun* about the assassination of Reinhard Heydrich on which the film *Anthropoid was* based.

One night we stayed up until about three in the morning chatting with John. He was telling us all about Ken Dodd's trial for tax evasion. He'd been there for the whole event. We were quite intrigued to know how it was that Ken Dodd had escaped conviction while Lester Piggott, the jockey, had gone to prison for doing something similar. John's view was that it was all down to the power of laughter.

Apparently when Eric Sykes got up to give evidence as a character witness, he was asked whether he wanted to affirm or take the oath.

'Eh?'

Sykes was pretty much stone-deaf at this time, so the clerk raised his voice and asked again.

'Eh?'

The prosecution counsel went over to him and asked loudly in his ear. 'Will you take the oath?'

Sykes did a double-take and said:

'I'm ever so sorry, but I can't work without me piano!'

The defence team managed to orchestrate the whole trial as a comedy festival. When Ken Dodd took the stand, he exclaimed:

'What a marvellous turn out for a Wednesday matinee!'

The judge tried to remind everyone that this was a court of justice, not a variety palace, but he had to keep adjourning because there was so much laughter. Judge, jury, barristers, everyone was having too much fun.

Dodd's counsel asked him to explain how his tax difficulties had come about.

'Well, unfortunately my accountant died...

'Did that matter?'

With perfect comic timing Dodd replied: 'Well... it mattered to him!'

It was a wonderful evening hearing a first-hand account of what went on at the trial, especially from such a funny storyteller as John. He was adamant that laughter trumps everything that life throws at you.

A few months later we were booked to appear on QM 2 again and flew out to join the ship in Lisbon. All of the embarkation problems seemed to have been ironed out and the security around the dock area was very tight. Queuing to get our documents checked, we noticed one man who looked really out of place.

K: He was a few people ahead of us in the queue, and completely on his own. He didn't look like a passenger: more like someone who had dressed himself up to fit in with what he thought cruise liner passengers look like. And he had based that idea on what he had seen in the film of *Titanic*. He even had a funny old-fashioned sailor's hat.

S: He had two suitcases, one in each hand, but they looked like 1920s cases, the old brown leather ones. It just wasn't right for someone who was supposed to be boarding QM2 for a week's holiday.

We watched him for a while, shuffling forward in the line of passengers. He was quite obviously a local who was trying to sneak on board and get away from Portugal. We imagined he must have been planning this new life in America for ages, working late into the night to forge his documents like Donald Pleasance in *The Great Escape*. When he got to the front of the queue and his papers were examined, we really wanted him to succeed, but he was turned away. He was so disappointed it was heart-breaking, and the last we saw of him was an expression of shocked surprise that his plan hadn't worked,

Cunard commissioned the QM2 to be ready to take over from the Queen Elizabeth 2, which was coming towards the end of its working life. We appeared on both of those ships around that time and the older Queen had certainly started to look very tired. There were buckets in the hallways collecting rusty brown water where the decks were leaking through the ceilings and they weren't allowed to dock at any American ports anymore because the original wood paneling didn't comply with fire regulations. There were problems with the old-style overhead flush toilets, and there was no system for chlorinating the water. It was ready to be taken out of service.

We heard a story of a magician who used to perform on the QE2 with his other half as his assistant, many years before us. They were a regular act on the ship, and when he suddenly died on board, she was consulted about the arrangements for getting his body home for a funeral. She decided that as he had spent so much time on the ship, what he would really have wanted was a sea burial, so that was organised for her. Unfortunately, when the ship next arrived in port his wife was there waiting to take the body home, because she'd somehow found out that he'd died. The company had no idea that the woman he was always seen with, wasn't actually his wife, and had to admit they'd already disposed of him during the cruise.

Unfortunately, people dying on cruises is just a fact of life. If you're ever on a cruise and the kitchens start offering special deals on ice cream, it's usually a clue that there have been more than they usually expect.

Sea burials are mostly a thing of the past. We did hear a story concerning one of the last overboard burials carried out on a particular line. The crew were mostly Filipinos who didn't understand English very well, so the captain decided it would be a good idea to have a discreet rehearsal the day before, so that nothing would go wrong at the ceremony. They cordoned off a section of deck, got a big sack full of potatoes to stand in as a pretend body, went through all that had to be said, and then released the sack into the water.

The captain was satisfied:

'That went really well. We'll do the real thing tomorrow at nine-o-clock with the widow in attendance.'

Some of the crew looked blankly at him, so he repeated it more slowly.

'Tomorrow we will do the real thing, with the widow here to take part in the ceremony'.

Then someone explained to him that they hadn't understood that this was just a practice; they'd released the body in the rehearsal. Next day, when they were supposed to be burying the poor chap at sea, they had to keep the widow away from the side so that she didn't see they were releasing a sack of potatoes into the ocean. She was crying her eyes out over a bag of Maris Pipers.

The QM2 has different levels of cabin and restaurant, but it isn't as extreme as the old QE2 in keeping people apart. That ship operated a definite class system: it was arranged so that the rich people never had to meet the poorer people, and that sometimes appealed to the real snobs of cruising. The only place where upper and lower class (Grill guests or non-Grill guests) could meet, was in the theatre or in the gym.

STEVEN

I went into the gym once and got onto an exercise bike and the first thing the man sitting next to me said was:

'Which restaurant do you eat in?'

He was basically asking me how much money I have.

The gym on board ship can be a good place to meet interesting people though. We were working out together in a ship's gym when an elderly American greeted us:

'Are you the guys that played the piano last night? That was the most amazing thing I've ever seen in my life!'

We recognised him straight away as one of the lecturers for that week, the astronaut Charles Duke, lunar module pilot for Apollo 16 and the youngest person to walk on the moon.

We had to say: 'No, Charles, it's NOT the most amazing thing you've seen. It really, really isn't'.

He's a wonderfully genuine man and we had a good laugh together about what he had just said. It gets us so annoyed when people claim that the moon landings didn't happen but it doesn't seem to bother him. He tells people they are entitled to think what they like, but he knows he was there. In his talk he showed film that he took himself of the moon rover trundling over the surface.

We did use the quote on our posters: "The most amazing thing I've ever seen: Charles Duke", but unfortunately not enough people know who he is.

KEVIN

I was in the gym once, wearing a T-shirt that said 'ARMY'. An American came over and looked at me closely. I thought it was a bit strange.

'It's good to see that, man. It's good to see someone promoting the army. That's really good.'

I wasn't sure what he wanted me to say.

'Really?'

'Yeah. The army, you know, they get a lot of criticism. It's good to see you're on their side.'

'Well... thank you...'

He leaned in closer: 'You see... I was in Vietnam.'

My heart sank. He wasn't congratulating me for wearing the T-shirt at all. He was just wandering the decks looking for anyone who would listen to his Vietnam stories. He'd found a link!

STEVEN

There are quite a lot of people who spend a significant amount of their time on cruises. Over the years we have become friends with two regular guests on QM2 called Brian and Yvonne, who come from Whitby. I should probably say they are regular guests in Whitby who live on QM2 as they spend far more time on the ship than they do at home. We often have lunch with them and we never fail to be the last table to finish; we rarely have dinner with them as they don't drink at all. They always support our shows onboard and seem to like our naughty humour. The staff and crew all love them as much as we do and they've acquired the nicknames The Duke and Duchess of Sleights. They are always the best and most imaginatively dressed guests onboard.

They are rather naive though. Once when they were about to leave home to join the ship they decided to get the captain a card for his birthday that was coming up. They were very friendly with him and Yvonne was keen to get a card that was personal and appropriate for the captain of such a magnificent ship. She found a card in a local shop with a picture of an anchor on the front. It also had a giant 'W' above the picture. Being naive as she is Yvonne thought it meant 'weigh the anchor' and she was quite oblivious to what the card was really saying.

We don't know what the captain's reaction was to receiving it but when Yvonne was told what the card meant she was absolutely mortified!

Several passengers had a real emotional attachment to the QE2 because it was their home for much of the year. They were very upset when it was announced the ship was being sold. One elderly lady told us she was booked onto the last voyage, and she had no desire to go on living afterwards:

'When this ship goes, I want to go too!'

We met her sometime later, on another ship, still alive obviously, and she greeted us with:

'When they handed the QE2 over to those Arabs – it was like watching an old lady being raped!'

A friend had suggested they go on the last voyage of the Saga Rose- a similar style of ship.

'But I said: "No Joy, I've been to one funeral this year, I am not going to another."'

We were booked to appear on the QE2 in Japan during its first visit there on a world cruise. These days when ships do a world cruise it is actually split up into several segments that people can book separately. Although the ship goes right around the world in one long voyage most people are only on board for short periods, and hardly anyone does the whole thing. Back then a world cruise meant the passengers were on board for the whole circumnavigation, which took four or five months. We were joining them at Osaka and stayed a night in the city before going aboard and Cunard arranged a really posh hotel for us.

We were checking in behind Jeff Stevenson, who was also going aboard the QE2. Jeff is a brilliant comedian; he was one of a group of people with a similar style who came up through the business at the same time, a contemporary of Shane Ritchie and Brian Conley. Show business was slightly over saturated at the time with his kind of comedian, but he had some success, appearing in *Bugsy Malone* when he was a boy and for a while he had his own daytime quiz show on TV. For years now he has had a very good career on the ships and he is one of the hardest working entertainers we know.

We heard him ask the hotel receptionist whether she needed a credit card. She said:

'No, QE2 are paying. It's fine. QE2 pay'.

KEVIN

We went up to the counter and said we were on the same booking.

No sooner had we got up to our rooms than the phone rang, and it was someone at reception saying:

'Mr Farrell, you didn't give us a credit card.'

The Japanese are famous for being very polite and not wanting any confrontation; I said:

'You told us QE2 are paying. So that's fine, QE2 will pay.'

That night we decided to try all the different cocktails because QE2 were paying. And then, overly refreshed, we went to the nicest restaurant in the hotel where we had our own personal chef cook Kobe beef for us at the table, because QE2 were paying. The bill was probably enormous, and the following morning, as remorse set in, we ran out of the hotel as fast as we could before anyone asked us to pay.

It didn't do us any favours. The office saw our expenses for that trip, and they didn't book us for ages after that.

When the ship leaves a port, a pilot comes on board to guide the captain through the local area and then returns to shore. This time, coming out of Osaka the weather forecast was so bad that the pilot had to stay on board. To start with the weather seemed OK, not calm but not overly alarming and Jeff was suggesting in his act that the pilot had probably brought his dinner jacket on board with him so he could stay for the formal dinners and have a nice time.

The second show of the evening had started and, as we were the only people out on deck at the rear of the ship, we decided to catch a bit of it from the back of the theatre. The very second that we stepped through the door a freak wave hit the ship. It felt like a tsunami, and everything and everyone went flying. The piano fell off the stage. In those days the seats in the auditorium weren't attached to the floor, so suddenly the entire audience went sliding with an audible 'whoosh' into one corner of the room and ended up in a huge pile of bodies. Several people were quite badly hurt but if we had still been at the back of the ship we would have been over the side and lost forever.

The guy in charge of the technical stuff like filming the concerts was called Casey and he had worked on the ship for twenty-five years. According to him the reason he had been kept on so long was that he made the old decrepit equipment work. He never asked for any new equipment, he just repaired and adapted the decades-old stuff that he had. This meant that the technical capabilities of the ship were stuck in the 1970s. For instance, if they ever filmed anything on board for the ship's TV channel it had to be done in a single take because he couldn't stop and edit it.

There was a daily programme about the ship's events and the travel itinerary, and letting people know about new cruises they could book. It lasted for about an hour and the channel played it on a loop all day. They would also do dedications for passengers and a 'Today's the Day' spot giving little interesting historical facts. We enjoyed one of those in particular:

'Today's the Day that thirty years ago scientists discovered AIDS, the disease that kills homosexuals... Also celebrating a thirtieth anniversary are Bob and Margaret from Deck Four...'

Because the whole thing had to be done in a single take it was always a nerve-wracking experience for the two girls who presented it every day, knowing that they would just have to start over again if anything went badly wrong. Usually you could see them gradually relax over the course of the show, and by about fifty minutes in they'd dispense with the scripts and grow more confident.

We were watching this show one day on that world cruise. In the final segment the girls started talking about another brand-new ship, the Queen Victoria, that was about to be launched, and Cunard's grand plan to sail the three Queen ships into New York. One of them closed with:

'The Queen Mary, the Queen Elizabeth and the Queen Victoria. It's a very exciting thing for us all to look forward to. So, until then, we would like to wish you a very happy voyage here aboard the Two E Q.'

As the film cut, it held a close up of her face frozen in a look of horror as it dawned on her what she had just said.

We quite liked performing on the QE2, but the auditorium left a lot to be desired because it wasn't originally designed for that purpose. It was right in the middle of the ship and was actually a shopping mall that had been converted. It had quite a small stage and didn't really work as a theatre at all. Wheelchair users were all put on an upper level because there was more space up there, and there were two long staircases coming down, one on each side.

During one of the shows on a different voyage, a brake failed on one of the wheelchairs, and it went careering down the stairs with a startled old lady in it. Looking up, the drummer from the band spotted what was happening, and instinctively went into a theatrical drum roll as she came hurtling down and hit the cymbals with a crash as she hit the deck. He was called in the following day by the Entertainment Director.

'I have to tell you that nobody is suggesting that what you did last night was not funny. Everyone who has seen the tape, the surgeon who patched her up, even the captain, everyone thinks it was funny, possibly the funniest thing that has happened on that stage since the ship was launched. But, I'm afraid there have been one or two complaints, and we're going to have to let you go.'

Once the weather cleared, our voyage on the QE2 from Osaka took us on to Nagasaki. On most of these long cruises, as the ship approaches a new city there will be a lecturer on board who will give a talk about the place the passengers are about to visit. With Nagasaki, of course, the focus was on the war museum, the dropping of the nuclear bomb and the horror that happened there. Through a translator we listened to a lecture by an elderly Japanese man who had survived the bomb as a child. What this man had witnessed, what he had been through personally was absolutely horrific: he had lost every one of his family that day. He also took us through some details of his life after the war, and in particular how proud he was of having been able to rebuild his childhood home. It was very moving.

At the end, the translator looked out into the audience and asked if there were any questions for the speaker. Immediately a loud voice piped up:

'So, Japan... Do they accept American dollars?'

Along with hundreds of the ship's guests we visited the war museum while we were in Nagasaki. We were in tears at some of the things we saw there: bicycles contorted almost out of recognition, accounts written by people who had been five years old at the time and spent days searching through the ruins for their families who had been killed, photographs of the destruction and of the radiation injuries. Thousands of innocent lives destroyed, literally or metaphorically.

Some of our fellow travellers saw it differently. Behind us a voice rang out:

'Well! If they hadn't bombed Pearl Harbour...'

We've experienced several examples of this crass tourist syndrome. For whatever reason we keep encountering people on cruises who have very little understanding of how different their lives are from that of the people they are visiting. It could be that living on a ship where everything is provided, cuts them off from reality, or perhaps they are so extremely wealthy they were already like that before they came on board.

On a trip through a floating market in Vietnam a woman told the local children on the boats alongside us to put their hands out and try to look like they were begging as she took their photograph. Another time we were on the tender boat carrying passengers from the ship towards the town of Honfleur in France. As the shoreline approached, a large gentleman in loud trousers declared:

'You know what? This really gives you a feeling of what it must have been like during the Normandy landings!'

K: I suggested that the troops had had a slightly different experience on the landing craft, as they weren't about to get off and have a nice plate of moules marinieres. They were going to get annihilated!

On another occasion during a week in Kenya, there was more odd behaviour from passengers. The cruise social hostess came to us just before we docked and asked if we would mind accompanying her to an orphanage that the cruise line was supporting. She didn't say why, but she was a bit bothered about the visit and would like some company; she was obliged to go along with the captain and wanted someone else there with her.

KEVIN

Steven had made other arrangements for the evening, but I said I would go. I thought it would be just the three of us and didn't realise that they had organised the visit as a trip for a few of the passengers until a people carrier van drew up. Just as we were about to set off one of the passengers called out: 'Don't go yet! We've forgotten the chocolate cake!'

There was a bit of a kerfuffle and eventually the cake was found and loaded on board the van, and off we went. This particular chap seemed to be very excited about having the honour of presenting the chocolate cake to the children, much more than being interested in what we were going to see.

Eventually we arrived at the orphanage and climbed out of the van. The place was in darkness, but a woman came out to greet us with a child. Apart from the two of them the place seemed to be completely empty and I began to share the unease that the hostess was feeling about what was going on.

'Oh no!' said our friend. 'We've left the chocolate cake in the van!'

The woman said: 'This is baby David. He's got HIV Aids positive'.

It was quite clear that she had no idea what she was talking about. She told us that the orphanage could hold up to three hundred children, so I asked where the rest of the orphans were.

She seemed most put out: 'There's a lot of red-tape before we can get there!'

Then a large silver Mercedes drove up. A man got out and introduced himself as the orphanage owner. It looked like some sort of scam was going on; it was an orphanage that had no orphans but was taking money from the cruise line.

Everyone was very disappointed. Chocolate cake man decided that maybe we shouldn't hand over the cake after all. Another lady passenger whispered to me:

'Oh dear, if I'd known they didn't have any real orphans I wouldn't have come on this visit. On one of the other trips, they take you to a home for the disabled where the people are quite clever with their hands.'

There was a moment of indecision about what to do next which the captain spent handing out 'Jesus Loves You' leaflets to some people in the street.

[S: On that voyage the captain's son was dipping the Filipino and Indonesian crew members into the swimming pool and baptising them. They really weren't happy about it.]

We all got back into the van and set off back to the ship. Suddenly cake man screamed out:

'Stop! Stop the van! There's another orphanage. We can take the chocolate cake there!'

The van stopped, we all piled out again and some rather bemused security men were eventually persuaded to open the gates and let us in. This place was a real orphanage and full of children and staff to look after them. As we got to the door, cake man asked me if I'd ever been to somewhere like this before.

'Ooh, they are wonderful these places! I came to one last year, and we gave them a cake like this. It's so marvellous to see their lovely black shiny faces all covered in chocolate!'

We were taken into this second orphanage even though the staff seemed a bit confused about why we were there and what we wanted. They proudly showed us around the dormitories, and it was obvious this was a very well-run establishment. Someone asked if they could take photographs, and a little girl was brought out to the front and all the passengers got their cameras out. The matron asked if anyone had any questions for her.

From the back of the group one woman shouted out loudly:

'Does she have Aids? Does she have Aids?'

The matron was seriously irritated.

'No, she doesn't have Aids. Now if you'll excuse us, this visit is at an end.'

And with that the security men ushered us back to the van. Despite what it looked like, I have seen reports since then that the empty orphanage wasn't actually a complete scam, although it did seem like something dodgy was going on there at the time. Maybe they just needed the money to get started.

[S: I was with some of the other entertainers on the ship when you got back from that trip and told us the story. We decided the people at the first orphanage could have made it more convincing if they'd brought over some out of work child actors who had experience in the cast of *Les Miserables* or *Oliver! Surely* Cameron Mackintosh could have helped them out. Or perhaps the Sylvia Young School of Acting.]

Chapter 9

In which we move to Scotland, Steven suffers a loss and we come to a realisation about fine wine.

STEVEN

Over the winter of 2004-05 we moved to Edinburgh.

In August 2004 we had made our first appearance at the Edinburgh fringe. We hired a function room in what was then the Scandic Crown Hotel on the Royal Mile and performed there. A friend of mine called Roger Cave looked after us and even paid the rent on our accommodation for the run. He has always been very supportive of our act right from the start. When we had those initial doubts about whether to book the Royal Opera House and launch a new career as a double act, it was his enthusiasm that convinced us it really was a good idea.

Roger decided that he liked having us around so much after that summer that he was keen for us to move to Scotland. He knew that there were theatres in Scotland that would book us and that there would be a market for us at private functions.

'Why not move up here? You spend most of your life flying off to work on cruise ships: it will be much easier to fly from Edinburgh than spending hours getting out to the London airports.'

It actually wasn't that difficult to persuade us that it was the right thing to do. We could see that there were opportunities for work in Edinburgh and it was certainly true what he was saying about getting to Heathrow and Gatwick. Every time we flew anywhere it was taking two or three hours to get out to the airport. We also thought it might be a bit cheaper to live away from London. But the main benefit we saw was that it would be a clean break. In London Kevin was known as a function pianist and a session musician and for writing music for films, and people knew me as an actor. It was probably better if we made a clean escape to the one place in the country where we were only known only as a double act. It was a chance for a proper start to the act, without distractions.

Scott had started to manage us by then. We were very lucky to have him: he gave up a proper computing job and would work ten-hour days contacting every theatre he could to get us bookings. A lot of them had never heard of us and wouldn't take a risk so it was a very frustrating job for him, but it was actually Scott that got our career going. He was doing so much more than dealing with our travel arrangements and getting bookings. Scott is multi-talented: he did all our photography, show reels, and all the promotion. His parents are in Falkirk which isn't far away, so all three of us moving to Scotland made sense for him too.

Roger saw a way he could have us live next door to him. His next-door neighbour was a chef called Tom and, in the same way as we were 'convinced' to move north, it was put to him that his prospects were much better down in London. That meant he could rent his flat to us. So we hired a big white van, emptied most of the contents of our flat in Manor Park and drove to Edinburgh. There were only two seats in the front, so Kevin lay in the back wrapped up in duvets for eight hours. I would phone him now and again to check he was alright.

[K: I wasn't bothered in the slightest. I slept the whole journey!]

It took us a while to make friends in Scotland. We found people quite reserved and wondered if there was a bit of mistrust because we were English, or perhaps because we had a bit of a profile after the Edinburgh festival run. Roger and his civil partner John Jarvis-Smith kindly introduced us to the society of 'old queens' in Edinburgh, and we went to lots of dinners and candlelit suppers with the gays in their big New Town flats and Georgian houses, but we didn't seem to be making friends of our own age.

Roger was very proud of John, especially because of his war record. In November 1944, when he was twenty, he was involved in a landing operation off the Dutch coast. His boat was hit and everyone else on board was either killed or seriously injured, leaving him the only man able to steer the survivors to safety. When he got back he was surprised to find that his parents had been told that he had been killed and that he had been given a DSC medal posthumously. He had to write in to let the authorities know that he was still alive and that it was a different man called Smith that had perished. After the war he went into a shipping business with Wallis Simpson's ex-husband Ernest. He was a very interesting man who died, sadly, a few years ago. Roger and John were together for more than thirty years.

The run at the fringe had generated quite a bit of interest for us in Edinburgh. For a while after we first moved to Scotland, it felt like we were flavour of the month. We were getting lots of bookings around the city at parties and gala nights, but we were performing the same routines to essentially the same small group of people. We looked around the audience one night at a charity event and realised that just about all of these people had already seen us doing the *Fur Elise* sketch three times in the last two months.

One of the best events was a party at Prestonfield House celebrating the twenty fifth birthday of The Witchery restaurant. It was an amazing evening in a huge marquee holding more than seven hundred people. Ewan McGregor's parents were there because his mother was involved with the charity for which we were helping to raise money. I had a very strange conversation with his father just after our performance. He told me he had been to see his son's latest film which involved some nude scenes. He said he was very pleased that Ewan had inherited his father's 'best bits'. I have no idea why he thought he should tell me that. His wife just walked off in disgust.

Although Scott was moving closer to his parents, both Kevin and I were now living much further from home than before, and that was particularly difficult for me. My Mum had been ill for a long time.

It started with a sore throat, around the time when Kevin and I began working together and then it got worse and worse. It was some sort of throat cancer and the prognosis wasn't good. She had always been a smoker so I kind of knew from an early age that one day she could get cancer, and I was right. It spread from her throat and she was having a course of radiotherapy. It was a horrendous battle over a couple of years. And it went on and on and on.

Her illness coincided with our career taking off and moving to Scotland, so I didn't see her enough that year. I couldn't be there much to help look after her and I wasn't there for the worst days. My sister Dawn was living in Burton at the time and she and my Dad were the ones looking after Mum while she was ill. Sometimes I feel that I should have been there more, but she wouldn't have allowed me to be at home.

She really wouldn't have wanted us to put a hold on our career. The one thing that Mum wanted was to see me have some success at last and I owed it to her because she had spent a lot of her life driving me around music festivals all over the country when I was a teenager. She was so proud of me winning most of them, but then she saw me disappear off to college and didn't see much of me afterwards.

My family were in Crete for the majority of the time I was at college and after I left, when they came back, Mum had to see me struggle doing this and that over the years. I was always eager for her to see me do well, but apart from the concerts with Peter Katin at the Fairfield Hall in Croydon there hadn't been many occasions when she could sit in the audience and be a proud Mum, until I started working with Kevin.

It was not long after the show at the Royal Opera House that she fell ill. She was tickled pink that we were booked for the QM2 and came to see us at the Wimbledon Theatre in a nice CBeebies kind of variety show with Chris Jarvis. But the wonderful thing is that she was able to come up for the Edinburgh festival in August 2004 when we were on at the Scandic Crown Hotel.

We were a bit naïve about how the Edinburgh festival worked and the need for publicity. We assumed we would get a review early on in the run and things would grow from there. We couldn't understand why the press seemed to be ignoring us. It didn't matter too much as our show was gradually building up quite an audience, getting busier and busier just through word of mouth.

All my family were there for the last weekend, and that one show was easily the best we did in that run. It was a hot summer's day, and we got the best reaction imaginable: the atmosphere was fantastic. Even though Mum was struggling she was actually in quite good shape that weekend. She sat on the front row with Dawn, and at the end she told my sister:

'Now I've seen everything I want to see.'

She never saw us play in any big venues, but at least she was with us in that one small room. It didn't matter that it was fewer than a hundred people. It was a stand-out show, and we've had useless shows with ten times as many.

By Christmas she was really very ill. We don't mind working at New Year, but we have always made sure we have Christmas at home. Family always comes first at that time, and this year I knew that it was close to the end. It would probably be the last time I would see her. After the Christmas break we were about to set off for a long cruise around the Antarctic on the Holland America ship Amsterdam. The chances of me getting back when she reached her last hours were virtually non-existent so taking my leave from the family home was always going to be an emotional wrench. Before I left, I went up to her bedroom.

She was lying in bed, and she took hold of my hand and said:

'I love you.'

And I said: 'I love you back.'

She said: 'I can't keep doing this much longer.'

'That's OK Mum, when you're ready you just need to go, because I don't think you are going to survive it now. It's probably got you.'

She nodded her head, and squeezed my hand.

'You can only fight it so much.'

When I was walking down the stairs I stopped, and turned, and thought about going back up, but then I thought:

'No. That's a good end to it all.'

So that was it. We flew to Buenos Aires to join the cruise which took us to the Falkland Islands and then to the Antarctic and all the way up the west coast of South America. It took nearly a month and fortunately there was no bad news from home. Finally we were dropped off in San Francisco, but we couldn't go home yet because we had an engagement on another ship a couple of days later back in South America. We flew to Las Vegas for a few days' rest.

We were staying in an awful hotel. It was a late decision to go there, and it turned out there was a big computer conference going on in Vegas, and everything decent was booked up. The place we had wasn't even motel standard, it was worse than a hostel and at quite a high price. When we took the hotel shuttle bus, everybody would be dropped off at their nice hotels like the Venetian, and we had to stay on for the walk of shame at the end of the route. And then when we got there, the door to the room fell off, so we did what anyone would do: we went out and got drunk.

In the early morning Scott phoned to tell me Mum had died. Even though I'd been half expecting it to happen all the time we were at sea, it was a horrible shock. I couldn't really speak to him, and I rather shut down and became quite withdrawn for a few days.

Kevin called Holland America. Even though we were between contracts with them they cancelled our next engagement and organised our flights home and paid for it all. There were a few connecting journeys to get back, and it seemed like every flight we got on, somebody wanted to talk to us. The last thing I wanted was to chat to anybody, so Kevin made sure we were positioned so he could deal with them.

[K: There was a stupid woman who kept asking if our show was 'clean comedy' because she only liked 'clean comedy'. On the main transatlantic flight back, there was a boisterous American man who was really annoyed that he couldn't smoke his cigars on the flight. He was furious that there were no flights that allowed that anymore. He was claiming to be Jackie Stallone's best friend and was going on about her for the entire nine hours. He talked at me non-stop, and Steven was just beside himself. It was quite exhausting, one of the worst times ever.]

We got back in time for the funeral in Burton, a dark and cold winter's day. When we left there, we went down to the flat in London, which Scott hadn't yet sold. The place was absolutely freezing even though a friend of Dawn's from Australia had been staying there for a while before.

When we switched on the light in the kitchen we all saw the same thing at the same moment. It was like a scene out of a horror movie where the camera closes in on a single object and in this case it was a bottle of wine on the table which had been opened and a small amount drunk from it.

We are both quite passionate about wines and this particular bottle had been with us for quite a while. For Kevin's 30th birthday somebody had wanted to buy him a really special bottle that would go up in value, that he could have as an investment. He asked the maitre d' at the Lanesborough Hotel what he would recommend buying, and he suggested a Chateau Clerc Milon, a very nice Bordeaux.

When Kevin joined Scott and me in the flat in Manor Park he brought this bottle with him, and we put it under the kitchen sink to keep it in the correct position and temperature. The idea is you let it sleep for about sixteen years, and eventually you have something that is either really valuable or is the best wine you've ever tasted. By the time we found it after Mum's funeral, it was already worth about £200.

Dawn's friend had left a note:

'Hi -. I fancied a glass of wine and couldn't find anything apart from this one under the kitchen sink. I'm sorry, I just took one glass out of it. I've left you the rest. Oh - and this.'

"This" was an Ernest Gallo white wine that would have cost her £4.99 at Oddbins, together with two bars of Dairy Milk chocolate.

I thought Kevin might be annoyed, but actually we all felt the same. We'd just got back from the funeral and it seemed pointless to be thinking about the value of something trivial like a bottle of red wine. Why keep something for a future you don't know will happen? And especially why keep it for monetary gain? Really the only question in our minds was whether it was drinkable or not.

She couldn't have organised it better. She had taken just one glass of wine, so there was plenty left. Thankfully, as the flat was freezing cold it had been preserved, even though it had been there over a week.

It was delicious. It tasted of damsons and blackberries and spice.

Wine is meant to be drunk; life is meant to be lived. And we have tried to do both of those ever since.

Chapter 10

In which we are represented in court by a pantomime villain, confess to smuggling honey into Australia and accept some free drinks through mistaken identity.

It should come as a bit of a surprise (being the easy-going people that we are!) that we have found ourselves embroiled in several law cases over the years. It's not something we enjoy at all, but it keeps happening to us. The first court case we were involved in was when we were sued for non-payment of debts by a videographer. Of course, we had a reason why we weren't paying him.

We decided that as well as selling CDs to our audiences after the shows, it would be good if we could make a film of a show and sell some DVDs. We looked around for someone to do it for us and eventually found a nice chap to come along and make it. The arrangement we came to with him was that he would not charge us for doing the filming itself, but in exchange he could have the rights to the footage. He had an idea he might be able to sell the film to PBS in America so it potentially benefited us, in terms of publicity, to let him do that.

The other part of the agreement was that he would arrange for the DVD copies to be manufactured. After he told us what he was going to have to pay we agreed a price to buy them from him. It all seemed fair: he was making a profit on getting them made, and we could make a profit over that by selling them at our shows.

Sometime later, before we'd fully settled up with him, but after we'd been selling the DVDs for a while, we discovered that he had lied about the costs of their production. We thought we had all agreed what profit he was going to make on selling them on to us, and it turned out he was making much more than that. So we stopped paying him, and eventually he took us to court for what we owed.

The case was to be heard at Swindon County Court and we needed someone to represent us. Of course we couldn't afford to pay for a lawyer, so we talked to a friend who is a barrister, and he agreed to help.

We had quite an outrageous night with this friend and his wife, drinking fine wines from their cellar until the early hours so, when we arrived at the court the next morning, we were all rather stinking of booze. The videographer was representing himself and it probably looked a bit much when we walked in with Neil Hamilton QC, a former Member of Parliament, (who after a bit of a fall from grace, was now making a living as a pantomime villain)!

We should explain how we came to have Neil Hamilton representing us.

We met Neil and Christine Hamilton when we appeared on a chat show called *Lunchtime with the Hamiltons* that they were hosting at The Pleasance during the Edinburgh Festival Fringe. This was quite a while after they had been shamed with the stories about brown envelopes of cash for asking questions in Parliament.

As a result of that scandal they had had to take to show business because they couldn't do anything more in politics: they had had to rebrand themselves. Neil got a part performing in *The Rocky Horror Show* in his Frankenfurter outfit. Louis Theroux had just done a fly-on-the-wall documentary about them, and they were getting a fair amount of TV coverage around the false criminal allegation against them that the publicist Max Clifford ambushed them with during that film.

A fantasist had gone to Clifford with an invented tale about them having been involved in a rape. He went out of his way to sell the story to the newspapers, and Neil and Christine even ended up being arrested by the police. It was very quickly established that there wasn't a shred of truth in the allegation, but Clifford wasn't really interested in that. They felt he just wanted to ruin them. He paid for it: they were the only people who successfully sued him before he went to prison.

They had suddenly gone from being widely hated to being really loved, or at least to being people the public loved to boo and hiss at. Commercially, they were a big commodity on the Fringe that summer, and for anyone needing to promote their own performances the Hamilton's chat show was the one to go on.

Everybody wanted a chance at it, except us. We weren't doing the Fringe that year.

The American comedian, Reginald D Hunter was an early guest. He was already a very good friend of theirs. His appearance on the show caused some controversy, however. During the interview he started to play the black race card with them. He said:

'I'm not the sort of person that you would invite to one of your parties.'

And Neil replied:

'Yes, we would. We always need someone to do the washing-up!'

Of course, within hours all the newspapers got hold of it and made a big fuss, not understanding that it was all pre-arranged. When asked by a journalist how he felt about the racist comment, Reginald replied:

'I wrote that line, and Neil delivered it beautifully.'

We got onto the show through a recommendation from our friend Michael Topping. He was staying at our house while he was appearing as part of an act called Topping and Butch, a camp duo wearing red leather. He knew the Hamilton's producer and suggested that if they were looking for musical acts then Katzenjammer would be good to have on the show.

KEVIN

Butch was a much younger lad than Michael, in his twenties, and with a beautiful body that men and women would lust after. He performed in just a pair of red leather shorts, with a red leather harness and Michael was in a tight red leather dress. Part of the show was a twelve-minute medley about online dating, which they called *Gaydar The Musical*.

I did the orchestration for it and it was a lot of fun: it went through every musical style. One of the songs that still makes us laugh, was called *Nobody is going to Rain on my Charade*. They were the darlings of the Fringe and received *The Scotsman* five-star award in 2004.

During one performance a drunken woman came staggering towards Butch carrying an unscrewed bright red lipstick. Michael stopped playing and over the microphone said:

'Excuse me, what are you doing?'

To which she slurred: 'I'm going to write my name with this lipstick on Butch's chest.'

'You're not." Michael replied curtly, 'I've seen what you've done to your face'.

Although we weren't appearing in Edinburgh that year, we did have a show nearby at the Brunton Theatre Musselburgh. Neil and Christine came out to see us there, enjoyed what we did, and so we were booked to appear on their show. We performed our song about the Pope and W*hy Does the Male Ballerina Make You Blush?*

Soon after the festival we were due to appear in Cheltenham, quite close to the Hamilton's home and they came to see us again. The friendship built up from there. When we first went to their house, they took us on a tour, and we went down into the cellar to see the wonderful wine collection they have. There were bottles of champagne dating from the 1960s, including one massive bottle that was reserved for a particular celebration. They told us it was only going to be opened when Max Clifford died.

S: The morning that it was announced that Clifford was dead, I sent Christine a text: 'Get down to the cellar!' She came back with 'We're already there. The bottle's half-gone!'

The chat show was an attempt to show their real personalities and was staged as though they were having a conversation with friends in their own home. It was all very charming, and everyone would be excited to see them. They would come on to affectionate jeers and cheers, and then behave the way the audiences wanted them to. They played up to everyone's preconceived notions that he's a buffoon and she's in control of him (whereas she really isn't!).

In 2011 they did another show called *High Jinx with the Hamiltons* and we played at the end of every one of their performances. We would do a *Land of Hope and Glory* British ending for them. As hosts they were charismatic but maybe not well equipped to deal with an awkward guest. They were quite excited to get Ruby Wax to come on for an interview, especially Christine who admired her. But Ruby was really vile to them, and it proved to be a very uncomfortable show.

'What is this?' she said. 'I know who you are, you're a criminal MP who ripped everyone off, but what is this show?'

She was so rude to them; it was really cringe-worthy. They accept that they are 'Marmite people', but this came across as much more than dislike. Ruby had always been very nice to us when we had met her before, but our involvement with the Hamiltons changed that, and she wouldn't speak to us after.

When Neil and Christine went back into politics there were suddenly people who had had an association with them during their show business phase who became deeply concerned about having had a photograph taken with them in the past.

We remain friends with them, and they have been very good to us over the years. They are fabulous people who we really like, although we can't bear their politics. They know we don't like their involvement with UKIP and such like but, to be fair, they probably don't like our politics either.

We're inclined to accept that they just have opinions that are different to ours, and their views on Europe are sincerely held. They have at least been consistent on the subject for decades; since the days of Margaret Thatcher their political aim has been for the UK to leave the EU so no-one can accuse them of jumping on a band wagon.

They are well aware that UKIP attracts some very nasty types and they hate how the unpleasant elements of the country have climbed onto the anti-Europe bus alongside them. They are not in any way racist themselves, and they are certainly not homophobic. In fact, they are very protective of their gay friends and Neil was once beaten up for trying to defend his friend Harvey Proctor.

Neil is a surprisingly witty man. He used to help Margaret Thatcher with her speeches, putting in some fun and warmth into what she was saying because she had no sense of humour herself. If you ever hear anything amusing in one of her speeches, the chances are that it was Neil that wrote the line for her.

Thatcher was a great political hero of them both and they call the rooms at the top of their house 'The Margaret Thatcher Suite'. They have a life-size cardboard cut-out of her so guests can pose for photographs with her in her prime, long after she died..

S: There's a nice photo of her with us sitting at the piano. There's even one of me dancing with her!

So when we were summoned to Swindon County Court, Neil Hamilton stepped in to help us. He is actually a tax specialist, but he was helping us as a 'McKenzie Friend' – a person who is there to help you represent yourself in court, but not necessarily legally trained in the area under dispute. It was maybe a mistake.

S: I don't think the Judge liked us as soon as we got there, because we turned up with Neil. It made us look like a pair of bullies.

Neil started off in full legal-loophole mode. He told the Judge that his court had no jurisdiction over this dispute because we were domiciled in Scotland and the matter should be heard under Scottish law. The judge was flabbergasted:

'Are you kidding me?! This gentleman is representing himself and won't understand the intricacies of the discussion. Are you really telling me he has to pursue this debt in Scotland? Is there any suggestion that Scottish law would treat the contract differently? '

Neil insisted that we had entered into the contract while we were in Edinburgh, so it followed that any question about the contract had to be heard in a Scottish court.

The poor judge had to go through the legal position with him. The whole thing was very technical, but he decided the matter was a question of where the contract began. Was it when it was sent from England or when it landed on our mat in Edinburgh? His decision was that the contract was entered into when it was agreed what should be in it and that happened when it was posted and that was in England.

We will never know if that made any difference to the outcome, apart from making the judge annoyed. His final decision was that even though he understood that we had only accepted the higher price because we were misled about the margin being made, nevertheless we had agreed to it, and indeed had been paying that price until we found out.

On that basis we must have originally accepted that it was a fair price, and we couldn't just decide later that it wasn't. We couldn't claim we had lost anything by not knowing exactly how much profit was being made, and we certainly didn't have a valid excuse for not paying up.

STEVEN

In hindsight we can see that the decision was right. If you agree to pay something, it doesn't matter how the price was arrived at. It was down to us to do our research as to whether the price was in keeping with what we'd been discussing previously. We should have checked what he was paying for the discs. We just trusted what he was saying. And you should never assume people are trustworthy.

Undeterred by this set-back we decided it would be nice to have a big event to launch the DVD and Steinway Hall in London agreed to let us hold it there. We invited lots of important people: friends like Lord Glendonbrook (Michael Bishop) who at one point was the chairman of Channel 4 and owned the British Midland airline, and Kevin Bishop who at that time was still the Producer of the *Royal Variety Show*. The list of people who said yes to coming along to our DVD launch was just amazing, and we arranged caterers to do the food and a big champagne reception.

If the launch went well it was highly likely that we could get onto the *Royal Variety Show* that year. There was going to be a great mood of celebration amongst all our guests the next day anyway because the day before London had just found out that they had been awarded the 2012 Olympics. We went to bed the night before really excited about what was to come.

The party was to be on 7th July 2005.

We weren't prepared for the horror of that day. Seven-Seven is now as carved into the memories of Londoners for the same reason as Nine-Eleven is remembered in New York.

We woke up on the morning of the day of our DVD launch and found that four terrorists had blown themselves up on the London Underground and a bus. More than fifty people were killed, and hundreds and hundreds were injured. It was a horrific day and, of course, everything had to be cancelled.

It was months later before we arranged another date for the launch, but very few of the people who were going to come in July could make it the second time. Perhaps people couldn't face being reminded of why the first party had had to be cancelled.

We didn't get the *Royal Variety Show* booking, but a little while later Michael Bishop, did invite us to appear at a special birthday concert for him in Sydney. The date almost coincided with us finishing a cruise in Australia so we accepted, even though it meant we had a few days to kill in between.

Our ship arrived in Freemantle, the port just down from Perth in Western Australia. We had a nice hotel and just across the road there was a lovely bar attached to the Little Creatures micro-brewery where they make very good craft beers. We thought we would go over to sample what they had. We were intending to be careful and not have too much to drink because we had a show the next day.

A couple of locals - big Aussie chaps - came over and offered us a beer which of course we accepted. They joined us for a while and we all got talking. The drinks were downed and, as we weren't quite ready to leave, we offered to get the next round in. They insisted that our money was no good in there and bought us some more beer. It didn't seem like an attempt at a gay pick-up or anything; they were just being friendly.

Even after they went back to their own table they kept sending more beers over to us. It went on all evening, and we were starting to wonder what it was that they wanted, and whether we would be too drunk to give it to them.

Towards the end of the evening, when we were absolutely rat-arsed, they came over again and the conversation took a turn towards horse racing, a subject about which we know precisely nothing. Eventually one of them popped the question. He leant in, and said:

'So... Can you give us some tips on tomorrow's horses?'

We must have looked bewildered, and then the penny dropped. They had mistaken us for jockeys because we're so short.

STEVEN

One afternoon in New York we called in to one of our favourite restaurants to make a reservation for an early evening dinner. The person on front-of-house wrote it down in the ledger.

When we went back at six-o-clock there was no-one about, and we couldn't actually remember whether we'd said six or half-past, or which of our names we had given. So we had a look in the book. They had written:

'6.00 - Two Gay Midgets.'

We tell the story about being mistaken for jockeys onstage sometimes. We put it into the act during a performance at the Royal Welsh Academy of Music and Drama, and everyone was laughing. To our amusement, a loud voice that we recognised rang out from near the front:

'They can't be jockeys – they're too fat!'

There was a gasp of shock from the rest of the audience, followed by a second wave of disgust when they realised that the heckler was: Christine Hamliton. They were probably all thinking: 'What an awful woman' – not knowing that she's a friend of ours.

With Michael Bishop's party coming up soon it didn't seem worth coming all the way home from Australia, and then going back out again, so we decided we would take a holiday in Thailand instead. And while we were there we stocked up on antibiotics.

When we are on our travels, because we are classed as passengers, we don't get free medical treatment like the crew do. They charge passengers an absolute fortune to be treated: a basic consultation is about $150, and then you have to pay for treatment on top of that. The drugs are particularly expensive, so we try to carry some pharmaceuticals with us.

STEVEN

We were in Malta one time and Kevin decided to try the local delicacy, which is rabbit. They do seem to eat a lot of rabbit there. Unfortunately, that night his neck swelled up out of all proportion: it must have been some form of allergic reaction to the dish.

KEVIN

I went down to the infirmary and the nurse there said:

'You need to see a doctor'.

I explained that as we were on the passenger manifest, I would be charged at passenger's rates and I simply couldn't afford that.

'But you do need to see a doctor.'

'I know, but we can't afford to pay the bill. '

'I'll put you on the crew list. Now, go and see a doctor.'

STEVEN

Kevin really didn't want to come out that evening; he was so self-conscious about his swollen neck. I was trying to be nice and pretended that no-one was going to notice. I was telling him that I could hardly see it just as he stepped out of his cabin. An American woman came along the passageway towards us, took one look at Kevin's neck and shrieked:

'Oh My God! You're not going to get a girlfriend tonight, are you?!'

What we learnt from that experience was that we should have our own medicines with us. Antibiotics can be picked up without a prescription over the counter in some countries like Barbados and India. We used to get them in Thailand too, so this stopover from Australia was a good opportunity to buy some more.

When we landed back in Australia, we realised that the customs people were checking everyone who was going through the 'Nothing to Declare' channel. Australia is always very strict about what they allow into the country. You can't get away with bringing in any food - even an apple - and they will lock you up for having drugs that haven't been issued under a doctor's prescription.

STEVEN

We were standing at the end of the queue with most of the contents of a pharmacy in one of our cases and we knew we were going to be in trouble when they stopped us and searched our bags. The obvious thing to do was to dump the lot somewhere but it was pretty obvious we would be spotted trying to do that.

We had everything: azithromycin, amoxicillin...mycoxaleakin.. We were like a pair of drug dealers.

KEVIN

I said to Steven:

'They're checking everyone anyway so let's go through the 'Something to Declare' line instead.'

I had no idea what we were going to say. We were the only ones walking through there and the security staff seemed quite surprised that anyone went down that channel.

'What do you have to declare?'

I heard myself talking:

'I have a bit of a quandary. We were here at this airport a couple of weeks ago and I bought some Manuka honey. Now, I've just noticed that you have posters everywhere saying that honey is banned, and that I can't bring it in. But I bought it here at this airport and I've had only one spoonful out of the jar, and it was very expensive.'

The security man looked at me blankly, so I tried again.

'I bought some Manuka honey at this airport, and you're charging $40 a jar for it, and I've only had one scoopful out so far. Can I keep it?'

'What else do you have?'

'Well...a few indigestion tablets...'

'Oh OK – go on'.

So, he let us through and we got away with it!

We managed to get back into Sydney to perform for Michael Bishop. Michael had just sold his stake in British Midland to Lufthansa. He is a hugely successful businessman and something of a rarity; a man prominent in business who has always been open about being gay.

His place is out at Darling Point in a quite spectacular setting overlooking Sydney harbour, just across the road from the church where Elton John got married to Renate. For his birthday, Michael had invited sixty of his friends over, all gay men, and asked us to do the entertainment. He hired a very good piano for us to play and it was a really lovely night.

He'd seen us play a few times before, and he said the one thing that he especially wanted us to perform was our song about the Pope. We had long since taken it out of our repertoire, so we weren't planning on doing it if he hadn't asked for it especially.

We told him that we really weren't keen because the song does offend some people. In fact, we said we wouldn't be doing it unless he checked that no-one who was going to be there was a practising Roman Catholic. Michael assured us just before we went on that he had checked and there were absolutely no Catholics in the audience, and that everything would be fine. So, we launched into the song about Joseph Raztinger:

Everyone was laughing apart from three guys in the front row who looked absolutely furious. We could see the men in the row behind them chuckling, but also drawing their fingers across their necks, gesticulating that we were about to have our throats cut! We couldn't understand what they meant so we continued singing.

It turned out that these three were the legal representation in Australia for the Pope! Michael had set us up for his own amusement!

Chapter 11

In which we become friends with a superstar, hang out with the Botox ladies of Tramp and Kevin plays at an unintended recital for the homeless.

When we are on the cruise ships the only thing we insist on is having two separate cabins. We really don't understand why people think that because we are a double act we will be happy with just one room. We don't want to be together the whole time, especially when we are in bed.

[K: I have a bit of a sleeping disorder and snore terribly, whereas Steven is quite a light sleeper.
S: You sound like a tractor when you're asleep.]

We kept on turning up at a ship to find we'd been booked into the same cabin and having to make a fuss about it. We can only assume that the agent who was supposed to be looking after our interests at that time, Jonathan Blackburn, was just accepting the work on our behalf without passing on our requirements.

S: Scott hated having to deal with him. He used to say he was the worst man he'd ever encountered in business, and that included Gaddafi!

We eventually had to sack Jonathan because he caused us to lose our work with one of the lines.

KEVIN

We had just done a run in Edinburgh followed by another short tour in England, and then had to catch a flight to Peru. Steven was shaking with exhaustion. All the long-haul flights were taking a toll on our bodies, so we decided we had to cancel one cruise over a New Year and have an extended Christmas break. We gave plenty of notice, but Blackburn didn't accept what we were saying and didn't let the line know. He sent us an email in block capitals telling us that he was the agent, and we had to do what he said. We replied (also in capital letters) that we weren't doing it END OF STORY, but he still didn't pass that on.

As it happened this cruise was an important one for the in-house booker as the owner was going to be on board. Jonathan Blackburn didn't tell her we had cancelled until a few days before we were supposed to be there, and she probably had a lot of difficulty getting another act in time. It was no surprise she didn't want to work with us again, and as it was our favourite cruise line back then it was hard to bear.

Arriving at a ship time after time and finding that we only had one cabin between us became a long-running problem, so we made it a condition that we would not compromise on. But it was while we were making yet another complaint about it that we struck up one of our most enduring friendships.

For this particular booking we were joining the cruise in South Carolina for a voyage up the east coast of America. As usual we went up to the desk to check in and they said they only had one room for the two of us. We were exhausted after yet another tortuous journey to get to the embarkation port and we were really not in a tolerant mood.

[K: I just remember shouting at the poor girl behind the desk 'We are NOT high maintenance!'

S: A smiling American lady waiting behind us in the queue tapped me on the shoulder and said 'Hallo! I wanna get to know you two!']

We had no idea who she was, but her being so amused at us getting irate certainly helped to defuse the situation and it was all sorted out. Later, when we went into the entertainments office to ask which days we were due to be playing, we checked the itinerary and noticed that Lorna Luft, Judy Garland's daughter, was on board. That seemed quite a scoop for them to have booked her as she had just finished a run in London of her show *Songs My Mother Taught Me*. For an American audience she was a very big name. We chatted with the office staff about what had happened at the reception desk and how we had been laughed at by a very pleasant lady.

Later that evening the manageress of the jewellery shop caught up with us and said: 'There's an American couple who have already seen you, but they would like to be properly introduced.' We were expecting it to be someone who had seen us on a previous voyage, but it turned out to be the lady from the check-in queue. And then they were introduced to us as Lorna Luft and Colin Freeman, her husband.

They were – they are – lovely friendly people. To be honest we had a bit of a problem being with them to start with. Although we're not prone to being star-struck, we were both very conscious that this woman is the daughter of Judy Garland, her Godfather was Frank Sinatra, she grew up living next door to Humphrey Bogart and Lauren Bacall, and she's had an amazing, and well documented, life. Colin is a fellow pianist and Lorna's musical director when she tours. What was interesting though was how quickly that initial feeling of awe disappeared. Within minutes we were just all being ourselves, and the more vulgar we were the more they seemed to enjoy our company.

We spent a fun ten days with Lorna and Colin on that voyage. As we called in at ports on the way they insisted on being our guides around the eastern American cities we didn't know. Lorna seems to live her life in a permanent state of detached amusement. When we were walking around the beautiful houses of Charleston she was pointing out the confederate flags, and commenting on how the civil war is still raging down there. We complimented one man on how nice his house was and on cue he came back with:

'Yes! It's a shame we lost the war!'

One evening, getting back on board the ship from one of these visits there was a steward checking identification who didn't recognise Lorna. When she showed him her pass, he was stunned into asking:

'Lorna Luft? Are you THE Lorna Luft?!'

to which she retorted: 'Hmm... I guess so!'

Over the years we got to know them very well indeed and it is evident, despite what the papers like to write, that she is very close to her sister Liza and to her brother Joey too. We've stayed at their nice house in Beverly Hills, and they've come to stay with us in our modest suburban semi-detached in Edinburgh. Lorna seems to hold on to a few friends around the world who she feels she can trust, and there don't seem to be that many. She says that her mother was the same and her half-sister Liza Minnelli is too, though perhaps their trust hasn't been placed in the right people.

On one visit to America our ship docked at Long Beach alongside the old Queen Mary which is permanently stationed there as a floating hotel. Having nothing particular to do for a day or so we called Lorna to see if she was home, and then caught a train from San Pedro into the centre of Los Angeles. Lorna met us at the Beverly Hills Hotel and took us out to her house. When we got there, we noticed photographers and press reporters hiding in the trees outside the house and realised how difficult it must be to live with that kind of intrusion constantly. Lorna was actually a bit miffed because this time the press weren't there for her; Britney Spears was going through another meltdown in the neighbouring estate.

KEVIN

We spent the night at Lorna's and in the morning I sent an email to Cedric Scott to say I was in town. I hadn't seen him for years so it seemed like a good chance to catch up. Cedric was no longer married to Lee Beberman's sister, and Lee himself had gone seriously downhill since the time I spent with him in Hollywood after Neil died. Lee (and several of his friends I met then) got involved with crystal meth, and his life spiralled out of control. Sometimes I wonder if, being as vulnerable as I was at the time, I would have been caught up in that scene if I had stayed.

Lorna wanted to know who Cedric was. I explained that Cedric was a Director and Producer who worked with Sidney Poitier; they both grew up in the Bahamas. Cedric had started out as an actor but realising that Sidney was more talented and there was probably only room for one major black star in Hollywood, he had turned to producing instead.

As soon as Lorna heard his credentials she said: 'I'll take you to meet him!'

We met in a Starbucks. Cedric came in, very chuffed because his studio had just won a contract to do some of the work on the *Pirates of the Caribbean* films. I had no idea what that meant and neither did Lorna but it was obvious he was going to earn a lot of money from whatever it was.

It dawned on me that we hadn't told Cedric who our chauffeuse for the day was. I'd just said: 'This is Lorna,' when he arrived. Lorna immediately leaned across and said,

'How's Sidney?'

Cedric was obviously a bit confused about her, especially as she kept interrupting his story with things like:

'You know, Sidney's always been so good to me and my family!'

I was racking my brains to work out how to let Cedric know who this woman was. He had just started talking about how much he loved Scotland and the Edinburgh Festival so I interrupted and said to Steven:

'Oh! Did you remember to tell Lorna about that show we saw on the fringe about her mother – *Over the Rainbow*?'

'Oh, he told me, I know all about it.' Lorna burst out: 'I had them closed down! They had no rights to it!'

[S: I was horrified. Just by telling her about the show I'd put all those lovely people out of work. It was one of the best things we'd seen on the fringe: brilliantly written! And now they had to refund all the tickets they'd sold.]

Cedric still hadn't got the point: 'A show about your mother...?'

Lorna looked around her and then leaned right over and did a stage whisper.

'You see, Cedric. My mother was Judy Garland.'

Cedric's mouth dropped. He would have seen the young Lorna singing *Santa Claus is Coming to Town* on her mother's TV show. Now it made sense!

And at that point Steven and I could see what was coming next. It was the car crash scene when everything goes into slow motion and you can't stop the inevitable carnage. He was going to say the one thing Lorna never wants to hear.

'And how's Liza!'

We had quite wanted to go to see West Hollywood while we were with Lorna, as it is the centre of the Los Angeles gay community and we tried to persuade her to take us. She wasn't keen maybe because her mother is such a gay icon that she feared she would be hassled by fans. She told us once that when he was quite young her son Jesse had asked her why they never went to West Hollywood, and then he had come up with his own theory:

'Is it because there are men there who like to dress up as various members of our family?'

We were wondering why she had given him that name and explained to her that in Scotland the word 'Jessie' is quite commonly used as a term for gays. We are quite happy referring to ourselves as 'big jessies' and innocently wondered whether giving that name to him was a reference to her mother's status in the community. She was absolutely horrified at the idea.

So, we set off for the gay scene of West Hollywood on our own, and found a place called The Abbey. We ordered two cocktails thinking they would be British-sized, but when they were brought over they were the size of goldfish bowls. We were pretty well sloshed by the time they were empty but unfortunately it turned out to be 'Happy Hour' and a second one each was free on the house, so we felt obliged to finish those too.

[K: Well, it would have been rude not to. As we came out of the bar, I bumped into a beautiful chap called Carlos, a South American TV presenter I'd met before in Palm Beach, but we were so trashed that when he invited me back to his hotel room, I turned him down.]

Instead of just going back to Lorna's or to a hotel, we hailed a taxi and asked to be taken out to the ship. And then we both fell fast asleep in the back of the cab.

[S: We thought it was just around the corner, but Kevin woke up and saw that the meter was already at $250. We had no idea how long we had been asleep nor where the driver had taken us, so we started screaming at him to stop.]

He took us into a parking lot where there were a few other taxi drivers hanging about and a huge shouting match started, us drunkenly threatening to report them all to the tourist police. That threat had worked before in Greece but possibly only because they do actually have a tourist police there, whereas California does not. Somehow our 'Pomp and Circumstance' performance worked, and we managed to get the driver to take us back to where we had wanted to go for $50, and then to shake our hands when he dropped us off. Exactly how that happened is lost in an alcoholic haze. When we spoke to Lorna later she couldn't stop laughing: her view was that we were lucky to be alive.

On another visit to America, we were with Lorna in a New York restaurant/bar called PJ Clarke's. There's a decrepit brick wall inside the restaurant where it's become a tradition that people put coins in through a crack. If you're unlucky enough to get a table in that area you have to suffer people coming up and interrupting your meal while they feed money into the wall. It's going to fall down eventually with all the weight of metal behind it!

Lorna told us a story while we were there about the American songwriter Johnny Mercer. Johnny actually wrote a song called *Lorna* specifically for Lorna when she was about eleven because she was a bit miffed that her sister already had her own song, *Liza with a Z*.

Johnny had had an affair with Judy Garland when she was still in her teens and according to Lorna, one of his most famous songs came into his head late one night in PJ's. The place was empty apart from him and a bartender called Tommy Joyce. Sitting at the bar, the first words that came to him were:

'It's a quarter to three: there's no one in the place 'cept you and me...'

He went home and did a bit more work on the song. Next morning the barman got a call.

'I'm so sorry. I've been writing a new song and you're in it. But I can't rhyme anything with your name, so do you mind if from now on you're going to be known as Joe?'

He was right: 'Set 'em up Tommy', wouldn't have worked so well for Sinatra's hit *One for My Baby*.

Lorna is a good source of such stories, especially about her mother. Judy Garland was involved in so many of the great show business careers. She discovered the Australian songwriter Peter Allen singing in Hong Kong and Peter eventually married Liza even though he was gay (he died of Aids). Lorna said to us that over the years she had disagreed with her sister on many things, but the one thing they were in complete agreement about was when Liza married Peter, because she absolutely adored him.

According to Lorna there was a time when Peter was on a plane circling over New York, waiting for a landing slot. He had a meeting to get to and was getting frustrated because the plane just was not going anywhere, and he was going to be late. A line came into his head: 'When you get caught between the moon and New York City'.

He tried to write the line into a song while working with Carole Bayer Sager but couldn't make it work. Then when Burt Baccarach was commissioned to write the score for the film *Arthur*, Sager, who was working as his lyricist, remembered the line and phoned Peter to ask if she could use it. When the song won the Oscar for Best Original Song in 1981, there was some controversy because four people were credited with having contributed (the other was Christopher Cross who sang it), and all Peter Allen had supplied was the one line. Mind you, the line is used nine times in the song! Since then the Academy have allowed only two people to win that Oscar, one for music and one for lyrics.

Many of our links to the 'upper echelons of celebrity' have come through Lorna. On one visit to New York, we called in to see her when she was staying with a person who had invented a famous dental mouthwash. He owns the brand, so he is worth squillions: in two ways he is minted. He and his wife and family have two floors of an apartment building in Manhattan and they really are quite crazy: very nice but crazy.

If you've ever seen *Different Strokes* you are on the way to understanding what they are like. These are very, very wealthy people. They have more money than God. When we arrived at the apartment and met the wife we genuinely thought Lorna had turned up with Liza Minelli, because this woman looked very similar at first.

[K: I think she'd taken a shine to Steven. As they took us through the apartment, she kept vanishing, and then she would reappear in the next room wearing a different outfit. In the end they showed us their piano room, and she turned up wearing just lingerie and sat down next to him.]

One time when she was over in Scotland, Lorna took us to see her friend Barry Manilow in concert in Glasgow. They are really close, like brother and sister. We did hear a story that Barry had an affair with Lorna's mother in the early days of his career, during the time when he was accompanying Bette Midler singing in The Continental Baths in New York, but it seems very unlikely and Lorna has certainly never mentioned it. She is immensely proud of him and when he tours, she travels with him on his private jet.

There were thousands at the concert, and we were right in the front row with Lorna and Barry's husband, Gary. You will be surprised to hear that we had been drinking before the show and had a couple more during the interval. Inevitably about twenty minutes into the second half both of us were absolutely busting for the loo. Because of where we were sitting, we couldn't just get up and leave: obviously, Barry would see us both go out, and it would have been really embarrassing if when we met him after, the first thing he knew about us was that we'd walked out of his show from the front row.

We met Barry afterwards and he was really lovely and extremely down to earth. If he had noticed the surreptitious peeing in the front row he was too polite to mention it. Gary, his husband, came in saying:

'Where are these British crazy pianists then, Lorna?'

What was interesting was there was no special celebratory atmosphere backstage after playing to so many thousands – it could easily have been a small concert for sixty by the way he was relaxing in his room. We're exactly the same, of course! Prince had performed at the same venue a few days before and Barry had been to see the show. He was complaining about the volume:

'Why does anyone need to have the sound turned up so loud?'

We had our photo taken with Barry but we weren't allowed to take a selfie. He has his own photographer travelling with him so he took it, and it was emailed to us a few hours later. Understandably when you're that famous you want to look good in photos and not leave anything to chance. We put the picture on our website and Facebook pages and a friend of ours, Jane, a really lovely woman who does an Annie Lennox tribute act on the ships, innocently commented:

'That looks like a mannequin?"

Gary is very protective of Barry and if he sees anything even slightly critical of his husband anywhere, he is straight onto it. Within moments he had replied to Jane's comment with:

'And you look dead!!!'

She was confused. She honestly thought we were just larking about with a doll or a cardboard cut-out, like we do with Margaret Thatcher at the Hamilton's house. This was before Barry had come out and revealed that he was married so she had no idea who Gary was or why he seemed so angry. Her first thought was we couldn't possibly be with the real Barry Manilow but then she looked up where he was performing and realised it was genuine.

It isn't all one way of course: we have introduced Lorna to lots of our friends too. She and Colin happened to be staying with us on the day of the Scottish independence vote in 2014: Lorna was doing a show about her mother's music at The Playhouse in Edinburgh. Like so many Americans Lorna claims to be descended from Scots, tracing a line up through her mother, and for that reason she says that she feels a great affinity with Scotland whenever she is here.

STEVEN

She always says Judy Garland was a Milne and she is very proud of her Scottish heritage.

That evening we told her we would cook some food to have when she came back from the show. While she was away we got her husband rat-arsed! Colin doesn't drink usually because Lorna doesn't drink at all now, not since the days when she and Liza used to go to Studio 54 in New York and get into a terrible state. She said she got to a point where she had to choose between that lifestyle and giving it all up to start a family and she chose the latter.

When Lorna came in and saw her husband, she was a bit concerned about him:

'Colin, are you sick?'

[K: I had to intervene - 'No, he's drunk. He'll be alright!']

We had a few other people round that night including one of our ringing friends. He is an impressive chap who is actually a Geordie, but looks like a Viking or someone who's escaped from the set of Braveheart, with a big beard and long mane of ginger hair.

He has a wonderful imagination and an endearing habit of making funny noises and fidgeting, and jumping into the conversation with a hilariously tangential outburst. We overheard Lorna exclaiming to another guest.

'Who is that guy?! He just burped in my ear!'

KEVIN

We usually put Lorna and Colin in my room when they come to stay. After they've gone it's really difficult to get me to wash the sheets. I just love the idea of having Judy Garland's DNA in my bed!

There was one friend of ours that Lorna got to know so well that, when he died quite suddenly, she asked to be allowed to sing at his memorial service. He was Brian, the manager of our favourite bar in Edinburgh.

We met Brian Crawford when we first came up to the Edinburgh festival in 2004. We were introduced to a very sweet old lady called Kate Doyle who said she would like to take us to a city centre venue that her son Kevin owned. She took us into The Dome on George Street, in the heart of Edinburgh's New Town. It is a magnificent building that started life as a nineteenth century banking hall but was converted into a restaurant and high-class cocktail bar, with a night club in the basement.

Kate was greeted by a towering man, a huge presence, affable and flamboyant. And this was Brian, the manager of The Dome. Her idea was that we might play the piano in the bar, but Brian wasn't keen on that until he knew our credentials and to be honest we didn't really want to play background music. We have both done enough of that.

We got to know Brian and the other manager Kate Bell very well and it has become so much of a haunt of ours over the years that they even have a cocktail named after us on the menu: 'The Boozy Pianist'. And because we knew all sorts of people they started including us on the invite list whenever they had some kind of function going on there. We took Lorna to The Dome a few times because it seemed like the sort of place that would really impress her.

Brian had a dual responsibility though because as well as The Dome he managed Tramp, the high-end club in London's west end that Kate Doyle's son Kevin also owned through his company. It's been very popular with the younger members of the Royal family over the years, although Prince Andrew doesn't remember going there.

Brian was back and forwards all the time, flitting between the two: at The Dome in the early part of the week and then off down to Tramp for the nightclub scene at the weekend. He was always back for Sunday lunch with his mother in North Berwick though, no matter how late he'd been working at Tramp on the Saturday night before.

At Tramp he was very much loved. He used to talk about his 'girls', a posse of famous women who just adored him and would almost fight for his attention: Cilla Black, Shirley Bassey, Rula Lenska, Cheryl Howard, that calibre of star. We were invited to a dinner at Tramp once with Lorna, and all the famous ladies were there fawning over Brian. There was also a collection of people who had had so much surgery done that they didn't look anything like they were supposed to.

KEVIN

I was talking to a woman who had a prawn stuck on her top lip, but because she'd had so much Botox stuffed in there, she had lost all sensitivity and couldn't feel it. At the time she was telling me she could introduce me to her surgeon if I wanted anything done. She particularly recommended a procedure where all her blood was changed by transfusion. The prawn was poised to fall off for a full five minutes.

STEVEN

I got into a conversation with a very glamorous woman about our pets. She was very much in love with her dog and wanted to show me a photo of it on her phone. She was quite tipsy and clumsy, and she accidentally scrolled too far and held up a picture of her with her tits out, a before-and-after for her boob job. I just said: 'Oh yes that's lovely!'

Sadly Brian got cancer in his early fifties and died of a heart attack while recuperating from treatment in Florida with his partner, Christopher. Two memorial services were organised for him, one in Edinburgh and one at St James Piccadilly in London. We were asked to play a short piece during the London service, and because Lorna and Brian had grown to be such good friends, she desperately wanted to sing as well. She chose *My Funny Valentine*.

[S: I rang the funeral bell for the service up in Edinburgh.]

KEVIN

Lorna asked me to accompany her singing. The musical arrangements for all her performances are done by Colin, but he was in America at the time and couldn't get over to play. He is a phenomenal pianist and I was petrified of Colin's chords because they are quite intricate. Apart from anything else, Lorna is so used to her husband's playing and what he can do, that I really was very nervous about doing it for her at all. It seemed like a good idea to have a rehearsal at the church in the morning.

The church authorities were quite happy to give us permission to do that but what they didn't mention is that it is one of those churches where they allow the homeless to sleep overnight. They hadn't left when we got there and there were dozens of down and outs still trying to get some sleep when we picked our way through them to get to the piano. Lorna was wearing a pair of those massive Hollywood-star dark glasses so tiptoeing between them was even more fraught.

We got to the piano and there she was, dressed as glamorously as possible, the daughter of Judy Garland, giving her most solemn rendition of *My Funny Valentine* to a largely unappreciative audience of snoring and farting homeless people. A particularly raucous hawking and coughing interrupted: 'Is your mouth a little weak?' and then as she got to 'Don't change your hair for me' she stopped and looked across at me:

'You know, Kevin? You couldn't make this sh*t up.'

Chapter 12

In which we tell you about the exotic places we have visited. Steven attracts some unwelcome attention in Costa Rica and we both risk our lives on a wet rope-ladder in the Faroe Islands.

Over the years our work with cruise ships has taken us to so many different countries we've lost count; from hot and sweaty islands like Tahiti to frozen places like Antarctica where the Emperor Penguins were the same size as us. As well as the normal tourist destinations we have been to lots of unusual and remote places. Wonderful as many of these experiences have been, it isn't all as glamorous a life as some people believe. At one time we had an idea to write a book as an alternative travel guide to the world called *Stay at Home! Don't Go Anywhere! The Whole World is Crap!* If we went somewhere really gorgeous like Bora Bora, we would take some photographs of rubbish dumps or dirty toilets.

Cruise ship entertainers are only engaged for short parts of the voyage, which often means we are having to make our way to places that are difficult to get to from our home, and return from others where it is just as difficult to get back. The cruise lines also try to save on the cost of transporting us to where we are needed, so sometimes we have to endure strange combinations of flights to meet a ship as it calls into a port.

Once we did two cruises for the same line that took us in and out of opposite sides of Morocco. We were joining one ship in Casablanca on the French-speaking Atlantic coast after leaving another in the Spanish enclave on the Mediterranean, and we had to cross the border before catching our connecting plane. Even though we were in the middle of a desert we were wearing suits because we were hoping we might get an upgrade on the flight.

[K: When we tell this story in America, we have to point out that whereas Americans might think this behaviour a bit odd, the British think it is perfectly normal to wear a suit in the desert.]

A lot of people were crossing the border illegally, but we had to do it properly because we needed our passports stamped and our paperwork signed. We queued up with our trolley cases amongst the sand dunes, and eventually we were cleared to cross over to the other side. As soon as we got over the border, we were spotted by a huge group of men who looked worryingly like thieves. They caught up with us and crowded around shouting aggressively, and it was quite clear we were about to be mugged. There seemed to be no police about and we had no idea what to do: we were in total panic.

And then strangely, and without discussing it or even really thinking, we both just suddenly launched into song. We started singing *Happy Birthday* to each of them in turn, waving our arms around and conducting to get them to join in. The angry shouting subsided into confused looks, so we followed up with a rendition of *Mac the Knife* from *The Threepenny Opera and* went into some improvised dances. And with that they gave up and all of them ran away. They probably thought we were mad.

[S: It worked! Even muggers have their pride!
K: Muggers' Pride. Best thing since sliced bread.]

It was really odd that we did the same thing automatically, but as soon as we started singing we became more and more confident, as though we had taken control of the situation. We must have looked very peculiar to them as we weren't playing our parts according to the normal set of rules for victims of muggers – fear, pleading, shock – so they couldn't compute what was going on and just gave up on us.

Some of the places that cruise lines have taken us have felt very dangerous. On one occasion we were dropped off in Dakar, the capital of Senegal. Ships go there to get cheap fuel and they warn guests to be very careful if they get off. On the morning we came into the port Martin Daniels, the magician, (son of Paul Daniels) came aboard in a terrible state, white as a sheet, having just travelled in from Dakar airport, so we knew what we might be in for.

Another bad omen was that the ship's hotel manager came down to put us into a van that would take us to a nearby hotel – normally we would be left to go out on our own. Officially, she had come down to warn us that luggage had been going missing between Senegal and Paris, but as she closed the door on us it had the same feeling as John Cleese's French waiter in *The Meaning of Life* tiptoeing away after persuading Mr. Creosote to take the 'waffer-thin mint.' It was as though she was expecting us to go out with a bang and closing the van door ensured we weren't the ship's problem anymore.

The van took us through some very dirty squalid streets to a hotel that had armed guards, and we waited there in trepidation until another minicab arrived to take us out to the airport. The car was in a terrible state. We could see the prop shaft and the road through the holes in the floor. The driver was grumbling to the hotel security staff, clearly unhappy about the fee he was getting for the journey, so we weren't all that confident he was going to be on our side in any argument.

We set off, through the most poverty stricken areas of the city, very conscious that everyone could see us in the back of the car in our nice suits. There were parts of the route where the driver had to go slowly because so many people were climbing onto the car, trying to break in. We were absolutely petrified and given the mood the driver was in we couldn't be sure he was really bothered about keeping them out.

[K: I had my head right down and I even started praying! In my best broken French, I promised the driver to double his fee if he got us to the airport in one piece.]

We really didn't think we were going to make it, so when we finally pulled up outside the airport building, we handed over about ten times the fare and ran for safety, feeling very lucky to have got out alive.

To be fair, every person we came in contact with in Dakar was very nice to us: the hotel staff, the people at the airport, even the driver once he'd been given a massive tip. And since then, we've heard from other entertainers who have been there that the Senegalese are very pleasant people. Adrian Walsh, a brilliant Irish comedian we know, told us that a young lad approached him on the streets there and asked if he had any money. Adrian turned out his pockets and showed him that he had nothing, and the boy ran off. A few minutes later the same kid caught up with him again and presented him with a handful of West African Francs. Confused, Adrian asked what the cash was for.

'It is for you, who has nothing."

It turns out that in Dakar there is a tradition that if you see a stranger, it is considered very rude not to welcome them on sight. So maybe the men on the car roof just wanted to greet us and give us some money.

On that occasion it did feel like there was a real threat. Sometimes you can sense danger even when there isn't anything obvious going on.

STEVEN

We were on a ship which docked at a port in Costa Rica. Having been on board for a few days we felt the need to get off and go for a walk even though it was a really run-down derelict area and there wasn't much to see. As we were going through the port gates there were several rather dodgy-looking men who seemed to be watching us. We walked into town and everywhere we went people seemed to be checking us out, staring at us and talking about us. A couple of them, separately, came up to us and said:

'Are you Steven'?

I said I was, and then they would ask: 'From the ship?'

'Yes.'

'You are the musician? You come with me.'

We are well used to people trying to sell us things in places like that, but this was different becuase they knew my name. We just waved them away and kept walking, but then a van stopped and the driver got out and he also asked if I was Steven. There were quite a lot of people around to witness what was going on and no-one actually tried to grab us, but we really didn't like how this felt so we started to make our way back to the ship.

At first we were walking briskly, then we broke into a trot and finally a run, and we got back on board safely. Apart from the odd questions nothing had really happened, but it felt like we'd had a really close shave. We went up and told the Entertainments Director what had been going on. The colour drained out of her face: she went white as a sheet. It was obvious she knew what it was all about.

On one of the previous cruises there had been a lad – someone we had met in fact – also called Steven who did look a bit like me and was a drummer in the band. It turned out he had taken some money from someone in Costa Rica to deliver drugs to Miami where the ship was going next. He picked up a load of cocaine, but he chickened out of going through the customs check as they were approaching the American coast and threw the whole lot into the sea. It was just as well because his roommate had got suspicious and reported him. The FBI went on to the ship at Miami and found traces of cocaine on his computer, but as he hadn't actually landed and he didn't have any drugs with him they decided to let him go.

Of course, he was fired from the ship and wasn't allowed to enter America; the FBI said he wouldn't be safe there anyway. As he didn't do the delivery at the other end there was also a bounty on his head in Costa Rica. As soon as the ship returned to the same port everyone in town was on the look-out for him, hoping for a chance to make some money out of delivering him to the drugs masters.

Bolting the stable door after we'd nearly been picked up and kidnapped the security team issued instructions to all of the staff not to go ashore wearing anything, uniforms or badges, that would identify them as being from the cruise line.

There have been other times when we have been completely happy with situations that others might think of as dangerous. For another voyage, we were booked to join the ship in Walvis Bay, Namibia. The easiest route there took us through Johannesburg. Unfortunately, whoever made the flight bookings can't have understood that Namibia is a separate country and not part of South Africa. They had only allowed twenty minutes between flights, which might have been a bit tight for changing to an internal domestic flight, but as an international change requires at least two hours, it was just impossible for us to make it. We missed the connecting flight and ended up being stuck in Johannesburg. Luckily, we weren't due on the ship for a week anyway and as no-one was answering our calls to sort it out, we booked ourselves into a posh hotel for five days and had a very nice time there. It just meant spending a few days in Johannesburg, instead of on the Namibian coast.

One morning, on a whim we grabbed a taxi on the street to take us to see Soweto. The driver was very doubtful:

'Are you sure about this?'

It turned out to be a wonderful outing: everyone seemed to just accept us walking about. There was no sense of danger at all, although we did feel very self-conscious carrying bottles of water as there seemed to be only one water pump for every hundred shacks in the township. One old lady called Agnes invited us in to see her home, which consisted of a single room with just a mattress and a stove.

Although South Africa is generally quite a cheap place for westerners to visit, Soweto proved to be quite expensive for us as we acquired lots of local works of art. The most touching piece that we bought was a very thin model of a woman, the artist's mother, carved from an ebony-like wood and framed in a wooden case. He told us he had made it in her memory just after she died, and for once his story seemed genuine. The only mistake we made that day was to accept the asking price when we wanted to buy something. It was very kindly explained to us that we were meant to haggle the price downwards, but we didn't bother.

When we got back to the hotel we discovered there were hundreds of carvings, just like the one we had bought, available in the gift shops nearby. We told the receptionist where we had been and he thought we had been crazy to take such a risk; he'd never heard of anyone doing that without a proper guide. He was even more doubtful about our sanity when a couple of nights later we took an even more adventurous taxi trip.

We wanted to go out for the evening, but by then we had seen everything that the area around Nelson Mandela Square had to offer. To tell the truth, we actually wanted to go to a gay bar, so after having had a look in *Time Out,* we ordered a taxi. A bullet-proof and hijack-proof taxi turned up and we got in and asked the driver to take us to the place that had been recommended. What we didn't realise was that this particular bar was in downtown Johannesburg, and we had been told at reception very firmly that the downtown area was somewhere we really did not want to go.

Within minutes it dawned on us where we were heading. We were passing loads of street fires and the taxi-driver wouldn't stop at any traffic signals. He just slowed down and crawled towards red lights, and then edged his way across the junctions in case someone tried to get on top of the car. It was quite obvious that he was just as nervous as we were, and to this day we can't explain why we didn't just ask him to turn around and take us back. But we had decided we were going to do this, we were committed, and we just let him drive us into the middle of this apocalyptic scene.

Clearly it had once been a thriving part of the city, but now it was just horrendous. It was the sort of scary setting you see in television crime series - boarded-up shops, burnt out cars, gangs of looters. All that was missing was Helen Mirren solving some grisly murder.

[S: It reminded me of *Escape from New York.*]

We were dropped off at the address we had asked for, but to start with we couldn't see any sign of the club we wanted. It turned out to be inside what looked like a derelict building with rubbish bins on fire outside. Our driver offered to come back for us and asked how long we thought we would be there. We thought that three hours would be quite enough.

We picked our way into this dark and dingy place and as soon as we got inside, a man behind a counter handed us two plastic bags. Puzzled, we asked what we were supposed to do with those.

'It's for your clothes. It's Naked Night tonight!'

It seemed rude to refuse to go along with the theme for the night, so we had to take our clothes off, but at least we were allowed to keep our shoes on. By now we were both seriously pissed off. We were in an area of the city that we definitely shouldn't have been in, and sat in a quite hideous bar, completely naked apart from our loafers. After handing over our plastic bags full of clothes to the man at the front counter, we went up to the bar and demanded two very large glasses of wine. He just shook his head and said:

'No, we lost our alcohol licence two weeks ago. You can have tea or coffee.'

It was the longest evening of our lives, stark-bollock naked, perched on grubby bar stools sipping tepid tea. And worse than all that - absolutely no-one approached us!

After exactly three hours we reclaimed our clothes and left the building. Fortunately, our driver was right outside, waiting for us, engine running. We thanked him profusely for coming back to get us so promptly, and said we hoped he had had a much better time since we last saw him , than we had.

 'I've been here all the time,' he said. 'I didn't leave.'

The knowledge that we need not have sat naked in that place for three hours, just tweaked the misery up a little.

The evening ended well though because when we arrived back at the hotel on Nelson Mandela Square, we bumped into a fitness instructor called John who we had met some time before on the QM2. We were so annoyed at having had such a wasted evening that the three of us tore into the alcohol very quickly and ended up wasted in another sense.

Next day we travelled across to Namibia and joined the ship on a cruise from Walvis Bay to St Helena, the remote island in the middle of the Atlantic. It takes five days to get there by sea and, as the airport had not yet been built, it would be another five days to get back. It is a beautiful island, a thousand miles from any other land mass and the people speak with a strange Cornish accent. What is especially noticeable there is the quality of the air. Colours seem more vibrant, and you can smell the grass and flowers as you walk about, because it is all so clean. It probably hasn't changed at all since Napoleon died there.

We have been to quite a few really remote places. Cruises across the Pacific take a very long time and there are only a small number of little islands to drop by. They are put into the itinerary to break up long periods at sea to give passengers, a break from days of watching the ocean go by, but some of these places don't offer very much of interest. Perhaps the most famous is Easter Island which is lusciously green but hot and humid.

The statues are awe-inspiring. Supposedly each one represents an actual person the ancient island people wanted to remember: a king, a queen or a local dignitary. The most surprising thing for us was that the statues don't look out to sea as we'd expected: they face inland looking towards the islanders. They weren't there to protect them by warding off invaders from the ocean; as far as the islanders of the time knew, there was no-one else in the world apart from them so they had no-one to fear.

On another cruise we visited a small island off Madagascar called Nosy Be. The water was very shallow, so we had to wade through the sea to get onto the beach there, and not many passengers made the effort and came ashore with us. The locals weren't wearing much in the way of clothes and for some reason they seemed very interested in our shoes. The island was absolutely beautiful, and the wildlife was amazing: lots of black flying foxes skimming through the trees. We thought it was well worth the visit.

STEVEN

Having had a look around, we sat down outside a beach shack and ordered a drink. It was a very pleasant afternoon and we had been sitting quietly looking out to sea for quite a long time when I suddenly realised there was something wrong.

'Kevin? Where's the ship?'

The ship had sailed away without us. There were only a couple of other passengers there with us, and one of them said he could just make out the funnel sailing away over the horizon. Obviously, there was no point in shouting or waving, and there was no phone signal.

[K: We were sitting in no more than a mud hut drinking some kind of fermented local juice that seemed to be hallucinogenic, and as time went on, the less and less bothered I felt about being stranded there. I thought 'We're supposed to be doing a show tonight, but I don't care!']

We assumed that eventually someone on board the ship would eventually miss us – but maybe it would be just before we were due to go on stage. We carried on drinking, the afternoon getting ever more hazy. At some point the bartender waded out into the sea and caught a couple of fish with his hands and then cooked them for us on the beach. We amused ourselves feeding bananas to the tame indigenous monkey.

Sometime in the early evening our ship reappeared and we were rescued. The show that night probably wasn't one of our best but it's hard to remember.

A rather exciting island we wouldn't want to get stranded on is Komodo, although there is talk of it being closed to visitors soon. We were lucky enough to visit a few years back but no-one was allowed to go anywhere on the island unaccompanied until the locals had fed the Komodo dragons with goats. Not long before we were there, someone had strayed off the beaten track, been bitten by one of the dragons and become paralysed, and unable to run away, had been eaten. Having seen what was left of the goats sacrificed on our behalf, we were glad the dragons we saw weren't hungry.

Perhaps the most remote place we've been is Pitcairn, halfway between Chile and New Zealand. The only reason to go there is if you're interested in knowing what the product of incest looks like. For that alone we would recommend a visit because it is full of very unusual looking people. We met a very nice man while we were there who claimed to be a direct descendant of Fletcher Christian, the leader of the mutiny on The Bounty. As there will have been so much in-breeding amongst his ancestors he is probably a descendant several times over. He and some other islanders came on board selling postcards and lots of old tat that no-one really wanted but felt obliged to buy. We bought a card from them and sent it to Kevin's aunt, even though we assumed the post office was just a scam. In fact it did reach her. Eight months later.

It must be a very odd life living somewhere so far from everywhere else. We have been taken to some really remote places in Europe too, and found that the people in the far north of Scandinavia have a different attitude to life from the rest of us, particularly in Norway. Maybe the fact that they spend six months of the year in darkness and six in near constant light has an effect on their mental health. Certainly the further you go up into the Arctic circle, the more popular suicide seems to be as a pastime.

On Spitsbergen, a really remote Norwegian island, about as far north as the ships ever go, we discovered that there is such a problem with alcohol consumption, the government control the liquor stores and limit the amount that locals can buy to one litre of spirits per month. Alcohol is hugely expensive and normal shops don't sell it at all, so there is almost a sense of shame around asking for it. Visitors can buy as much as they want to though if they produce a passport.

Of course, everyone knew when the cruise ships passengers were coming ashore, so every week a scene played out that was a reversal of what happened in our teenage years when we used to ask pensioners to buy cans of lager for us. Here there were old men hanging about outside the booze shop asking young tourists to buy bottles of vodka for them.

But darkness and restrictions on alcohol aren't the only problem they have to contend with.

[K: I was attacked by an arctic tern there (that's a bird, not a cabaret act). The terns nest on the ground, so when we were walking along a coastal path we must have strayed a bit too close to a mother bird's chicks or eggs.

S: You were running along the path with a huge bird pecking at your head, blood streaming down your face, just like Tippi Hedren in The Birds. It was really funny!

K: It was really scary, you mean. I had little prick marks all over my scalp.]

Our friend Spencer Cousins toured the northern parts of Norway once and told us that he came away with the feeling that the Scandinavians have a healthier view of sex than the rest of Europe, and we discovered for ourselves that he was right. One night we were in a bar in Helsinki and got talking and drinking with a couple of local guys for a few hours. Their English was impeccable, much better than our Finnish, and we were all getting on very well when suddenly one of them said, with no warning, and quite casually:

'OK – now we go have fun together?'

We hadn't realised it, but right in the middle of the bar, there were some little rooms where anyone could nip in and get to know each other (a lot) better, in between pints of beer. It rather explained what we had been hearing.

[S: 'Up a bit, just there!... No, left a bit...'

K: I just assumed it was two people putting up a rather heavy picture together.]

One lesson we have learnt the hard way is to ensure that we always have at least one free day, between travelling to a venue and the day of the show itself. On that northern cruise we had cut it a bit fine. We were meant to disembark on the Faroe Islands just a day before we were due to play at the Chichester Festival. As we approached the port at Torshavn the weather was atrocious and the captain announced that we were going to be at sea for at least another two days before we could have another go at docking.

This was very early in our career and it looked like it was going to be disastrous. Chichester would have sued us and we would have damaged our reputation just as we were starting out. It must have been pretty obvious what a panic we were in because the cruise entertainment director took pity on us and got the captain to call up a pilot boat. We were given ten minutes to pack our things and be ready to get off.

In the roughest of seas imaginable the pilot boat came alongside, but it looked tiny beside the cruise ship. Its deck was at least twenty feet below us so there was no chance a gangway could be put across: there was only one way we could get down to it. Gripping the handle of our suitcases with one hand, and the slippery rungs with the other, we were lowered over the side of the ship on an old rope ladder, as the two vessels crashed into each other on the waves. We didn't have lifejackets because the crew said they wouldn't be any help in those waves, so one slip would have been the end of us.

We were accompanied on this perilous descent by an ageing American comedian known as 'The Mirthgiver' who seemed to be really enjoying the experience. Part way down, a head popped out of a porthole. It was a Dutch hotel manager who we had met on board the night before. He offered us some chocolates from a tin of Quality Street.

'Would you like a toffee finger?'

We threw our bags onto the deck of the pilot boat, grabbed some caramel swirls and green triangles to take with us and carried on down. Fortunately, we caught our flight back, and just made it to Chichester in time.

As it happened we had a great time at Chichester. It turned out Patricia Routledge, the actress famous for the sitcom *Keeping Up Appearances*, was in the audience to see us and we ran into her the next day. We had noticed that there were only two people sitting up in the balcony at the show. Apparently, she had gone up there with the woman responsible for the bookings and no one else was allowed to follow them. We said we were very pleased to meet her, and she responded in full Hyacinth Bucket mode:

'I was very pleased to see you do some Gracie Fields songs last night!'

In our Katzenjammer routine we did do some Gracie Fields songs like *Nice Cup of Tea in the Morning* and *Everyone Keeps Pinching My Butter*, but we changed the lyrics. Somehow, we managed to get 'prosthetic knee' to rhyme with 'cup of tea'.

Believe it or not, playing the Faroes and Chichester on consecutive nights is not the most outlandish itinerary we have committed ourselves to. For a long time, there was a section in our show where we told the audience that it was Kevin's birthday (even though it hardly ever was). It's a nice trick to get the audience on your side, and many performers before us have used it through the years. Gene Pitney would have a birthday cake brought onto stage every night during his tours. Unfortunately, there are some members of our audiences on ships who are inclined to sit with their arms folded, determined they aren't going to put any effort into the process of being entertained. Strangely if you tell them it is your birthday, it provokes a human response, especially with British people. They reconnect with empathy, and they are suddenly committed to enjoying themselves.

[K: It was part of quite a good joke that we used to do, but it doesn't seem fair to play that trick on people when we're on land, where the audience have paid to see us.

S: We used that section in Cape Town recently when it actually was my birthday, and we did the joke the other way round. It was very strange doing each other's lines.]

Even though we were rarely actually performing on Kevin's birthday, quite often we were away on a ship or travelling to one. Scott was managing us for a while, and there was a long-standing joke between the three of us that Kevin never got to celebrate his actual birthday at home. One year we were in the middle of a tour of the UK, and it appeared that for once there were actually going to be some free days around the birthday so that we could go home and celebrate.

About a week before the day, we were about to set off to perform at the Pitlochry Festival Theatre (in the middle of Scotland), when Scott took a phone call. Smiling, he told us he'd managed to get us a booking for Kevin's birthday:

'It's just 48 hours on the QE2'.

'Where are we joining them?'

'Oh, I forgot to ask. I'll call the agent back.'

When he came back, he was laughing. 'It's in Papua New Guinea!'

We agreed to do the concert, but getting there was absolutely exhausting. Even though it could be done in three stages, Cunard had arranged a cheaper schedule that took six flights and an overnight stay in Manilla. The fifth flight took us to Port Moresby, the capital, and from there we were due to fly further east to Rabaul on the island of New Britain to catch up with the QE2 sailing up from Australia.

There are several active volcanos near Rabaul, and when we arrived in Port Moresby one was threatening to erupt. The local airline didn't want to risk their plane in the ash clouds, so having flown all that way it looked like the last flight was going to be cancelled and we weren't going to make it to the ship. To start with, sitting in the airport, we were really hoping that the flight would be reinstated so that we wouldn't have to turn around and go all the way back, but then someone started telling us some worrying stories about the place we were trying to get to. One was that cannibalism had only recently been outlawed in the country, and that it was probably still going on in some of the more remote islands like New Britain. There was also a tale that two women had been lowered into the volcano recently, accused of being sorcerers. It started to sound like it might be a blessing if our plane was cancelled.

The most plausible story was that some of the islanders were addicted to chewing betel nuts that produce hallucinations, and when we were eventually cleared to fly and arrived in Rabaul our taxi driver was clearly off his head on something, and his teeth were all blackened. We were scared that after such a horrendous journey - six flights, an overnight stay in a grubby hotel in the Philippines, and an erupting volcano - we might actually die in a crashed car in the last mile, on Kevin's birthday.

We made it to the ship though and did our show and then got back to the UK just in time to resume our tour. So, the schedule for that week was:

Pitlochry Festival Theatre.

Newark Palace Theatre.

Papua New Guinea.

Berwick-on-Tweed.

Chapter 13

In which we star in a Canadian play in Austria and endure a weekend with an American deity.

Whenever we meet Canadians or Americans after our performances there will usually be someone who asks us if we have heard of, or seen, the play *Two Pianos, Four Hands.* When this first started happening we didn't know what they were talking about, but as it kept getting mentioned to us we became aware that it was very big in North America. In fact, it is Canada's most successful play ever, and one of the most produced plays in the USA. Since it was first performed in Toronto in 1995 it has played to over two million people in one hundred and fifty cities on five continents.

It tells the story of two young pianists, Ted and Richard, who each dream of becoming classical pianists. They compete with each other at competitions, but gradually come to realise that neither is going to have the musical career they wished for. We could see why people made a connection between that story and us, but to be honest we were getting sick of hearing about it.

And then we were asked to get involved in a production of it.

KEVIN

As so many episodes in my life do, this started with a conversation with someone on Gaydar. This chap had no profile photograph and I usually ignore people like that, but for some reason I engaged with him and he told me he was working in theatre. It turned out to be Paul Iles who was running the Richmond Theatre in North Yorkshire, and was also the manager of the Blackpool Grand.

As a result of that conversation Paul gave us a try-out at Richmond, and then said he would book us for Blackpool. He really was a great help to our career, because once he had taken the risk and we'd been seen at the Grand, other theatres started to ask us to appear.

[S: He was a lovely chap, and he also had a lot of respect for Scott who was managing us in those days. He's also the friend we mentioned earlier who would drink wine all day, very slowly. Only four glasses of wine a day, but each would take him several hours over each. Sadly, he died a couple of years ago.]

Before going to Richmond, Paul had set up the Festival Theatre in Edinburgh which was now being run by John Stalker. John had put on a production of *Two Pianos, Four Hands* during his time in Birmingham but hadn't managed to find anyone in the UK who could perform the play that time. He had had to get the original authors, Richard Greenblatt and Ted Dykstra, over from Canada to do it for him. Paul knew that John was still hoping he might find someone in Europe who could do it in Edinburgh.

STEVEN

The play involves lots of different characters, but they are all performed by the two actors. When the focus is on one of the characters the other actor plays the parts around him. It also involves quite a lot of music so what is needed is two concert pianists who can also act, or two actors who can play the piano to a very high standard.

They don't just need to be able to act a bit, they have to be able to play a lot of different people convincingly and do a variety of voices and accents. The chances of finding that combination are pretty close to nil; most concert pianists can barely speak to their audience! That probably explains why a lot of the productions have involved Richard and Ted. They've performed the play several hundred times.

Paul Iles got in touch with John Stalker and said:

'I've found the two guys you've been looking for.'

John had actually been keeping an eye out for people for about ten years, so on Paul's recommendation he asked if we would perform at a variety show he was putting on at the King's Theatre in Edinburgh to give a demonstration of what we could do. John was responsible for both the Festival and the King's Theatres in Edinburgh.

He offered us the chance to open the show and explained that he was going to get Allan Stewart to organise the rest because he does the pantomime at the King's every year and is one of Scotland's best known variety performers. John had asked us to do the first half, but Allan cut that down to only fifteen minutes. It seemed like he felt a bit threatened by us being the opening act, and then he told Scott that we would have to be cut down even more. Scott said that was out of the question; we would have to pull out. John was still very keen to see us in a performance situation, and had our slot reinstated and of course the show went down very well.

Allan's response after the show was to proclaim on his own website that it had been a brilliant night, and he gave his own critique of each act. His wife, he said, had sung beautifully and brought so much class to the evening. All that he could say about us was that 'Katzenjammer added style' – an ambiguous phrase of very faint praise.

Since then Allan Stewart has produced a similar variety show almost every year. He knows that we are based in Edinburgh, but he has never once asked us back, even though he has brought other piano acts up from London to appear. Our friend Roy Walker, of *Catchphrase* fame, once asked Allan why he doesn't make use of us since we are local, and apparently the reason is that we aren't Scottish.

Allan is Scottish, of course. He lives in London, as does his daughter Kate who has appeared in the show.

John Stalker was very happy with what we had done at the Kings and took us over to Canada to meet Richard and Ted, which was very exciting. They needed us to audition for them, which we did at the Yamaha offices in Toronto (as Yamaha pianos were sponsoring the play). Then Richard Greenblatt came back to this country to direct us in a short portion of the play, which we had to perform in front of some potential funders and Michael Harrison, a leading tour booker in the UK involved with the London Palladium and Lloyd Webber musicals. This version of the play lasted about forty minutes, but we had only a few days with the author to put it together.

After the performance we were taken to an Edinburgh club by a cigar smoking Richard without knowing what the outcome of the funders' deliberations was. He told us:

'Michael's very impressed with your commitment. You guys are going to be very wealthy!'

And then all the funders arrived at the club, and it was obvious that everyone had pound signs in their eyes, and it looked like a long tour of the play was going to be organised.

The tour didn't happen.

However, word had got out that we might be able to perform the play. The English theatre director Julian Woolford got in touch with Julia Schafranek who runs the Vienna English Theatre to say he had heard of two guys who could be cast in *Two Pianos, Four Hands* , and wondered whether she was interested in taking us on. Julia had been carrying on her own long search for someone to perform the show and had almost reconciled herself to the idea that she would just have to wait until someone brought the play to her.

Julian came up to Scotland see us performing as Katzenjammer at the Brunton Theatre in Musselburgh and took us out for drinks after the show. He was selling us the idea that we would have a lot of fun if we went over to live in Vienna for a couple of months to do the play with him as Director. And then he slipped into the sales pitch, almost as an aside:

'There'll be hardly any money, but you'll have a great time...'

STEVEN

Kevin said: 'Oh well. If there's hardly any money available, I'm not interested.'

And then turned his back on Julian and talked to someone else for the rest of the evening.

The next morning Julian phoned me:

'I think I may have made a bit of a twat of myself last night with Kevin.'

But to be fair to Julian, he was actually being honest. The Vienna English Theatre is well known for not paying very well. Famous as it is, they usually only do dramas, and rarely stage commercial shows like musicals. Even though it's a theatre of only two hundred seats, they quite often don't manage to sell out. And when they did get around to making us an offer, the money proposal was just horrific. There was no way we could give up our other work for two months for what they had in mind.

They assumed that everyone was desperate to get a chance to work at their theatre. When we auditioned for them we had just been recording *Friday Night is Music Night* for BBC Radio 2 with the opera singer Willard White. They got us to read a bit, and play a bit, and then we started to talk about money. The play was going to open the autumn season in 2009, and they wanted us to understand that the first production of each year rarely sells well. We told them we couldn't possibly do it for their first offer, so they upped it a bit and we turned that down too. After the third offer we told them we would have to go away and think about it and left them to stew for a while.

Of course, in the end we decided we would do it.

We had just started rehearsing with Julian in London when, out of the blue, we got a phone call asking us if we would go to Chicago for the weekend. As it happened the following Monday was a bank holiday so we weren't due to resume work on the play until the Tuesday, but it did mean we would have to miss the Friday to catch an early flight. We asked permission from the producer, promising that we would learn our lines on the transatlantic flight.

When she heard our reason, she said it was the most unusual excuse she'd been given, but she certainly wasn't going to be the one to refuse a request like that. We needed the time off because we were being asked to perform with Mickey Rooney!

Apparently Mickey had seen us performing on a Youtube clip. Back then if you received a million hits you were probably in the top ten most viewed. These days it would take about three hundred million hits to even get noticed. We had one successful clip on Youtube at the time: a film of us performing *The Simpsons* theme tune. A friend of Mickey's had seen that and shown it to him, and that was enough for us to get the chance to perform with him.

STEVEN

We phoned our friend Lorna Luft because we knew Judy Garland had been close to Mickey Rooney, and she would know what he was like.

'Don't do it!' she said. 'He's skint! He invested all his money in a "Hair-in-a-Can" product in the fifties and lost the lot. You won't get paid!'

We told her we knew we definitely would get paid. We'd already agreed a fee of three thousand dollars with his manager Kevin Pawley. He had promised it would be covered by Mike Schwimmer, a friend of Mickey's, who had made his fortune by inventing Glowsticks. He still held the patent for them so he was worth millions.

The flights were arranged for us (business class which was lovely) and when we arrived we were checked into a nice hotel and generally treated like royalty. On the Saturday morning Mickey and his entourage came round in a car to pick us up.

The odd thing about Mickey Rooney was that he seemed quite insecure and kept dropping the names of famous people he knew into the conversation. While we were all in the car a John Williams musical score came on the radio and he shouted out:

'That's John Williams, I know him!'

[K: We just thought: 'Well of course you do. You're Mickey Rooney. We assume you know everyone!'

S: It was as though he constantly needed to impress us, which became a tedious nightmare quite quickly.]

He was eightynine and it really did seem sad that he had got to that age and still needed to show off to people he'd never met before. It was also quite obvious that he and his manager Kevin Pawley hated each other, but at the same time they both desperately needed each other. Kevin kept asking us questions, but it seemed like he was only doing it to annoy Mickey rather than because he was interested in us, and Mickey was constantly trying to butt in to bring the conversation back to him. The experience was difficult to deal with, but also fascinating.

Mickey was really nasty to everyone around him that day, apart from us. We quickly decided that if any of the unpleasantness came our way we were going to tell him where to go, and he seemed to sense that we weren't going to take any nonsense. And he needed us to do the show.

On the Saturday night we were picked up in a people carrier with blacked out windows. Mickey had decided that we would all go to see his friend Tony Bennett performing at the United Center Stadium, in front of twentyfive thousand people. There was constant bickering between Mickey and his people as we drove along, and then they couldn't find anywhere to park. The police were trying to move us on.

[K: I said – why don't you just wind down the window and tell them who is in here?']

When the police saw it was Mickey in the car, they just guided us through. It was as though their god had come amongst them! And as we walked into the stadium everyone seemed ready to worship him. We sat down for a meal, and fans were gathering around the table all wanting to shake his hand. He was paranoid about germs so he just kept fist-bumping people rather than risk them touching him properly. The more people crowded around the more irritable he seemed to get about it, behind a fixed smile of course.

Mike Schwimmer tried to calm him down:

'Mickey, they're only coming over because they love you.'

To which Mickey shrieked in response

'Yes! But they won't save you!' which seemed a very odd thing to say.

[K: Mickey couldn't even go into the toilet without someone getting a phone out to film him having a pee!]

Tony Bennett called round to meet Mickey's party. To us he seemed a bit (shall we say) 'preoccupied', but he managed to deliver the most amazing concert nevertheless. He didn't forget a word and didn't go out of tune once. The support act had been a woman singing very badly, and we couldn't think why she had been chosen to open the show for Tony Bennett, until she finished and the announcer said:

'Ladies and Gentlemen, please give a big round of applause. You've just been listening to Miss Antonia Bennett!'

We were thoroughly enjoying Tony's performance until part way through, between songs, he told the audience:

'We have Hollywood royalty with us here tonight! Cary Grant and Laurence Olivier both described him as the greatest living screen actor in the world! Would you please welcome...Mr. Mickey Rooney!'

Mickey loved this kind of attention and everyone in the stadium started screaming. Because we were sitting next to him we stood up when he did, out of respect. A close-up image of the three of us flashed around the screens in the stadium, and we realised that we were all pretty much the same size, and that everyone must have assumed we were somehow related. The Americans behave quite differently from British people in that kind of situation. It really felt like these people were in a frenzy of wanting him so much that they might actually eat all of us.

The 'love' that was being poured on Mickey was quite frightening and, unused to this adulation we both suddeny had an overwhelming feeling that we had to get the hell out of there. Fortunately the security team came over to protect us from the fans and escorted us out, but people were reaching over the policemen to get a piece of us all, even trying to pull our hair. We were directed out through a safe exit and left the stadium while Tony was belting out *I Left my Heart in San Francisco* and that was the end of us enjoying the Tony Bennett concert

On the Sunday we did two shows with Mickey in St Charles, Illinois, which is a town about forty miles west of Chicago. We performed the first half of the show, and Mickey and his wife did the second half. When he went on stage after the interval, he opened with

'This is all that's left of Mickey Rooney!'

and in that moment, you could see how fragile he was.

After the second show we all went out for another meal and it was all great fun. Kevin Pawley was telling us he'd not seen an act get such a reaction for ages and he could arrange for us to get a show in Las Vegas if we wanted it. It was our first appearance on land in America and the sky seemed to be the limit.

We all left on good terms, and Mike Schwimmer said our fee was waiting for us in our room at the hotel. Exhilarated at the weekend's experience and the prospect of a cheque for $3,000 to take to Vienna with us, we got back to our room.

STEVEN

It didn't matter that we weren't going to be paid much for acting in the play now; with that amount of money we were going to be able to live like kings in Vienna.

We went into the room and looked around, but there was no envelope anywhere. All that was different from when we had left in the morning was that someone had put a suitcase just inside the room. For a moment it crossed our minds that perhaps we were being paid in cash, but then we opened it.

Inside: twenty kilos of glow-sticks.

No cheque, no money. Just twenty kilos of Mike Schwimmer's glow-sticks, some novelty glasses, things for waving, and necklaces that glow. That was our fee. We'd been diddled.

KEVIN

I phoned Kevin Pawley: 'We agreed on that fee'.

'No, we didn't' he said, 'I never confirmed it.'

'Oh, come off it, you know what was agreed. Why have you done this to us?'

'To give you an opportunity to perform in America.'

'We don't need the opportunity, we're already busy. We interrupted rehearsing a play to come over here.'

I slammed the phone down.

STEVEN

We took the glow-sticks and they lasted us years for children's Christmas presents. We can laugh about the whole thing now and we probably wouldn't exchange the experience we had for the world. But it took us over ten years to admit to Scott that we hadn't been paid for that weekend.

The next time we saw Lorna Luft she said:

'So. How did it go with Mickey?'

We had to admit we hadn't received our fee.

She laughed. 'Hello? Of course you didn't get paid!'

Over that weekend we must have spent about four hours in the car with Mickey: it just takes forever to get anywhere over there. When he found out we knew Lorna very well, it was as though he could finally stop trying to impress us. We were no longer fans, we had become part of what he regarded as his extended family. He had been very close to Judy Garland, and also to Liza Minnelli at one point.

Lorna tells a story about Mickey getting up to speak at her father's funeral. Sidney Luft was Judy Garland's third husband and the producer of the remake of *A Star is Born*. A projector failed during the eulogy presentations and Mickey stood up and offered to fill in while it was fixed. But instead of talking about Sidney he launched into a series of stories about himself and Judy which Lorna finally had to interrupt by shouting out:

'Wrong dead person, Mickey.'

On the trip back from St Charles a misty-eyed Mickey told us that Judy had been the love of his life, but she just wasn't interested in him.

'Judy and me,' he said, 'we weren't lovers. We weren't husband and wife, we weren't brother and sister, but what we <u>were,</u> was magic'.

That sentiment resonated with us. And so we felt the weekend had been worth it, even as we lugged all those glow-sticks onto the plane.

We got back to London and returned to preparing for Vienna. Julian proved to be a brilliant director and he let us put our own stamp on the play. As written, the play finishes with a rendition of Bach's D Minor concerto which unfortunately brings the atmosphere right down. We said we would do a bit of the Bach and then go into our usual routine playing together on one piano, to cheer people up before they left. It was good that he let us do that, because it went down a storm every night.

As Julian had promised, we did have fun during our two months in Vienna and we became very good friends with him and still see him from time to time. The theatre put an immense amount of publicity behind the show, supported by the Canadian Embassy in Vienna, and it became their best seller in forty years. We probably made a fortune for them, but not much of it came our way. They did allow us to ship over and sell our own merchandise though. We made more money from selling our own CDs and DVDs than we were paid for the performances.

As the run there had been hugely successful, it looked like the original plan to tour the play in the United Kingdom might be resurrected. However, the backers didn't want Julian Woolford to be our director, even though he had done such a good job for the Vienna season. Instead they brought Richard Greenblatt, one of the authors, back over; and Ted Dykstra was to be involved too. John Stalker arranged a two week run at the King's Theatre in Edinburgh, and following that it was agreed there would be two weeks in Perth. Assuming all was going well, we said we would think about venues in England.

As soon as we started talking to them Richard and Ted made it clear they didn't like the alterations we had made with Julian. They wouldn't budge on anything; even minor changes we had made to the way the characters were played were thrown out despite the fact that we knew they worked. They were especially strict about us doing the ending exactly as they had written it, with the full Bach D Minor concerto and without our coming together on the one piano as we had in Vienna.

The concerto is very difficult to play and certainly a striking piece to finish on, but it isn't everyone's cup of tea. We knew that the impact it has in Europe is somewhat different to how it goes down in Canada; over here audiences hear such works pretty regularly and aren't as easily impressed as Canadian audiences can be. The thing about Edinburgh audiences is that they have a huge influx of culture every year at the Festival, so they have seen everything the world can offer.

It wasn't only the ending that we felt wouldn't work in Scotland. When we had been over in Canada, we had heard about Jeremy Sams who had directed the play when it was first performed in London. He had also had a lot of reservations about the writing, not least that the play was far too long. For the first UK version he had cut about a third of the dialogue and honed it down to a one act play. In doing so he left out a lot of the cultural references that meant less in Europe than in North America. He thought the success of the production in London was largely down to his having adapted it for a British audience. Apparently, Ted and Richard hated what he done and declared that his version would never be performed again.

We felt we knew what would work best in Scotland and could see the merit in cutting anything that would leave our audiences bemused. We knew for instance that all the references to Jewish life would not resonate here because there just isn't such a large Jewish community in Scotland. We were sure we had a much better idea of what was right for Edinburgh than they did and that our local audiences would never buy in to the schmaltz and the cheesiness that Richard and Ted could get away with Stateside.

KEVIN

One scene particularly grated on me. In it, I was playing the father of Steven's character and trying to persuade the son to practise. The line was:

'Look, I love you and I want you to do well.'

I was going to explain to Ted and Richard that in this country that line doesn't ring true. That particular generation of fathers in Britain just wouldn't tell their sons that they loved them. Before I could get it out, they started telling us that Jeremy Sams had said the same thing. Ted described him as an arsehole who doesn't know fathers love their sons.

We had a blazing row with Richard on the first day of rehearsal. He was insistent that we had to finish on the Bach, so we asked if we could do our Vienna ending as the encore. But he wasn't having that either:

'You will do *Sheep May Safely Graze* for the encore.'

[S: We said we'd rather commit suicide. It's a wonderful piece of music but no good as an ending for the play. We wanted a strong Scottish cheddar ending, not mild Canadian cheese!]

He got quite unpleasant and insisted we do whatever he told us to. I pointed out that actually we could do whatever we liked as an encore, because he wouldn't be there to see it. I'm afraid we were screaming at each other!

STEVEN

We came close to it but I'm glad we didn't walk out on them, because we did do it rather well. But the reason the show wasn't the huge success it could have been in Edinburgh and in Perth, was down to Ted and Richard being too stubborn. John Stalker had wanted to produce the Jeremy Sams cut down version, but they seemed to think they had written the equivalent of an Ibsen play, and it just wasn't that good.

We did perform the Bach concerto in full, but then naughtily went into our rendition of *Highland Cathedral* - usually played on the bagpipes - as the encore. We chose that piece because it gradually builds and builds towards a conclusion. We started it on the two pianos and then part way through came together on the one keyboard, just as we had in Vienna. Richard came to the last performance of the Edinburgh run and was quite taken aback when he saw what we had done, but it was too late to stop us.

In *The Scotsman* the production was awarded four stars, even though there was some harsh criticism of the play itself. The reviewer disliked the assumption that Edinburgh audiences would be interested in all the Canadian references, but recommended people see the 'magic that Katzenjammer bring to the stage'.

After Perth they wanted us to go out on a tour as had been originally planned. It would have been a great opportunity for us, but we asked again about putting our own stamp on it and making changes for the British audience and were told we couldn't. So that, sadly, was the end of that. It's never been performed in the United Kingdom since.

STEVEN

I did wonder at the time whether we were cutting off our noses to spite our faces. They were proposing to put us into Number One Theatres – the biggest venues across the country. But I'm sure we did the right thing. The way it was, we were never going to get anything better than three-star reviews and that wouldn't have done us any good.

Chapter 14

In which we move into the world of mobile phone apps, and spend hours deleting nude photographs of men.

About a year before we got involved with *Two Pianos, Four Hands* and Mickey Rooney, we were with Lorna Luft at the Waldorf Hotel in New York. That night she started telling us about yet another approach she had had from someone to be allowed to perform Judy Garland's music.

'Oh my God, there's this crazy nutcase who wants to do my Mum's concert at the Carnegie. He wants to reproduce her whole show there!'

She was talking about Rufus Wainwright, although she'd never heard of him. We hadn't heard of him either so we all got on the internet together and looked him up and to be honest we weren't any the wiser. One man doing the whole Judy Garland concert in a huge venue like that seemed absurd to her, but it was such an interesting idea that we managed to persuade Lorna to at least go and meet him the following day.

Off she went, and when she came back she did an impersonation of his singing. She didn't understand why anyone would want to try such a thing, but she agreed that it could be fun. She had decided that she would give him the rights to do the show, and that she would get involved to give it a seal of approval. Being a part of it would give her the opportunity to keep a watch on him and maybe pull the plug if she didn't like the way it was going. The idea appealed to her because it could be a good opportunity to introduce her mother's career to a new generation of people.

We didn't see the show but it has now become a famous occasion, helped by Sam Mendes filming it. A while later we heard a first hand account of the night from a young man who had been there, a person who became hugely significant in our own lives.

We were at a party near our home with Marek Kukula. He was then an astronomer lecturing at Edinburgh University, and went on to be Public Astronomer at the Royal Observatory Greenwich. He had brought along one of his protégées, a young man called Steven Elliott who was very keen on Judy Garland. We all got chatting and it turned out he had been at the Rufus Wainwright show at Carnegie Hall. We had the conversation about having been there with Lorna at its inception and he could tell us all about how it had gone on the night. We all hit it off.

After that he became a close friend, coming over from his home near Glasgow to stay with us at our house several times. We liked him a lot: he was young and clever and we admired his general enthusiasm. He was a computer professional doing some work with Glasgow University and conversations often turned to the idea that one day together we could come up with an internet-based business that would work.

Scott had given up working as our manager and was working in IT as well so he and Steven Elliott could talk the same language. Scott had had an idea that there was a market for a discreet computer repair business where people could go if they had concerns about the likes of PC World finding 'dodgy content' on their hard drives and search history. He had got as far as drafting some advertising ideas and setting up a website but didn't think he was going to pursue it. When Steven Elliott decided to move to Brighton, Scott happily let him make use of what he had done to try to get a similar business off the ground there.

Another idea we tried was 'Ship my media'. It was a way of getting the merchandise that cruise acts like to sell after their shows to different countries without them having to lug suitcases of CDs and DVDs around themselves. We knew that sometimes people had to take a lot of stuff with them if they were doing back-to-back engagements, and also that they often ran out of stock while they were away, so it would be good to have a system whereby they could order up what they needed and have it meet their ship.

It didn't really work out but we carried on musing about other ideas over a period of time. While we were performing *Two Pianos, Four Hands* in Vienna, Steven Elliott came over to have a short holiday and to see us in the show. The three of us went out for a few drinks in the evening: nothing too heavy as we were performing six shows a week.

STEVEN

We were in a bar in Vienna. Over the week before that I had been thinking about the possibility of us all coming up with a gay dating app for smart phones. At this time, the late summer of 2009, the only smart phone that was available was the very first iPhone. The only dating sites that existed were Gaydar which was desktop computer based and becoming a bit stale, and for the iPhone Grindr had just become available.

Grindr wasn't that great. The main reason it had taken off in the UK was because it received some very useful publicity on *Top Gear* when Stephen Fry was asked by Jeremy Clarkson what apps he recommended and he described Grindr and what it was used for. Everyone laughed because it seemed such an outrageous thing to exist but him talking about it sent its profile through the roof and it couldn't cope with the demand for a while.

Sitting there in Vienna, we were sure that we could design something that was better than Grindr. We were really very excited and we knew that the first thing we needed was a good name. Between us we didn't know anything at all about how to go about writing the software for an app, but we did know that the key to success was going to be what we called it.

We needed a name that would attract attention but we also knew there might be a problem with using anything too explicit. It may not be the same now but back then Apple would not sell anything in their app store that had a name that was too suggestive. Any kind of sexual innuendo and they were likely to reject it. But then it came to me.

I said: 'How about "Bender"?'

We all agreed immediately that was a name we could get past Apple. In the UK a 'bender' is a slightly derogatory term for gays but the word also has other meanings. Anyone intending to meet up for a drinking session might talk about 'going out on a bender', it's just a common term for getting drunk and having a good time. 'Bender' seemed to be a perfect name; and because it was ambiguous Apple should accept it. We were all very excited about the idea and agreed this was something we could work on together.

Steven Elliott was eager to take on the programming if we could help with the design and lead the marketing. He admitted it was going to take him some time to learn how to program for Apple apps but if we could buy an iPhone and a computer for him, he would get straight on to it.

At the time that was all we agreed to do for him financially because we really didn't have much money. We were just finishing a very successful show in Austria but we hadn't been paid very much for it and we had been ripped off by Mickey Rooney and his friends. Everybody had been making money from our efforts over the last few weeks, apart from us.

KEVIN

I remember saying that I hadn't really been bothered about the other business ideas, but I really thought this one was going to make us huge amounts of money. We were just about at the end of our run in Austria and when our last payment came in, we put it together with some money from the merchandise and sent Steven Elliott the money for a secondhand Apple Mac on eBay and an iPhone on which he would work at the new idea. It was all the money I had in the world at the time: we paid up and wiped ourselves out financially.

Young Elliott got to work immediately and learnt Apple programming very quickly, as we knew he would. He's a real go-getter and we were sure with his computer knowledge he was going to succeed. It felt like we were all on the brink of something very big.

A few weeks after we got back from Vienna, Steven Elliott sent us an email:

"We need to get something in writing that just states in basic terms how we all fit together with this. I'm obviously going to be the developer, at least for the foreseeable future ... and you guys are going to be a mixture of investors/marketing gurus etc. To get something up and running, I'll probably be investing hundreds of hours programming, and then when it is running ... there will be constant work to improve it, deal with issues etc. So, to reflect that ... and also to safeguard my control over the application that after all that time will probably feel like "my baby", I said to Steven and Kevin that my only condition would be I have a controlling interest so that if in five years' time for example, if it's a massive success and some investor offers you guys a fantastic amount of money to buy you out, but I don't want to ... I can't lose control to them because your shares add up to more than mine. So, what we agreed on the other night was that I have 51%, and the other 49% can be divided up between you three however you fancy."

That seemed a very reasonable summary of what we had talked about except that he was assuming that Scott would want to be involved as well, and he hadn't decided if he was really interested. Normally we don't bother entering into formal contracts with anyone – not even agents – we just work on the basis of trusting people at their word, but we didn't have any problem with Steven Elliott writing it out like that nor with him having just over half of Bender.

The initial version of the app was ready as early as the following February but it was quite basic. We gave him more ideas and advised him on design all the way through and he regularly came up with new versions. Sometimes when we had been away working we found ourselves a couple of versions behind; he was that quick at getting things done. We were on the phone all the time when we could and there were hundreds of emails backward and forward discussing it with him. And eventually we had something that we could take to market.

We decided that to get it out there and known we would make it available to use for free for the first year and collect money from adverts embedded in it. Every time someone clicked on one of those adverts, we would get a penny. If enough people downloaded the app and either deliberately or accidentally clicked on an advert those pennies would pay for the whole thing while it was getting established. Later on if it was successful, we could introduce a nominal annual subscription to get access without adverts. We thought it could be 99 pence per year, surely no-one would object to that. Our creativity for design and marketing, his ability to make it work - it was going to be a winner.

STEVEN

We three got together towards the end of July 2010. A friend of Steven Elliott's had come up with a design for a logo and we all thought it would be best to get it protected as a trademark, to stop anyone else copying our idea. I found the form that you have to fill in to register a trademark online and completed it as best I could. One problem I had was that when it came to whose name it should be registered under, there simply wasn't room to put all three of our names, so I just put 'Benderapp.com' as the name of our partnership. As two of the three of us lived in the same place I used our home as the address, and Kevin paid the fee.

After a couple of months we got an acknowledgment that Bender was a registered trademark, so we felt a bit safer from being copied. At the same time we also took our usual precaution of sending a copy of what had been created to ourselves by recorded delivery to protect the intellectual property, just as we would with our music.

At first we thought we would launch the app in Brighton, to where Steven Elliott had moved, put out a few flyers in the gay bars and let it grow from there. But in the end we decided to release it just before the Edinburgh Festival in August 2010. It took off immediately; within three days we had a thousand users who had downloaded the app onto their iPhones. Over the three week period of the Festival we were working hard at getting everyone we met to download it. Having a lot of friends helps and word of mouth through them led on to a huge network of people, all interested in the idea, so it grew quite quickly. After the Festival, we went for a holiday in Gran Canaria and that was a brilliant opportunity to spread the message. We got hotels to promote it, we got clubs to mention it and it started to do as well in Spain as in the UK.

The same happened in Gibraltar when we went there next. We strolled into a gay bar meaning to ask the owner to push it for us and the moment we mentioned the app he started complaining that it had ruined his trade because people weren't coming into the bar to look for dates any more. They were getting all they wanted from Bender.

Although we weren't involved in the coding Steven Elliott gave us access to all the data electronically, so we could see how many users there were and how much money was being made. A million messages had been sent between Bender users by the third week of September and not long after we were already the tenth biggest social networking app in Spain. Buoyed by the initial success we all thought it was worth him starting work on a version for Android phones as well. Another obvious development would be to clone Bender and produce a lesbian and a straight version.

[K: It came to me that the obvious name for the lesbian version of Bender would be 'Brenda'! And then playing about with similar words I came up with 'Banter' for a straight dating app. Steven Elliott said he liked that because straight people are all talk.]

The only problem was it was giving him - and us – huge amounts of work. Because Steven Elliott was doing everything on coding and fixing bugs and adding new features on his own, he was working so many hours on the app that he was losing out on income from other things. He started asking us for money to support him and we would send him £200 a month when we could do it. Bender wasn't quite big enough yet to be able to employ people to run it but it was too much work to be able to do it as a side-line to everything else. We were all getting overrun with the work needed to keep it going.

Every time a user uploaded a photograph it had to be rated because Apple would have shut us down if there was anything obscene visible. Someone had to look at every image individually as it came up to check it was acceptable, so we had to go through hundreds of pictures every few hours and rate them. For months every time we would log on there would be another thousand to rate, and it seemed like every waking hour had to be spent on this task.

At first it was quite titillating looking at all these gay boys but it very quickly became a terrible chore and there were some pretty shocking things we had to look at. No nudity was the main rule we had to work to but most of the pictures were nudes, hundreds and hundreds a day. Scott joined in as well, even though he didn't really want to be a part of the project. It was really quite difficult because the photograph had to be examined quickly for fear of Apple finding it before we did.

In the early days we were still rehearsing and performing *Two Pianos, Four Hands* so we had very little free time, and then after that we were back on ships and having to log on while we were in the middle of the ocean. We were running up big internet bills on ships because we were spending so much time online doing this work. Steven Elliott did the lion's share and got some of his friends to help and we had to get our friends involved too.

[K: My friends Jane and Dinea in Bingham spent their Christmas rating willies!]

The other great concern was keeeping an eye on what was going on, especially in relation to the age of the users. For instance, one afternoon we spotted messages that made it clear an under age boy was going to meet some men at a caravan park. We managed to put a stop to it but it was a warning that we couldn't just turn a blind eye to what the app could be used for. There was one user who complained that there were fourteen year olds on the site, and when we investigated his messages we found he was only fifteen himself!

Bender was getting good ratings apart from a few reviews that were tracked back to people working on Grindr and another new rival called Qrushr. Apart from the amount of work involved, we were all very pleased with how Bender was growing. It was obvious we should all make a lot of money from it eventually.

Chapter 15

In which we get involved with a trouser-dropping impresario and decide not to be "Two *****s on a Stool'

While all of this was going on we found we had to come up with a new name for our act. We appeared as Katzenjammer from 2003 until early in 2011 but we were forced to give that name up because a Norwegian girl band came on the scene and used the same name. We discovered that although we had the European rights to 'Katzenjammer', they had registered the name in America the previous year without letting us know. It didn't seem likely that there wasn't going to be much of a cross over between our audience and theirs but then one night they were performing in London at the same time as us. We took advice and were told that we would have to change our name if we wanted to work in the States or on cruises with Americans on board.

STEVEN

'Katzenjammer' had been a great name for us and it was a struggle to think of something else that encapsulated what we do without being too obvious. We should probably have asked our friend Dillie Keane how she and her friends settled on the name 'Fascinating Aida', because it doesn't really mean anything and doesn't mention their names but somehow describes what they do. Three educated women of a certain age singing rude songs in an operatic fashion.

We spent ages trying to think of a new name. We even posted on Facebook asking people to suggest something for us. There were some horrible names like 'Double Digits', 'Norfolk and Good', and 'Fruit and Fibre', but most people were quite unimaginative. One name kept coming up, and from people who didn't know each other all suggesting the same thing independently, but it was so obscene we couldn't possibly put it on a poster and hope to sell out the

Usher Hall, unless we wanted to get a completely different kind of audience!

In the end we went with 'Worbey and Farrell' which is pretty bland and sounds like a firm of solicitors. Even if some of the other suggestions were just as accurate it is undeniably who we are. One idea that had been under serious consideration was 'Well Strung', and although we eventually rejected it as the name of the act, the title of our show in 2011 was 'Worbey and Farrell Are Well Strung', so maybe we hedged our bets a bit.

At the time we became 'Worbey and Farrell' we were starting to reduce the comedy sketch element from our show and even though it was forced on us, changing our name was the start of a process of evolution. The Katzenjammer act had really been a musical slapstick routine. There were a lot of those acts around when we started out but they had fallen out of fashion over the years. The ones that didn't change couldn't survive unless they moved to Germany; you can always get away with slapstick in Germany.

We knew there were parts of the Katzenjammer show that didn't fit well together. The song about the Pope seemed incongruous when it was following a beautifully played piece of music. The same could be said of a ditty about our old College Director Michael Gough-Matthews, entitled '*Why Does the Male Ballerina Make You Blush?*' We used to launch into that immediately after *Jupiter* from Holst's Planets Suite.

STEVEN

There was also a terrible sketch to end the show based on an ENSA group that Kevin had performed with.

[K: ENSA could stand for Every Night Something Awful.]

What we were doing was sending up the romantic notion that it was the patriotic songs that won the second world-war. We set the audience off on a jolly singalong of songs like *The White Cliffs of Dover* and *We'll Meet Again*, and then suddenly horrified them. The screen displaying the words changed to pictures of Hiroshima being bombed. It was a bad idea and definitely the wrong way to finish a show; moving so quickly from pantomime to shock just wasn't entertainment. We might have got away with it if we'd used that kind of material for the whole act, but this was too muddled and we sent people away with the wrong memory. We know that now.

So, we abandoned Katzenjammer and relaunched as 'Worbey and Farrell'. We did lose some offers after the name change: booking agents just assumed we'd stopped working altogether because we were no longer Katzenjammer.

[S: Maybe they got a Norwegian girl band they weren't expecting instead.]

That process of evolution in our act probably wasn't really completed until we met Geoffrey Durham and invited him to be our Director. Geoffrey appeared for years as The Great Soprendo, a big camp Spanish magician, very popular on the Friday tea time children's show *Crackerjack*. Geoffrey was also Victoria Wood's husband and even though they were divorced by then, if you listen to the episode *of Desert Island Discs* when she was the guest, you will hear her say about her success:

'It was all Geoffrey'

We would say the same thing now.

Before we talk about what Geoffrey did for us we need to explain that he came into our lives through a larger-than-life character called Michael Vine who became our manager.

When Scott got a 'proper job' we started looking out for someone to promote and represent us and get us into areas of the business that we hadn't really reached yet. It proved to be quite difficult to find someone that suited, more because of the nature of our act than there being a lack of candidates. We weren't a serious concert performance and we weren't really slapstick comedy anymore, so we didn't really think anyone would want to take us on.

Eventually a flautist friend of ours, Clare Langan, said she knew of someone who would be ideal for us and offered to get us an introduction. We didn't hear anything more and left it for a while because we were quite busy, but then we thought that maybe we should get in touch with him ourselves. He's a very busy man, but within minutes of us sending an email, he replied. It was really quite surprising:

'Hello! I've been waiting for you two to contact me.'

Michael Vine was the manager that people wanted: especially magicians. He started out performing a magic show himself, as part of a variety troupe. It's well known that his act was pretty awful but somehow after every performance flopped he was the one in the ensemble who was getting rebooked; such was his ability to talk himself up. We can imagine him saying to the bookers:

'It didn't go so well tonight, but I just know I'll nail it next time'.

It soon became obvious that he was more suited to representing people than performing. He first became known as the manager who transformed Joe Pasquale, rehearsing his act in his own front room. Before they met Joe used to come on to the stage wearing his underpants and vest, hit a boxing punch ball and let it hit him in the face. Michael's advice was that if you are a clown you don't dress like one, so he had Joe wear suits and boots. They did very well together but at the height of his fame Joe decided he wanted to get more serious gigs than pantomime and left Michael's management.

Once we got to know him Michael told us the story of how he came to be so successful. He and his friend Andrew O'Connor noticed how well David Blaine's act was going in America and decided that there was a market for a mentalist based in the UK. Well aware that the way to make British businessmen agree to things is to take them out and get them drunk, they invited several commissioning editors and executives from Channel Four out for lunch, plied them with wine and then told them that they had met a new David Blaine type character, a mentalist, and offered them the chance to commission a series from him. Michael had the magician's gift of being able to work people and the sales pitch was so good that they agreed to have a look at this potential star.

The only problem was they didn't actually have anybody at that stage, so they quickly set about auditioning people for the show. A mindreading artist called Mark Paul was considered as was the comedy actor Andy Nyman. Michael was very keen on Jerry Sadowitz, but he told them that it wasn't for him. He did, however, suggest someone that he had seen doing close up magic in Bristol. And that was Derren Brown.

Michael's philosophy has always been that if an act is worth promoting then the thing to do is to throw money at it. There is no point in skimping on making something as good as it can be. Mark Paul told us sometime later that he met Michael during the week that Derren's first Channel 4 show was due to go out, and he told him that it was a make-or-break night for him. He would either be bankrupt or make a fortune: he had thrown all his money at getting the show up and running. Of course, together Michael and Derren were a huge success and the fortune was made.

Derren didn't really have any experience of doing theatrical shows; all he had done up to the time of recording the TV series, was close up sleight of hand magic at restaurant tables. After the TV shows a West End theatre run was arranged, and Andy Nyman and (eventually) Geoffrey Durham were brought in to help Derren with his live performance.

Having made contact we arranged to visit Michael in his offices in County Hall in London, a magnificent building that used to be the home of the Greater London Council.

'Come and see me at my office at...oh dear what's it called?... big place...there's a tower with a big clock just opposite on the other side of the river...'

When we arrived we realised he had been describing the House of Parliament and Big Ben. As we went into the room, he got up to greet us and immediately tripped over the carpet and fell down in front of us. It was so obviously done on purpose that we were completely confused by what was going on.

[K: He said: 'Now. Your names. Is it Kevin with a PH and Steven with a V? Or the other way round?"

S: My first thought was: 'Oh God, what have we got here?' Which is probably what he wanted: magicians work on having people around them feel unsettled.]

He is a very clever businessman but he's also legendary for his odd sense of humour. He has a magician's mentality; he plays tricks on people all the time. You would be in a crowded bar and all of a sudden there would be a flash and a bang. Everyone would be startled and look around wondering what's just happened, and it would turn out he's lit a firework and let it off. He gets away with some outrageous stunts, and people have said to us that at times they feel as though Michael is the act instead of them. He's his own client.

The first meeting went well. He seemed quite interested in us for the very reason we had thought that no-one would take us on, because we had several things on the go at once. Not only were we doing our own show which involved playing in several different styles of music (jazz, classical...) and doing some comedy, we were also composing and had been acting in a serious play in Vienna. He was also intrigued by us being a part of one of the fastest growing iPhone apps in the Apple store.

We went out for lunch and it was evident he enjoyed behaving like a multi-millionaire, and was truly generous at the same time. The unsettling eccentricities continued though. In the restaurant he insisted on paying for everybody's drinks and meals. Not just us, everyone in the whole restaurant.

STEVEN

He called the waiter over to pour the wine for him and said:

'Now don't let me see what the wine is, and don't tell me anything about it.'

And then he held the glass up and sloshed the liquid around, took a sip, and made a big performance of swilling it about in his mouth for a while, and then looked up, and asked:

'Is it white?'

When we left, an old homeless woman was asking him for money. Michael told her:

'Mother! You've got to stop following me about! I'll give you some money, but please, do go away.'

We've frequently seen him just giving money away on the street: fifty-pound notes even.

Although he was interested we didn't get any commitment from him that day that he would become our manager. Time went on and we weren't any clearer about what was happening, so we arranged to go out with him again.

KEVIN

We were out for a meal with him one evening and I got quite frustrated at one point because although he was saying all the right things, he wasn't committing to doing anything for us. I asked him straight:

'Are you interested in taking us on?' To which he said in a whisper, so Steven couldn't hear:

'I am interested in you... just not the other one.'

STEVEN

And then Kevin went to the toilet and Michael leant across to me and said:

'I think maybe you need to get rid of that chap. You've got a big career ahead of you'.

And then later on he said to us both:

'You two are good together, but you really need to drop the piano. It's getting in your way.'

Despite this game-playing he did eventually commit to helping us and invested a lot of money (and quite a lot of his own time) in us. He filmed showreels, told us how to dress on stage and quickly arranged a spot on ITV's *This Morning* with Eamonn Holmes. The whole point was to get ourselves seen and the new name well known and this seemed like a fantastic opportunity. It cost us a lot of money to go on the show however, because we had to hire a suitable piano.

KEVIN

It turned out they had another piano act on the show that day so we could have split the cost. And then Eamonn Holmes kept pronouncing Steven's name as "Wor-brery".

He did it about five times, and there's a golden rule of theatre and stage that you don't show anyone up. We would have made him look unprofessional if we had corrected him live on television, so we almost had to stick with Wor-brery and Farrell.

The power of television was wonderful. After just a ten minute appearance on ITV, our first shows under the new name sold out completely. The downside was that the moment we came off set, our phones were going Ding! Ding! Ding! Not with offers for work; it was all begging emails. And then the letters started coming. People assumed we were rich because we'd appeared on the telly. One of the letters was asking us to give money to set up a parrot sanctuary. It was a very odd experience.

One thing we learnt from that time has stuck with us. Michael always said:

'When you're out there on stage, remember that everybody who is professional can have a performance that can 'go well'. Going well is a given. What you have to do is 'absolutely kill the show', you have to go down a storm every time. You have to be brilliant or you don't get to come back.'

He tried all sorts of things to make us famous. He had an idea that it might be possible to use us for two things at once and invited us out to meet a producer called David Fricker who was interested in revisiting our performances of *Two Pianos, Four Hands*. Michael was getting very excited about the idea of us touring the play at the same time as doing our own show so we could put on both two hour shows at the same time.

[S: For some reason during that meeting, I casually mentioned that I didn't think I'd ever eaten oysters. It turned out Sheekey's shellfish restaurant was one of Michael's favourites so we went there for lunch.]

It's a very posh restaurant in Covent Garden that specialises in oysters. As we went in Zara Phillips was sitting there with her husband Mike Tindall so you can tell what kind of place it is.

Michael went up to the head waiter' and said:

'I can't remember what they are called but do you happen to have some er...' and he started gesticulating and miming oysters.

'They're like rocks ... kind of black and white ...you open them up and scrape the insides out'.

The waiter said: 'Do you mean oysters?'

'THAT'S what they're called, yes. Do you happen to have any of them?'

'Of course.'

'We'll have some of them and to drink...Four vodka and lards'.

'I'm sorry..?'

'Have you not heard of them? They're the latest thing. You pour out the vodka, and then you heat some lard up to the right temperature and you pour it over the vodka. It's just delicious.'

These waiters are all trained at a high level, but he still went away and asked the head chef about it and then came back and said, 'I'm sorry we don't do that here.'

'OK just get us some champagne then. But is it warm?'

During the meal he launched into another routine. In a stage whisper he started talking loudly behind another guest, telling us:

'So, what I did was, I knocked down the wall that was here and made it into a bit of a bistro area.'

And when the waiter came over to check everything was OK with our food, he asked him loudly:

'Yes, and how's everything going on your side today? Is everything working well, out there?' I think everyone's enjoying their food.'

The man for whose benefit this was being done was nudging his companion and mouthing: 'That's the owner of Sheekey's on the next table!' Michael interrupted them and said:

'I hope you're enjoying yourselves. Come and join us for some champagne when you're finished.'

[S: Invariably those routines would end with Michael's trousers falling down, accidentally-on-purpose. And he would be standing there in ragged old underpants refusing to acknowledge what had happened: 'Don't you try that one on me'!

K: I'd heard about him years before from another agent complaining: 'Joe Pasquale's stupid manager turned up in the green room last night. He's an idiot. You're talking to him and then suddenly his trousers will fall down.']

The idea of a dual tour rather fizzled out but Michael hadn't lost interest in us. He arranged for us to perform at The Pheasantry in Chelsea, one of London's leading cabaret venues. It was to be our last show performing as Katzenjammer. We did a week there and received great reviews. Everything was really looking up for us.

Michael was delighted with how the week had gone and turned up to take us to dinner at another of his favourite restaurants –PJ's in Covent Garden. On a lovely summer's evening we piled into the back of a taxi, and Michael started off on another of his routines.

'Now. We're going to Covent Garden. How much do you think this is going to cost?'

And as the cabdriver looked back to answer he carried on:

'No. I'll tell you what - I'll pay you now' and handed him £60.

The journey is only a couple of miles, so the driver told him that was way too much.

'No, it's all right, it's all right...' said Michael.

'Is there a particular route you want to take?'

Michael thought about it.

'I don't mind really. Just avoid the fog!'

Our relationship with Michael was riding high. We'd been on national TV, we had the manager everyone wanted, we had a good team of PR people behind us and our shows were selling well. Michael was confident we were going to be big stars and have a West End run. He just loved telling people that not only were we famous piano players, we were leading entrepreneurs too: we were the inventors of the app Bender which was getting more and more users. He told us that Derren Brown was interested in meeting Steven Elliott to develop something, and perhaps he could introduce him to Stephen Fry too?

Because we had had such a success at The Pheasantry we decided that we should try a three week run at the Edinburgh Fringe Festival. Even though everyone knows it's virtually impossible to make any money there, it is a wonderful chance to get noticed. We were booked into one of the very best venues: the Cowbarn at Udderbelly.

Michael was quite happy to put his own money behind us and in the weeks leading up to the Festival several people were brought in to help us 'improve' the show we had performed at The Pheasantry. But we had to pay for the venue, the piano hire and the publicity. He had already got us the services of a public relations company, but it was costing us about £750 a month even when we didn't have anything to promote and it was making us skint.

For that run at the Edinburgh Fringe Festival we paid for a billboard to advertise the show. In those days (it's probably the same now) although you handed over £1,000 for a very large poster you were never told exactly where it was going to be. We searched all over Edinburgh to try and find out where our main publicity had been positioned.

[S: Eventually I found it on the bus shelter right outside the clinic for sexually transmitted diseases. For that show we decided not to ask the audience how they had heard about us.]

As it turned out our bubble had already burst. As we prepared to go to Edinburgh we discovered that we had been cut out of Bender. We were about to embark on years of litigation to try to get it back.

Chapter 16

In which we are deprived of our rights and learn a lot about stagecraft from The Great Soprendo.

In a way we had seen it coming. We just hadn't wanted to believe what was happening. The first hint of trouble was a conversation around Christmas 2010 about the film *The Social Network*.

STEVEN

I met Steven Elliott in London one evening and, just as a part of a normal conversation, he asked what I thought of the film about Mark Zuckerberg and his friends setting up Facebook. I told him I hadn't seen it yet.

He said: 'It's quite scary. It reminds me of us!'

KEVIN

Steven told me about this conversation, so when I was on the train going back to my mother's house for Christmas, I downloaded the film and watched it, and grew more and more alarmed. If you haven't seen it then we're not going to spoil it for you, but it was plain that our young developer was quite intrigued by the idea of cutting us out.

STEVEN

When Kevin came back after Christmas he said:

'He's going to run off with it.'

Until that point, we hadn't had any trouble at all. There had been no disagreements and we were all working really hard at getting Bender up and running. We had been sending money as and when we could, to keep him going. I remember saying to Kevin:

'No. He's not that type of person. There's no way he's going to do that to us!'

But then I went out clubbing with him one night and we seemed to be getting on fine to start with except that there was obviously something he wanted to say. I was telling him about our plans for the New Year when he suddenly launched into what he described as a new plan. He said we should set up a limited company.

'I'm going to have 80% of this and you're going to have 20%'

I said: 'Why on earth would we agree to do that?'

'Because I've done all the work!'

He drew up a business plan that all looked very good apart from the percentages. We continued sending money to him through the spring of 2011 even though paying for the PR company and everything involved with launching with a new name was making us absolutely broke.

But as the new upgrades and versions of Bender came out we seemed to have lost our ability to log in and see any information about the number of users and how much money was coming in from advertisers. We asked about that and he sent what seemed to be friendly emails about what was going on, including that the owner of Qrushr had been in contact to suggest a merger which he had rejected.

It turned out he had gone ahead and set up the limited company without telling us and, perhaps in a reference to the film he liked so much, he called it Bender Social Networking Ltd. We didn't get the 20% of shares that he had been talking about. Instead he was proposing that we receive a royalty from the company instead of a share of profits. We thought about it and decided that could probably work out.

In April 2011 we missed sending the monthly money to support him. We just couldn't afford it as we had bills of £15,000 to pay for the Edinburgh run that was coming up. Obviously he was annoyed about that as he depended on it to pay his rent.

He told us that he was going to get a solicitor to draw up a couple of alternative agreements based on the royalty idea that he thought would be fair to everyone to supersede everything we had agreed previously. We could have two weeks to choose which one we wanted to sign which seemed completely reasonable to us.

But the agreements never arrived. In the second week of May, out of the blue, we received a letter with a cheque attached. He had totted up everything we had put in so far, added a bit of interest and sent it all back to us claiming that because we hadn't sent him any money that month it meant the whole arrangement was over.

STEVEN

We were completely flummoxed because we were expecting him to send the two alternative agreements for us to think about. And attached to the letter there was a note addressed just to me that said:

'I'm sorry how all this has turned out. I wish things could have been different. I wish you all the best. Lots of love xx '

We didn't cash the cheque because we thought that would indicate that we accepted what he was saying, and we didn't.

Michael Vine wanted to get involved on our behalf. He even arranged for Sooty and Sweep's lawyers to come on board and help but the first letter sent to Steven Elliott cost us £2,500 and that was just a simple 'cease and desist' instruction. He took no notice at all of anything the lawyers sent to him and he blocked us and all of our friends from contacting him in any way. He seemed to have people working for him now so it appeared that Bender was making enough money to pay them. We looked around to see whether there was anyone who might be able to help without charging a fortune – law students even - but nobody seemed to know anything about intellectual property. The only legal case that there had been at this point on anything similar was the Facebook case that the film was about.

We were cut off completely. All access to the app was deactivated and there was nothing we could do because we had no money to pursue him legally. The worst of it was that we felt so betrayed by someone who we had thought of as one of our very best friends. Scott says now that he never trusted Steven Elliott and that was the main reason why he decided not to have anything to do with the Bender idea, but both of us had had complete faith in him, both in his abilities as a computer wizard and in his integrity as a friend.

KEVIN

I think now that if he had come to us and said it wasn't working for him and offered to buy us out for the few thousand pounds that we needed then to pay for the Edinburgh run, I would have been willing to accept that. But instead he just shut us out and left us with absolutely nothing.

It was a hugely distressing time. What had happened was eating away at us both and far too much of our energy was being taken up with worrying about that and what we could possibly do to restore our share in the app. And this was exactly at the time when we should have been concentrating on preparing for the Edinburgh run. The 'help' we were getting with the show turned out to be a case of too many cooks spoiling what we had, and we were quite unable to concentrate sufficiently to be able to see what advice we were being given was worth taking and what was not.

As a result we really weren't at our best when we opened in Edinburgh, and the first reviews were not good, one of them came from a website that had reviewed our show in Chelsea and tipped us to be one of the best acts on the Fringe that year. When Michael saw the show, he wasn't impressed at all and decided it needed a bit of sprucing up.

And that's when we met Geoffrey Durham: Michael paid for his time and advice.

Geoffrey arrived in the middle of the run of Edinburgh Fringe concerts. Before the show he gave us what we now understand is his standard line:

'I don't know whether there's anything I can do for you.'

But of course, he can help anybody. He's the oracle of theatre!

After the performance he said he wouldn't tell us anything until after the Festival was over but we insisted that we needed to know about anything that he could see needed fixing right away. He actually seemed quite impressed that we thought we could make alterations immediately and not be phased by doing so, and we did incorporate a few changes for the very next night. A couple of small adjustments made a massive difference.

The first of these was to focus the audience's attention on us. That might seem an obvious thing to do, but Geoffrey could see that we were doing things that actually stopped that happening, and the main one of those was something we had introduced ourselves because we thought we were helping people see what they seemed to want to see.

When we first started out we came to realise that people are quite interested in our hands and what we are doing on the keyboard. At first it didn't occur to us that playing over and around each other is quite intriguing for the audience. It certainly wasn't intended to be a gimmick, but we noticed that if there was space people were moving to one side of the theatre so that they could see our hands more clearly. Based on that we had come to the conclusion that what we should do was to have a camera pointing at our hands with a screen above us all the way through the concert so that everybody in the hall could see what was going on. When Geoffrey saw us doing this for the first time he was absolutely horrified.

'You're upstaging yourselves! There's always a problem with double acts at the best of times because you're splitting the audience's focus and they don't know which one of you they are supposed to look at. And in your case, you've got a piano which splits the focus even more, and now you've got a screen which makes it even worse.'

Focus is crucial for a magician. The key to Geoffrey's act is for people to look at his face and not his hands, and not see the trickery going on. In his view we were making the same mistake as too many magicians:

'You think the focus should be on the hands. It's not, it's on the face. You think, like a lot of magicians, that it's your hands that are going to make you famous, but it isn't your hands you want people to remember, it's your face. You can give the audience everything they want but you have to do it on your terms. Don't give them the screen until well after they have had a good look at you.'

After that we stopped turning the screen on at the start of the show and now it's only introduced part way through. Geoffrey still hates us using it at all. After we made that change people who'd seen us before, started shouting out:

'Where's the screen? We want the screen!'

We found that rather hard to cope with but Geoffrey's advice to deal with this heckling was to tell the audience:

'We haven't put it on yet – but you'll see why later!'

And, of course, they never did see why later but it didn't matter because they'd just forgotten about it.

The next thing that he noticed was that the position of the piano was wrong. We had assumed that the best place for the instrument was centre stage; it's what all concert musicians do. Geoffrey showed us that even when the screen wasn't on, we were being upstaged by the piano. To make us the stars of the show we had to put ourselves right in the middle which meant the keyboard was at the centre with the bulk of the piano to one side, and a big open space behind us.

It felt completely wrong to do this at first and we really weren't comfortable, but as soon as we made the change we could see the audience were watching us rather than staring at the big black Steinway or whatever. It is a trick that Victoria Wood always used; watch her shows and you see that the piano is positioned well to the side and angled away, so that she is the natural focus. It was Geoffrey that did that for her.

STEVEN

Before we came on stage and as the audience were filing in, we used to have a slideshow of photographs of famous pianists. It was very tongue in cheek because amongst pictures of Chopin and Beethoven and other famous composers, we had Rolf from *The Muppets* and Mrs. Mills and Liberace. Just about anyone who is associated with the piano.

Bobby Crush saw the show quite early in the run and came backstage to ask why we hadn't got a picture of him as well, so we put one in the next day. He's such a lovely man, why wouldn't we?

Geoffrey wanted to know why we had these pictures of famous pianists up at the start of the show before we came on.

'The show's not about them, it's about you!'

And he told us off for saying 'well done' to the piano at the end of the show (it was just a silly joke):

'It's like me, as a magician, asking the audience to applaud my cups and balls!'

Up to that point in the run our show had had rather mixed reviews in the papers. Fortunately, Kate Copstick, the reviewer from *The Scotsman*, came to see us the very day after we had made the changes and she gave us a wonderful write up. Unfortunately it didn't get printed until the final weekend of the festival, but the last two performances sold out.

After the Edinburgh run Geoffrey made us get rid of most of the comedy routines and songs and told us to concentrate on the music. The comedy is still there but our act is much more music-based than it ever was when we were Katzenjammer. He told us:

'Just stick with what you're really good at. And that's the piano playing!'

Meeting Geoffrey was easily the best thing that could have happened for us. He's taught us about focus, about order, and that any show needs direction, in fact it needs a Director. He's been our guardian angel ever since and become one of our closest friends. He has helped us understand not only how to stage our act but also what we should be doing in the show. He's a very clever man and a wonderful generous human being.

He took the piano stool that Steinway presented us with when we became a Steinway ensemble and redesigned it, building secret compartments into it so that we could hide the gin and tonic bottles, glasses, ice and cocktail umbrellas for the *Fur Elise* routine. It's typical of a magician: they have secret compartments for everything. Michael Vine came by once and noticed all these things attached to the piano stool.

'What's this?'

Geoffrey said, 'It's all the equipment for the gin and tonic sketch. I've designed the stool to hold it all.'

Michael laughed: 'You sad old magician you!'

As Michael is an ex-magician himself he really appreciated what Geoffrey was doing for us.

STEVEN

We wanted an excuse to take our jackets off after the first piece in every show but we had nowhere to put them other than to throw them on the floor of the stage, which would look really messy. Geoffrey always wants a reason to do something; every move on the stage has to have a motivation, something the audience can understand, so if we wanted to take our jackets off there had to be a bit of stage business around us doing that.

He said: 'What you need is a hat stand.'

'We can't have a hat stand on the stage with us!'

'No. But I've got a special hat stand.

KEVIN

He designed it and had it made and gave it to us for free, saying:

'I can afford it. I'm a rich old queen!'

Even though he's not a queen at all.

It really was very clever. We would announce that we were taking our jackets off and Steven would get up and turn the stool slightly, open it and take out an oak hat stand. The stool was perhaps only four or five inches deep but a six-foot stand would emerge from inside it. The feet and the top are proper solid oak. It's not telescopic and it's made from some clever material. Between the top and the bottom is...

Well, we won't give away how it is done but it would just astonish the audience as this thing appeared from inside the stool, and the whole process took only about four seconds.

STEVEN

I needed lots of lessons in how to do it and there was a complicated rigmarole for putting it away.

Geoffrey had a very small flight case made for it which we used to travel around with. We were passing through Heathrow Terminal 5 one day and this case seemed to be causing a lot of confusion at the X-ray machine. One of the security team said to Kevin:

'Is this your case sir? What's in it?'

'An oak hat stand'

'What?'

'An oak hat stand'

Kevin called me across and whispered: 'They've got the case. This is going to be a fun moment!'

' Would you mind opening it up?'

So I took the case and opened it in the right position –they had to be in front of me, which they didn't really like - and then I started unfurling the hat stand from the case and they all gasped.

The supervisor came running over to see what was going on. One of them said:

'Let me introduce you to Mary Poppins!'

They were all very nice about it and made me do it twice so their friends could see.

Another thing that Geoffrey designed for us was a set of ivory keys that flew off the keyboard. We would be playing something incredibly fast and then suddenly there would be ivory keys flying everywhere as though we had broken the keyboard by being too fast and vigorous. We would have them on the top octaves and we would go into a glissando and the keys would whoosh off the end into the audience. It should really have been hilarious and we loved doing it, but it came as such a shock to the audience that it just seemed to frighten people.

 Over the years Geoffrey has taught us so much about the dynamics of theatre. After that Edinburgh run he came out to see us at some other venues. When he walked into our venue in Leicester he could tell, just from the shape of the room that we weren't going to go down well.

He explained that if the stage is too high or there's too much gap between the stage and the front row, it's hard for the audience to connect with us. We have found recently that it's just like that at the Usher Hall in Edinburgh. There's a wide front aisle, the stage is too high, and the pricing encourages people to sit twenty rows back.

After the Leicester show he said,

'Am I right in thinking that because they were a bit of a shy audience that you backed off from them?'

We nodded in agreement.

'No,' he said. 'You need to throw the ball even harder!' The more forceful you are with them the more you'll get out of them. Never back away from them'.

Michael Vine did his best for us but there is no doubt that under his management we also lost some good opportunities, one of which was the 2012 Olympics in London. Someone called Michael's office and asked if we would do a very small spot during the Olympic opening ceremony. Without consulting us, Michael's brother told them we would do it and that our fee would be £10,000. Honestly we would have paid the organisers ourselves to have the chance to be in the Olympics ceremony, but that conversation was the last anyone ever heard of us appearing.

Another chance lost was to be on children's television. The BBC were looking for new acts for CBBC and were thinking about a musical version of Ant & Dec's show. We were asked to audition for a commissioning editor and a producer. We probably should have gone along on our own but Michael said he would be with us to guide us through it all.

When we arrived and went in to discuss the idea the executive producer was being rather grand and precious about what they were looking for and this seemed to irritate Michael. He put his feet up on the table and went down his usual route of trying to throw them off their stride.

'I'm asking because this is children's television, but what swear words can the boys use?'

She said: 'They can't use any!'

'No seriously', he said, 'what can they use? We will need to know'.

She tried to continue, but then he interrupted again.

'Here at the BBC, in this building in Wood Lane, do you have email? I'm just interested.'

She had no idea what he was up to. The trouble is that when Michael gets bored and lapses into taking the piss out of people if things aren't going his way, that attitude can backfire on his clients. The BBC were interested enough to come and record us rehearsing at Steinway Hall but nothing ever came of it after that.

After introducing us to Geoffrey, Michael lost interest in us a bit and started to disappear from our lives. We weren't making much money for him (certainly not compared to Derren Brown), but he was still taking a split commission with our agent for our cruise work so we were giving away 20% of everything we earned on the ships, even though we got most of the work on our own anyway.

We understood that this was the way things work in show business, and Michael had probably put more money behind us than we had made for him, but nevertheless we weren't showing much of a profit either.

Working with Geoffrey made us a bit more confident about how to construct a show on stage and we had a better idea of how 'Worbey and Farrell' would be different from 'Katzenjammer'. We should have been in good shape to start anew but the situation with Bender was eating into us, knowing that we had been involved in the invention of something that was getting more and more successful, but had been cut out of sharing in its future.

[K: We were on a plane one evening and I was getting upset about it again. Steven said:

'Don't worry about it. We're nice people. One day somebody will come to our rescue.']

Clearly it was affecting our performances and our enthusiasm for work, and bookings started to dry up. We decided we were too distracted to perform at the Edinburgh festival the following year and thought we should take a chance to do some research, to observe for ourselves what the people who we regard as our audience were going to see that year.

It turned out the act that was appealing most to those whom we regard as the demographic for our show was a performance by two musicians playing Mike Oldfield's *Tubular Bells* on their own, picking up and putting down a huge variety of instruments and playing back some of the tune on a recorded loop. Musically they were very good but there was absolutely no charisma and they made no attempt at engaging with the audience, so we concluded we could have done quite well that year.

It also brought out how truly dreadful side two of that album was!

Chapter 17

In which we remember some interesting characters we have met on ships, fail to recognise several people and experience a buttock-clenching half hour.

Cruise ships have taken us to all corners of the world and we have seen some fantastic places. When you have to travel so much for a living you do get a bit jaded at the prospect of another long haul flight, at the end of which there will be yet another beautiful sunset. Apart from the chance to do what we love – playing top quality pianos and making people laugh – for us the greatest thing about being on the cruise ships has been the chance it gives us to meet some really interesting people.

On one occasion we joined a Silver Sea ship for a two week voyage from Tower Bridge to Monte Carlo. When we walked onto the stage to do our show we were greeted by the most bizarre sight. The two front rows were taken up by two people and eleven teddy bears. We heard later from several guests that they would have wanted to be in the front row, but couldn't do anything about the bears being there because each teddy was a fully paid-up passenger. Silver Sea is a six star line and the couple had paid for each bear to have a suite of its own at £8,000 a time, complete with full turn-down service in the evening. They were called Charlotte and John and they apparently trusted stuffed toys more than they did people.

We were rostered to have lunch with them one day: we couldn't turn them down. There were four seats at the table and all the bears were arranged in highchairs around us. Charlotte went round them all feeding them caviar from spoons made of mother of pearl.

[K: And that night at the show she kept interrupting us, shouting out that the tiny one dressed in leather was in love with Steven!]

It was a shame for the other guests, many of whom don't travel on the bigger ships because they don't like the more commercial stuff that goes on. They're people who have had high-profile positions, retired judges and the like, and they take the smaller-ship luxury cruises to get away from spoiled nutcases like Charlotte and John. To start with everyone thought they were quite sweet and funny but as time wore on people were getting sick of them, and they were trapped with them for two weeks.

The ship was quite small: about sixteen thousand tonnes. To put it in perspective that is about a fifth of the size of the big Cunard liners. One night, the seas were very rough out on the Bay of Biscay, and the engines stopped, causing all the electricity to go off. All the lights failed, the alarms started sounding and with no engines or steering we were just bobbing around on the huge waves. One woman was so scared that she was trying to phone her children to say goodbye to them. Several people believed they wouldn't see the morning.

We were all right. In fact, when things calmed down the next day it was reported to the captain that Katzenjammer had been seen going to the bar just as it closed, and securing a couple of bottles of wine to see them through the night.

Unfortunately during this crisis Paddington Bear felt a bit seasick so Charlotte and John called the infirmary for help; a qualified doctor was dispatched to tend to him. The bill for the consultation was $80 but there was an extra $180 for the injection they insisted on him having to deal with his nausea.

Years later we were having a conversation with a percussionist friend about strange guests we had met. He said he'd met a couple who would beat anything we could possibly come up with, and then launched into his story about the teddy bears. We had actually reached the point where we were no longer sure we were remembering them correctly and our minds weren't playing tricks on us, but his experience of them was every bit as weird as ours.

Perhaps the most luxurious and exclusive line we've worked for is Seabourn. It's another six star luxury liner company catering for people who have done very well in their lives. There's only room for between three and four hundred people on board and the atmosphere is very relaxed and non-competitive, simply because just about everyone on board is at the very top of their profession and money is no object to them.

They have top quality chefs who get off when the ship comes into port and go to the local markets to pick up the very best fresh ingredients they can find. You can ask for whatever you want and they will cook it. And as we were guest entertainers we were treated just the same as everyone else.

We had been quite keen to perform on Seabourn Legend for years but when we finally got the chance it was for a nine day voyage and we had quite a lot of work to do preparing our next show. We vowed that, even though everything was available for free, we were not going to drink on this trip. We were going to use the time to rehearse all day and really get a lot of work done, arranging new pieces and writing the new show.

Nine days enforced solitude seemed absolutely perfect for getting a lot done so, as soon as we had put our cases in our rooms, we thought we would go for a quick lunch and then get on with it. We even decided not to go to the main restaurant and make do with the outside lido-style dining area.

As soon as we sat down, the waiter came over and offered us a choice between Sauvignon Blanc, Pinot Grigio and champagne.

KEVIN

Steven said he would have a bottle of Pinot. And I had the bottle of champagne and we were 'happily hydrated' for the whole nine days. We said every day that from that morning we weren't going to drink, but as soon as we sat down at half twelve for lunch the waiters kept plying us with the very best wines imaginable.

STEVEN

It got so ridiculous that whenever we got into the jacuzzi the waiter would bring us a bottle of champagne and so that we didn't have to get out, without asking, he would bring us another one in about thirty minutes.

When I got home from that cruise I was due to go to the doctor for a check-up. He took my bloods and found that my cholesterol level was really high, which it isn't usually. He couldn't think what was going on with me but I realised straight away what the problem was.

'That will be because of all the caviar I eat.'

He had a good laugh at that, but I said:

'No, really: I've been eating caviar non-stop for days now. '

He still didn't believe me so I had to explain that I really had been eating caviar every day for over a week on Seabourn. He agreed that was the likely cause so I stopped eating so much of it on ships, and it's gone back down to normal.

On that trip we met a chap called Richard Beck, a retired schoolteacher who spends his life travelling the world on a shoestring. He never buys anything he doesn't actually need: staying in hostels and being very careful with what money he has. On this occasion he was travelling as a guest of a violinist called Chris Watkins and seemed to be completely in awe of the whole Seabourn experience, how you could order lobster or caviar at any time of the day or night. Within a few days he'd fitted in so well that he had become quite demanding. We were having a party outside on deck and Richard was there complaining about the wine.

'It smells like smelly socks!'

Like so many people we meet at sea Richard has become quite a close friend. These days, during the Edinburgh Festival, Richard is the EdFringe Editor of the website Broadway Baby which for a while was reviewing more shows than anyone else. We introduced Richard to the owner of the site Pete Shaw, because he fancied doing some reviewing in his retirement and eventually Pete handed over the editing reins to him and he's very good at it. Pete's idea for a website reviewing all the Fringe shows came out of an evening of drinking with us back in 2004 when he was helping with our show, the first time we were in Edinburgh.

Originally there were going to be two websites: Broadway Baby and another one to be known as Bag o' Sh*te.com. Anything that received only one star on Broadway Baby, would automatically receive five steaming jobbies on Bag o' Sh*te.

The people on the Seabourn ships are a class apart and we do feel we have to exude confidence more with them than with audiences on other ships. Most of these people are multi-millionaires and oddly they aren't as judgmental and demanding as some people simply because they know their status in life. Everyone we have ever met on those particular ships has been very pleasant, interested and engaged. But what they expect from everyone around them is to be the best you can be, whatever your field. They can look at us and know that they could never do what we do on the piano even if they took lessons, but they still expect a performance that surpasses their imagination. If we can do that it puts us on a level with them, but these are people you can't really surprise: they've seen everything and they don't have a need to applaud

To some extent all of the cruise lines are selling a level of luxury that a lot of people never see at any other time. There are the formal evenings where everyone has to dress up, there are elegant tea-dances in the afternoon and then there are copious amounts of top quality food. It is not surprising that some guests feel the need to fit in and act up to this image of how the upper-class behave. But true class doesn't need to show itself: it's why the super wealthy don't need to spend a lot of money on designer clothes and watches. There's no need to be ostentatious when money means literally nothing to you.

STEVEN

We overheard two couples checking in on the QM2 once. They'd just got on and met in the queue and they were obviously trying to outdo each other with their conversation.

'I was saying to my husband today,' one lady said, 'as we were alighting the ship, I said to him (didn't I George?) it's so very important in one's life that one has a sunny interlude during the winterval.'

'Oh yes, we agree. It is so important!'

Over the years we have seen some really amazing acts on the ships, good and bad. Probably the worst one we've ever seen was The Argentian Devils: a man and his daughter who had a rope each with a knot on one end. They would just run around the stage whirling their arms and cracking the ropes on the floor and screaming.

KEVIN

This went on for forty-five minutes. I'd never seen anything so bad. I had to stuff my mouth with a handkerchief and I couldn't really see the show because tears of laughter filled my eyes! I was trying to be discreet because it was actually a very luxurious ship with only about a hundred and twenty people on board and people might be able to see us.

And then the Cruise Director came over and said drily: 'This is their good show...'

It's sometimes surprising how some of these acts get booked. There was a juggler who'd been appearing in Las Vegas on the Golden Strip for ages as part of an entertainments troupe, who was given a spot on the QM2. Just after he went on board the Cruise Director, Paul O'Loughlin, told him:

'Your first show is tomorrow: forty five minutes. I've not sorted out the rest of the programme yet. You'll get another forty five minutes later in the week but just to warn you, we might give ten minutes of that to the dancers so you would have to cut it down to thirty five.'

The juggler looked astonished and Paul thought he was going to complain about cutting his act down, but he shrieked:

`Forty five? Forty five minutes? But I only ever do ten minutes! That's all I've got!'

'In that case', said Paul, 'as the ship is about to leave I suggest you get off, and we'll try to sort out something else.'

The juggler left, shell shocked. A few minutes later there was a knock at the door, and his head reappeared.

'How about I do two sets of five?'

One of the most excruciating experiences we had in an audience on a cruise ship was our own fault. Early in our career we were on the QM2 when Kitty Carlisle-Hart came on as a guest. She was an American stage and screen actress and she was well into her nineties when we saw her doing an hour long lecture, talking about memories of her life.

We had done our own performance the night before and the whole theatre had been absolutely ram-packed. Realising that most of the guests were going to watch the sail-away from Canada, the Cruise Director, Paul Beck thought that he had to step up our promotion. As a non-revenue part of the ship, it's important for the entertainments department to have as many as possible watching the show. So Paul advertised us as 'Katzenjammer, the Royal Family's favourite act!' and that was enough to get us a huge audience.

Unusually we were on a long contract of two weeks on the ship - it was the maiden voyage into Canada - and we were going out of our minds with boredom because we had just finished another two weeks on a Holland America ship. We had been away from home for over a month. We were in our early thirties and really wanting to be out and about in bars somewhere on land, not just watching the sea go past.

We wandered into the lunchtime show in the theatre and found it was the lecture by Kitty Carlisle-Hart. She had been married to Moss Hart, the playwright, but before that she was in an affair with George Gershwin and claimed to have had relationships with Irving Berlin, Kurt Weill, Oscar Hammerstein, Bing Crosby, Lerner and Loewe... and several other people who were no longer alive to deny what she was claiming. If you think our name dropping is bad you should have heard her! She got a standing ovation when she came on just for still being alive!

KEVIN

Then she announced she was going to sing. Steven said:

'Oh dear I don't think this is going to be good.'

And he was right; it was the typical old lady singing routine. She was singing *Something Wonderful* from *The King and I* and the performance consisted of lots of theatrical warbling, ending with a throaty croaking noise.

Because everyone had been to our show the night before everybody knew who we were, and during the daytime shows they tend to keep the lights on. In those circumstances we were committed to the show; we didn't want to be seen to be disrespectful, so we were stifling our laughs as much as we could.

And then suddenly we were having to control something else.

STEVEN

Just before we went into Kitty's show we were wandering around bored, and found ourselves in one of the shops. I picked up a bar of laxative chocolate and said to Kevin:

'Have you ever had any of this?'

We thought we would try it to see if it works and had half a bar each; it was quite delicious. We didn't feel any different though so we carried on wandering around and eventually ended up in the theatre.

In the second verse of Kitty's warbling the laxative chocolate kicked in. We were sat in agony, clenching our buttocks, and holding on to our stomachs. The beneficial effect was that we could no longer laugh for fear of sh**ting ourselves. The downside was that we had to just sit there, we couldn't get up and leave because there were sixteen hundred people in the theatre who knew who we were and it would have been all over the ship that we had left in the middle of Kitty's show. The moment Kitty's rictus grin stooped for a bow we ran for it. It had been about half an hour of being desperate for the toilet. Still - we found out that it works!

For that performance Kitty was accompanied by one of Cunard's best in-house piano bar players called Campbell Simpson. We've met him loads of times and he's a wonderful player, so imaginative and he gets a lovely colourful sound from the instrument. He has the demeanour of Herman Munster, a big gentle giant with an amazing deep voice. Everyone loves him.

One of the first times we went into the 'Commodore Club' bar on the QM2, Campbell was in there playing. There was an American woman there, dressed in a big hat and a polka dot black and white dress.

'Campbell, we love your playing! What inspired you to become a pianist?'

'I wanted to really annoy my parents, and I didn't have the guts to tell them I was a homosexual!'

He isn't gay; he's just an outrageous and wonderfully eloquent person. If you ask him which tunes he put together into one of his intricate medleys he is quite likely to tell you:

'It was a blend of chardonnay and sauvignon blanc!'

We saw a raconteur called Barney whose main attraction was a trick with a cigarette. He would roll it up, loose tobacco in paper and light a match behind his head. Then he would flick the match up in the air and try to get it to land on the cigarette and light it in his mouth. His whole forty five minute show was him trying to get the trick to work, and he would carry on doing it until he succeeded.

He aimed to get it done after forty one minutes but the stressful thing for him wasn't the fear that the trick wouldn't work by the end of the show. It was that he'd accidentally get it right five minutes in, at which point he had nothing more he could do., except start again.

Jim Coston, a superb banjo player who we met on a ship, told us that over time we would get to know everyone's acts very well and see when they were on top of their game – or not. He recalled a legendary ventriloquism act that he used to see regularly on cruises. Watching from the wings one night he could tell that something was going wrong.

Like many ventriloquists this performer was known to have arguments between himself and his dummy, but backstage after the show, neither was speaking to the other. Jim decided to call his friend to invite him out to lunch the next day and the dummy answered and took down all the details. Jim waited an hour at the restaurant but Ray never showed up because the dummy hadn't passed on the message.

KEVIN

I was engaged to help a ventriloquist called Bertie Pearce with some songs that his dummy was going to sing. Bertie was quite well-to-do himself, rather posh, but his dummy (his alter-ego) was a slutty American doll called Angel. I had to go along to try to get the key right for some songs that Angel was going to sing.

He didn't bring the actual dummy with him to the rehearsals so Bertie would sit quietly beside the piano as though he was just there to listen. But then Angel would sing, belting out *I will Survive* while he sat there with a blank expression. I was in the room with a brash American broad, but the voice was coming out of nowhere. They really are a very odd lot those ventriloquists!

One of the most impressive acts we have ever seen was Fred Chernow, a well known lecturer on ways to improve your memory. He's written books on the subject and he gave a very interesting talk about brain patterns and memory control. To demonstrate what could be done with memory he would ask audience members their name as they came into the theatre – five or six hundred people - and would then be able to remember everyone's name later on. As a feat of recall it was really quite astonishing.

We were invited out for a meal with him and his wife to a nice restaurant serving Japanese-American fusion food. He was very interested in how we construct our pieces, and also how we work together. We are still surprised sometimes that people might want to know how what we do comes about. He was probably interested in how we are using our minds during the performance, and the feeling of telepathy is something we are very interested in ourselves.

KEVIN

He was asking loads of questions, and we were enjoying explaining it all. But we really wanted to understand how on earth he manages to remember everyone's name in his lectures. He said he studies the features of the person's face and then takes an imaginary pen and writes their name on their forehead. In that way whenever he sees them again, he recognises the face and also sees their name written large.

'When I look at you,' he said to me, 'I see not only your eyes, your nose, your mouth, I also see the name KEITH.'

At first I thought he was joking. But Americans have a habit of overusing your name and he kept on doing it:

'How is your meal, Keith?'

'Can I top up your glass, Keith?'

'Could you pass the salt, Keith?'

It became quite obvious that the world's greatest memory expert had forgotten my name.

We were trying hard not to laugh every time he did it. We came to the conclusion that his memory system works but only if you can read your own imaginary writing.

[S: It was very awkward and we didn't dare put him right. I think his wife cottoned on eventually, because there was a certain amount of kicking going on under the table.]

We used to see a talented American comedian called Marty Brill who had also had brief success as the lyricist for a Broadway musical called *Café Crown*. When we knew him he had a reputation for telling wonderful stories that turned out to be not quite true. In fact there was an unspoken agreement that if you were at a dinner table with other acts and Marty was around, out of respect for the others there, no-one would get up to leave on their own, because Marty would take the opportunity to sit down in their place and start in on another of his tall tales.

STEVEN

There was a wonderful story he told us about how when he was a young lad he was working as a cleaner at Carnegie Hall. Vladimir Horowitz was going to come out of retirement to play there and one day he came in to rehearse. Marty said he was clearing up and hid behind some chairs and listened to the wonderful playing. We were interested in someone having heard not only that famous concert but also the rehearsal for it, but when we checked the story out it wasn't true at all.

And then he told it again and this time he claimed Horowitz had been at a comedy gig he'd performed, and the great man had come up to him after and told him he was the funniest man he'd ever heard. Marty told Horowitz how he had heard him rehearsing all those years before. The punchline was that although Horowitz was mad at him for hiding, he'd then asked:

'Was I any good?'

KEVIN

He also told us that he had once been a concert pianist himself. We looked for evidence of that but there is no trace anywhere. His story was that he had performed Rachmaninov's first piano concerto somewhere. We would have been very impressed if he had played the first concerto publicly, it's a very difficult piece which we wouldn't attempt.

According to Marty's version, just before he went on stage Rachmaninov's sister visited him and told him a story about Rachmaninov on his deathbed. The great man told her that he had decided to write a letter to God, saying:

'Dear God, it is an absolute pleasure to have been Sergei Rachmaninov.'

A more widely known account of Rachmaninov's death in 1943 was that he was in a terrible state with cancer, and his last words were:

'My poor hands.'

Rachmaninov's sister died of diphtheria in 1883.

Another claim Marty made was that he had written for the TV series *MASH*. We looked it up, and there was no mention of him in the credits.

He was, however, a very talented comedian and of course the stories you tell on stage as a comedian don't have to be true, just funny. Like so many comedians to whom storytelling comes naturally Marty had a problem with switching it off when he came off stage.

It is important to remember that so many of the entertainers that we meet travel the world on their own, and there's an inevitable tendency to become a bit self-obsessed. It's very difficult for them to stop performing when they come off stage especially as the only people they meet in the bars of the ship are actually the audience for their show. It's a bit easier for us as we don't have the piano with us when we go for a drink afterwards, but it must be particularly hard for comedians who are fighting for attention all the time. As soon as you meet a comedian they try to tell you a joke, and if you say something funny they see it as a challenge and will try to upstage you.

The good (and bad) thing about being on a ship for days at a time is that everything is very intense. You can meet people and get to know them very well very quickly, because you are thrown together in a small environment. Many of them have become very dear friends for years, but some were only close for the few days we were together.

We got to know the actor Robert Powell when we joined a ship in Rio de Janeiro, although we had met him briefly on the Isle of Man when we played there. He had <u>almost </u>featured in our lives over the years without ever really getting to know him. He was on board performing his one-man show, a wonderful celebration of the life of Charles Dickens, which included him bringing many of Dickens's characters to life.

[K: I was first aware of him when I was playing a duet with Gerard Kenny, who wrote *I could be So Good for You*, the theme for *Minder*. Robert and his wife and friends used to go to Gerard's shows, and I remember looking out into the audience and seeing Jesus of Nazareth sitting there.]

We got chatting to Robert and his wife in the bar. Robert said that of all the roles he played the one he totally respects was playing *Jesus of Nazareth*. So many comedy programmes have approached him asking him to do a spoof on that role and he always refuses to do it.

One night, returning to the ship after a meal out, we met Robert and he beckoned us aside, and asked if we had enjoyed Rio. We said we had. He said:

'I'm not sharing this photo anywhere but was this wrong of me?'

And he showed us that he had been up to the statue of Christ and taken a selfie in front of it.

A year later Scott was with us, celebrating his birthday while we worked on a cruise around the UK. Robert was on board again with his wife Babs and came to see our show. They persuaded us that we should all go for a drink together. We met for a pint at lunchtime and as sometimes happens, that one pint turned into an absolute riot of afternoon drinking.

Babs is a really lovely woman and she has her own line of stories. One time a couple of Jehovah's Witnesses knocked on her door and asked if she'd like to meet Jesus. She replied that she didn't need to as she was already married to him and closed the door.

She told us that just before she came on the cruise she had gone to the Royal Free Hospital for a check-up for the travel insurance. The nurse taking down her details said to her:

'I've just noticed your address. I walk down that street every week. Did you know there's a famous actor lives on that road? Robert Powell'

Babs said: 'Yes I know. I'm married to him.'

But the nurse went on: 'Did you know he married one of the dancers from Pan's People?'

'Yes, that's me.'

'My favourite in Pan's People was Babs.'

'That's me. I am Babs!'

'I remember her clearly. She used to have beautiful blonde hair.'

'Yes, I did!'

This bizarre third person conversation continued with the woman telling Babs all about herself without understanding who she was. It was probably difficult for her to think of Babs as having a real life away from the black and white images she remembered from her days in the *Top of The Pops* studio.

Similarly, we find that if you've met someone once at a theatre or in a variety show, or particularly on a ship, it can be difficult to remember exactly how you know them when you come across them again in a different context. If a face is familiar the first thought that goes through our minds is: 'where did we work with this person?'

STEVEN

I find it particularly difficult to remember where I have met someone before. Over the years we have come across rather a lot of famous people, not just those who were performing or lecturing on cruise ships. There have been quite a few show business parties too.

We were at one such party at the Actors' Church St Paul's in Covent Garden, when Judi Dench was unveiling a new sculpture by Bruce Denny. There had been a service beforehand and then there was a lovely reception for the unveiling. There were a lot of well known people there and I spotted someone I thought I hadn't seen for a while.

I had had a couple of drinks, so I bounded up to him and said:

'Hello! How are you?'

He looked at me a bit cautiously and said in quite a sombre voice: 'Hello?'

I said: 'We know each other, don't we?'

'I don't think so.'

'Yes, we do. We've worked together.'

'I don't think we have.'

'Yes, we have. We've trod the boards! You're an actor, aren't you? Or a magician?'

'No. I'm not a magician.'

I left it and mingled for a while. And then it came to me, so I went back.

'You're a trombonist, aren't you?'

'No. I'm Rowan Williams...I'm the Archbishop of Canterbury.'

He was very nice about it. My problem is I don't watch much television. I have no idea about reality shows or pop music. We were once at one of Derren Brown's parties; you have to assume that everyone at one of his parties is famous or in the entertainment business.

I had been chatting to a group of very nice young lads for nearly an hour before I got around to asking what they did for a living. One of them said they were a pop group, so I asked the name.

'We're called McFly.'

Of course, I'd never heard of them, so I asked if they had any gigs coming up.

'The next ones are Wembley Stadium and the O2.'

[K: You came over and asked if I'd ever heard of a group called McFly, and I immediately knew. I thought: ' Oh no, he's done it again!]

[S: Well, you did something similar at Cap d'Antibes...'}

KEVIN

It was New Year's Eve and Scott Williams, a very good director, invited us to a rather posh function at Cap d'Antibes. There were only about a dozen people there, and as Scott knows so many successful people I should really have thought that everyone around us would be well known in their field.

We were introduced to a Scottish man called Graham Lyle. The name didn't mean anything to me, so I asked him what he did. When he told me that he was a composer I immediately felt sorry for him because every composer I've ever known is barely scraping enough money together to live on. I was one, so I know how hard it can be.

'What sort of thing do you do?'

'Mainly pop songs.'

The penny started to drop: 'Anything I might have heard?'

'Do you know *What's Love got to do with it?* Tina Turner sang it.'

And then we went on to talk about the people who have recorded his songs: Stevie Wonder, Michael Jackson, Rod Stewart. He was really nice to me but I should have realised and not jumped to conclusions, especially as I'd just been talking to one of the other guests who was Director of the Performing Rights Society.

Of all the people we have met on cruises one person stands out. We were asked to be on board the QM2 for a couple of days during Cunard's week-long celebration of the Queen's Diamond Jubilee in 2012. We hadn't really taken much notice of who else was appearing as we were there for such a short time but we knew the BBC royal correspondent, Jennie Bond was doing some lectures about the royal family.

We were sitting in our favourite little bar on the ship, the Commodore Club. It was one of the formal nights that Cunard have on board so we were dressed up in our dinner jackets and bow ties. A rather dapper man in his mid sixties and dressed in the Scots formal wear of kilt and jacket, came across to our table.

'Are you Worbey and Farrell?'

We admitted that we are.

'I phoned my friend Dominic John and read to him the list of entertainers that are on board this week and you two have come up, on his recommendation, as the best people to go drinking with.'

He introduced himself as Herbert Kerrigan QC, and said he was engaged for the week to do a series of lectures on criminal cases. Dominic John is a concert pianist we know quite well and if he thought that we were suitable as drinking partners for this imposing gentleman then we were very happy to accept the challenge. We were just about to go down to dinner, so we arranged to meet for cocktails later that night and it was the start of a very long friendship.

Herbert – Bert - is one of the top criminal lawyers in the country, appearing at both the Scottish and English bar. He has defended some very high-profile criminals, the serial killer Robert Black for instance. He is an expert in forensics and is a human rights advocate. He also likes his wine as much as we do and lives only a couple of miles from our house in Edinburgh so we regularly visit each other for a meal, and he's come away with us on some of our trips abroad.

It was now about a year since we had had any contact with Steven Elliott and inevitably the conversation that first evening got round to us telling Bert all about how Bender had been taken from us. We said we were on the point of giving up hope because we had spent all the money we possibly could on legal representation. The whole thing had rather dried up because Steven Elliott just ignored anything that was sent to him. It looked as though we weren't going to be able to continue and would have to accept what had been done to us.

STEVEN

I said to Bert: 'It's not really the money we're concerned about. It's the principle.'

At this Bert got most indignant and went quite red in the face.

'No! Stop right there. It's never the principle we deal with in law, we deal with logic. You've had money stolen from you and it is logical that this should be rectified. Leave it with me!'

Since then, I've always been very careful with using that phrase: "it's the principle."

Because he's right. It never is the principle.

Chapter 18

In which we start running up huge legal bills, Steven finds us lots of new friends and we come to a new arrangement with the cruise lines.

STEVEN

By the time we met Bert in the Commodore Club we had very little work coming in for the next few months. We were so demoralised about the situation with Bender that we needed a recovery period.

This was when I got involved in bell ringing again. I was chatting online with a young lad called Simon Westman and noticed a picture of him holding a bell rope on his Facebook profile, so I told him that it was something I used to do when I was young.

He was living in Edinburgh for a while so he invited me along to a practice at Edinburgh Cathedral. The sessions there were run by a lovely couple from Wolverhampton called Bill and Helen Brotherton and they were really welcoming. Bill seemed to be almost completely deaf but it didn't affect his ability to ring a bell.

I told Bill that I hadn't been in a belfry ringing bells for goodness knows how many years - at least twenty - but I had been to the cathedral once before with Derek Jones. Helen got out the old book that listed visitors and I found my name signed there. As soon as I rang a bell it all came back to me. It's just like riding a bike; you never forget how to do it.

After that I got the bug again. I went to the other churches in Edinburgh and around Scotland and I developed a whole new set of friends all involved in campanology. And then I joined a society of gay ringers called The Friends of Dorothy and I've had some lovely weekends away with them.

KEVIN

It changed our lives, our complete experience of Edinburgh. Until then we didn't really have many good friends in the city apart from the old queens in the New Town, and many of them are no longer around. One thing you can say about bell ringers is that they do need to quench their thirsts after all that pulling on ropes, and the people that Steven was mixing with quickly became very close friends of mine too because I could share an interest in alcohol with them.

It turned out their pub sessions after ringing practices are longer than the ringing itself and I have got into the habit of joining them all as they come out of the belfry and head for the pub, and we've had a great social life in Edinburgh ever since. They are a lovely set of friends who have helped and supported us in our career, and these are the people we go on holiday with now.

Amongst this bell ringing group there was a rather unhappy middle aged lady called Sue. Every time we saw her, we'd say:

'Hello Sue, how are you?'

'Awful. Dreadful. Really bad.'

Although she meant what she was saying, she always said it with a smile. We knew that she was divorced, and perhaps she was estranged from her family as well, but at the same time she was always out and about, and she just loved culture. She had been studying as a mature student at Edinburgh College of Art and was always going to concerts and shows, ours included. Whenever we did a BBC Scotland live show she was always there in the audience. So although she always said she was unhappy, people didn't think of her as clinically depressed.

STEVEN

We were all very fond of her, especially Scott.

One Friday evening there was a special bell ringing practice at Edinburgh Cathedral to which people from all over Scotland came. Sue was there and was in a really good mood, and she came to the pub afterwards and sat chatting with everyone. I remember leaving the bar thinking that she had really turned a corner, and that it was so nice to see her doing so well.

A couple of days later we found out that she had taken her own life sometime over the weekend. We realised that when we saw her on the Friday evening she had made her decision and had come out to say goodbye to everyone, without telling anybody that's what she was doing. It explains how happy and relaxed she seemed that night. I really felt annoyed at not noticing the signs and that experience has taught me a lot about the nature of depression.

KEVIN

It wasn't long after that Helen Vint, Neil's youngest sister came up to see me in Edinburgh. She wanted to know about Neil's last day and I found myself describing how ordinary it had felt that last morning I spent with him. I had been going off to work with a drag queen in Brighton and Neil was going to the party his parents wanted him to play at, and we had been giggling a lot that morning.

'Giggling'!?

She seemed shocked to hear that. She had always imagined that Neil must have been in a completely depressed state and perhaps she thought that someone should have known what was about to happen.

Having seen it with him and with Sue, I've come to the conclusion that there are some cases of suicide that just can't be prevented. These people are in a place where they believe that they are such a burden to their friends and family that it is going to be a great relief to everybody around them that they will no longer exist in the world. They have made peace with themselves and become happy about what they have decided to do.

It is tragic how wrong their perception is that they don't understand how loved they are. There were nearly two hundred people at Sue's funeral.

Apart from our new bellringing friends the main change in our social life that year was Bert. We were regularly going over to his place for meals and he was coming round to our house to share good food and wine. When we talked to him about our problems with Bender on the QM2, Bert said: 'Leave it with me', and he was true to his words.

Within a couple of weeks of the Jubilee cruise Bert had arranged for his friend Andrew Smith to become our advocate. Andrew studied under Bert as his 'devil' and like Bert, he can act as a QC in both the English and the Scottish courts so having him on side was a great advantage. He's also a very handsome man. We found ourselves in the Edinburgh offices of the law firm Simpson and Marwick meeting Gavin Henderson, one of their partners and Marco Rinaldi, a solicitor. Andrew had arranged for them to act on our behalf in pursuing our rights to a share in Bender.

When we arrived their first question was

'How would you describe this app?'

STEVEN

I said: 'Well, basically it's a satnav for perverts.'

I don't think they'd ever dealt with entertainers before so they started laughing. Their second question was:

'What are you after?'

And Kevin said: 'Death?'

We told them the whole story from start to finish. It took about ninety minutes to go through everything that happened: how Bender came into existence and how we had been shut out of it. When we finished someone commented that it was quite obvious that we were telling the truth just from the fact that we hadn't referred to any notes and not corrected each other on any detail. Our body language showed that we hadn't made anything up as we told it to them.

When they said they were going to take the case on we were relieved that somebody actually believed what we were saying.

Next we had a meeting with them and Andrew Smith in his chambers, just off the Royal Mile in Edinburgh. The rooms are very old-fashioned and quite intimidating. He held up the document that had been prepared about our claim, declared that we had a very interesting case and went into it in great detail, giving us all the legal reasons why the law was on our side. We were definitely going to win.

There was another advocate called Peter Barclay sitting in the corner with a quill pen, who looked like he had been there since the 1890s. Andrew was in mid-flow when Peter suddenly put down his quill and said:

'Can I ask you something? How did you two come up with that arrangement of the Gershwin?'

There was an awkward silence and then Andrew, somewhat embarrassed, said:

'We've all been watching your YouTube videos.'

It was quite funny, and it happened again at another meeting. Whenever someone new was brought onto the case, Andrew or Marco would show them our videos to bring them up to speed with who we are, and what to expect when they met us. Lots of these lawyers are enthusiastic about music so it was quite a charming way to introduce us, and maybe better than starting off by meeting us face-to-face!

Gavin Henderson sent Steven Elliott's lawyers a letter pointing out that we had been denied our rights as 49% partners in Bender for the past two years. According to Elliott's own website the app now had over a million registered users and it appeared in the top twenty of social networking apps in the Apple app store. Gavin suggested that we wouldn't take Steven Elliott and his company to court if he agreed to pay us our share of profits past and future, together with an acknowledgement that all three of us had had a part in inventing Bender.

A few weeks later we heard back from his lawyers. They started off by being insulting about Scottish law, went on to say we had waited until Bender was successful before making a 'desperate effort to net themselves an undeserved windfall gain', and that we had given up any chance of a claim by not making any attempt to contact Steven Elliott since he sent the cheque. And anyway, they said, Bender was making a loss. So there.

They also let it slip that the Bender trademark, that we had registered at our address, had been transferred into his new company without us knowing about it. We couldn't really understand how something with a million users could not make a profit, but someone explained to us that the accounts of the company would look like it was making a loss if Steven Elliott was paying himself everything that was coming in as a Director's salary.

No-one seemed surprised, or concerned, that he hadn't just given in straight away. The lawyers thought the next stage in the campaign would be to try to get Steven Elliott to come to a meeting with us chaired by a professional mediator.

While they planned that, we went back to work devising a piece that would be at the heart of our next show. Seeing the two musicians perform *Tubular Bells* the previous summer taught us that there was a market for doing something experimental with a piece that everybody knows. It could get everyone talking about us. We started tinkering about with the famous *Caprice* by Paganini and eventually came up with twenty four 'deviations' as we called them, and that was the idea behind *Deviations on a Caprice* that was the centre of our 2013 run in Edinburgh.

Geoffrey was very nervous about the idea because at twenty four minutes it was far longer than anything we had ever done before. He thought it was probably too much of a risk, but he let us go ahead anyway, saying:

'I might be wrong...'

To minimise the exposure a little we decided to take a slightly smaller venue than we had had two years before, and also committed ourselves to doing only a two-week run, instead of the full three weeks of the Festival.

We made the arrangements for hiring the Assembly Rooms on our own this time. We also asked Claire Smith, a reviewer at *The Scotsman*, if she could recommend someone Edinburgh-based to be our public relations representative, and she suggested Fiona Duff. We arranged to meet Fiona for a coffee at The Dome, conveniently just along the street from the Assembly Rooms. A glamorous woman sauntered into the bar wearing dark glasses and a mink coat, quite evidently hungover from the night before. From this first sighting we knew she was our sort of person and she has become one of our dearest friends. Sshe's also fantastic at what she does for us.

[K: Claire Smith warned us that Fiona is quite posh, but when she's had a few glasses of vino that aristocratic voice goes up to another level.]

When we told Michael Vine's assistant, Corrie McGuire that we were only doing two weeks at the Assembly Rooms, and that we'd arranged for Fiona to do our publicity, she said:

'You won't be able to get Fiona Duff: she doesn't do it anymore'.

'That's funny, we had coffee with her this morning, and she's happy to work for us.'

'Well, you won't get the Assembly Rooms, because they won't let you do only two weeks.'

'But that's not true either; we've sorted it out with Tommy Sheppard already. We're getting the one hundred seat studio for two weeks.'

Tommy Sheppard used to run the Stand Comedy Clubs in Scotland and for years he was the producer of Assembly. He is now the SNP MP for Edinburgh East.

One afternoon just before we were due to go on stage, we had a call from Gavin Henderson checking what time our festival show was on.

'Can you be at Simpson and Marwick's offices at 9.30 tomorrow? I'm taking you somewhere.'

It was like a magical mystery tour. He took us to an industrial estate somewhere near Glasgow and we were led into the headquarters of H Morris and Company, a high end furniture business who used to supply furniture for prestigious hotels and Cunard ocean liners. We were greeted by a man with a Scottish-American accent called Robert Morris. He came in with a loaf of bread which he'd just baked himself and offered us: 'Tea? Coffee? Whisky? Whatever?'

He took us on a quick tour of the factory and then we got down to the business of why we were there. Robert said his hobby was getting involved in other people's legal cases. His proposal was that he would approach Steven Elliott and say to him something along the lines of:

'You're being sued for a large amount. There is a way to make all that go away, and it won't cost you. If you take me into partnership instead of them, I will pay those pesky kids off and you and I can make Bender even bigger than it is now.'

He takes on cases that he is pretty much sure the other side (i.e. our side) is going to win. We don't know what figure we were going to be offered, but he told us of another case where that plan had worked and he had given the litigant a six figure sum, so it was probably going to be a big sum of money.

It was an interesting proposal. We thought seriously about taking him up on it but in the end we felt we wanted to follow it through and go ahead with a court case if necessary. So many people were now involved and investing their time in what we were doing and they were doing it for free.

We saw Robert on the QM2 a few years later, sitting on the front row of our show with his wife Penny, and we spent the week with them. He is quite a wonderful character, but he still insisted we were making a big mistake not taking him up on his proposal because the matter might drag on for years.

The sixteen performances of the show, *Deviations on a Caprice*, completely sold out and, as we actually made a profit (which few people do at Edinburgh) we turned out to be Michael and Corrie's best-selling show that year. Geoffrey graciously told us he had indeed been wrong about the *Caprice*.

KEVIN

I think Corrie McGuire was quite amused by the fact we'd taken things into our own hands and she was really pleased how well our ticket sales went that year. She had been genuinely concerned about us doing such a short run. Michael had told us when we first met him that anyone doing the Edinburgh Festival should always go through Corrie, as in his mind she was an absolute genius when it came to anything to do with the Fringe. She had been involved with the Festival since being a student at Edinburgh University, so she knew it inside out.

Everyone was telling us that we should extend our run and do another week. We were booked to perform on a cruise ship during that third week but we remembered that Michael had said in advance that he would be very happy to cancel the cruise if we did well, not really believing that we would. As it happened, the American comedian Scott Capurro had to cancel his run because he was ill so the Assembly Rooms management were actively looking for someone to fill his spot and were keen for us to stay on. We went to Michael and said we had been offered the chance to extend and asked him to get us out of the cruise booking.

'I can't suddenly cancel work on a cruise ship. They're going to think you're a pair of tarts!'

So we went on the trip, and abandoned the chance of a third week in Edinburgh. It made us think seriously about whether the cruise line would have been more sympathetic if we weren't approaching them through an agent. After all, Holland America were very good to us when we had to cancel at short notice when Steven's mother died.

Being allowed to deal with the cruise lines direct was actually quite a big deal. Normally when an act leaves an agent that has an arrangement with a company, the line will not book them again for at least a year, out of coutesy to the agent. Increasingly acts have a signed contract with their agent so they are afraid that if they fall out with them and leave, the work will dry up.

Some of these agents have an exclusivity clause in their contract with the cruise companies they deal with because it's simpler and cost effective, and greener, for the lines to have acts brought to them. Cruise lines take carbon emissions very seriously and are very environmentally friendly. Unless you're a very well established artist, it can be impossible to be employed except through an agent, and that means there are still some lines we just can't work with.

Since we have represented ourselves, we've found the entertainments teams of the cruise lines (their booking consultants) are really lovely people who can be very accommodating if you have a problem. Very often the bookers are retired dancers, actors, and other people who have performed on ships themselves. Some of them knew us during their professional careers onboard and it helps when they remember us as friends, or just people who treated them with respect.

It always pays us to be nice to the nice people – and really it's not difficult! It is also refreshing when people go out of their way to be nice to us too. We were extremely grateful, for instance, for all the work our lawyers were doing on Bender, apparently just because they believed in us and didn't want to see us cheated and without any real expectation that we could pay them.

By the time we went to the mediation session with Steven Elliott there was £107,000 worth of legal work racked up, but we hadn't been sent a bill. On the day of the mediation session we were introduced to a man called George Clark from a company based in Aberdeen called Quantum Claims. After only the briefest of conversations he said his firm were willing to finance our legal fees if we agreed to give them a percentage of anything we won at the end. He was so sure that we would win that he was quite happy to take the risk.

KEVIN

The mediator was a lady called Marjorie Mantle. Obviously her role was to get us to negotiate and come to an agreement and she told us she had a ninety percent success rate and that if we all remained calm we would come up with a solution that satisfied everyone.

I'm afraid I thought of her as a Claire Rayner figure and found it all rather patronising. At one point Gavin Henderson asked me what I made of her and trying to be tactful, I said:

'Well, she doesn't need me to like her.'

She didn't seem to be on our side at all and was downplaying our involvement in Bender as 'a bit of advertising'. I got the impression she was quite friendly with Steven Elliott's new lawyers, Brodies. But maybe it looked the same way from his side too.

To start with we were all in the same room. This was the first time we had seen him since the period when we thought of him as one of our best friends and it just seemed to emphasise how much had changed since then. We had been told that mediation usually starts with a statement from each side about what we thought about the dispute, so a few days before we had sat down with our lawyers and put together a letter that we read out.

When it came to his turn Steven Elliott said he hadn't written anything but he wanted to speak from the heart. He then went into a speech about how we had wasted two years of his life and made him very ill for no reason other than greed.

After that we were split up. He was in one room with his lawyers, we were all in another, and Marjorie Mantle was trotting to and fro between us. George Clark seemed particularly irritated by Steven Elliott's speech:

'Lads, if you want to leave now you have my full backing. I have no worries about you not winning this case. I'm not used to dealing with this sort of behaviour. Emotions!?!'

The first question Marjorie put to us was:

'Steven Elliott wants to know what you want.'

Gavin Henderson said: 'It's a ridiculous question. Let's treat it with the contempt it deserves. We want five million pounds.'

'Are you being serious?'

'That's half of what Bender is currently being valued at, as far as we can gather.'

She came back a few minutes later.

'He's offering you £2,500. And you can have the seven-year-old laptop back.'

The rest of the day didn't go any better. After seven hours of getting nowhere, Marjorie Mantle popped her head in again.

'Mr. Elliott would like to know what the relationship is between Mr. Clark and Worbey and Farrell.'

George wasn't pleased.

'Now listen, lady. Go back and tell them it is none of their business. Get them to negotiate something reasonable and sensible. At the moment it is four'o'clock and I'm getting the 4.30 train back to Aberdeen so you've got five minutes.'

She looked kind of shocked but came back quite quickly this time.

'He's offering £50,000 and £10,000 to Simpson and Marwick for their legal costs.'

[S: We all stood up, put our coats on and minced out past the room that Steven Elliott and his team were in. We saw him look up horrified; he couldn't believe that we were leaving.]

We discovered later that before coming to the meeting he had put £127,000 into his current account, so if we'd stayed he was going to cover our legal fees and offer us £20,000 to go away. That's as far as he was prepared to go.

After that there was nothing else to do but take him to court. Technically we had to demonstrate that he was <u>legally</u> required to pay us our share of the profits he had made from the joint idea. That meant more months of meetings with the lawyers, going through all of the emails and texts there had been between us and him, and preparing statements that ran to hundreds of pages that detailed everything that had been said and done over the period between us first talking about Bender that night in Vienna, right up to the time when he sent us the cheque to get rid of us.

We were ready for the hearing at the Court of Session in Edinburgh and decided to take a short holiday in Gran Canaria before it went ahead. We had only been there a couple of days when we had a phone call from Marco Rinaldi.

'It's all over! Steven Elliott has backed out and he's cancelled the court case. He's not going to defend it and his lawyers have told him they aren't going to act for him anymore!'

We're still not sure whether he knew that by pulling out he was actually conceding that we were right, but it meant that we had won and it was time to celebrate.

But if any of us (him included) thought that we wouldn't have to go to court at all, we would have been wrong. Saying that he wasn't going to defend our claim didn't mean he was settling up straight away. The judge awarded us an interim amount but said that Steven Elliott still had to produce all his financial information, so that a decision could be taken about how much money he owed us. It was still going to drag on.

Chapter 19

In which we tell you about the Edinburgh Fringe Festival, we create a marvellous deception and are deceived ourselves.

During the 2013 Edinburgh Festival our friend Bert Kerrigan overheard a conversation outside one of our performances that amused us so much that we told our PR guru Fiona Duff about it, and she phoned up the editor of *The Times* Diary column. The incident was reported the next day.

Two ladies of a certain Edinburgh type had been good enough to buy one of our programmes before going to see the show. As they queued to get in they were reading what we had to say and spotted amongst the list of acknowledgements, that we wished to give our sincere thanks to Dame Margaret de Lumiere.

'Dame Margaret de Lumiere?' said one.

'Oh yes, you remember! We heard her playing last year. A wonderful performance!' replied the other.

And now you are probably thinking: 'What's funny about that?'

Dame Margaret was our pet Yorkshire terrier.

STEVEN

When we were living in London Scott and I thought it would be nice for him to have a little dog to keep him company when I was away from home so much. We knew exactly what we wanted: a little Yorkshire terrier girl-dog. And she would be called Margaret.

We did our research and eventually found a litter for sale, including just one girl, at an address in Worksop. We drove up and found this grubby two-up two-down terraced house which turned out to be absolutely full of dogs. The rather dodgy looking owner tried to persuade us to take a male but we insisted that we only wanted the lady dog and eventually we came away with this tiny little creature, no bigger than the palm of my hand.

We absolutely adored her. At the time we were living in a building called Lumiere, and as Margaret grew older she started to affect the airs and graces of a dowager duchess so she became known as Dame Margaret de Lumiere to us all. And of course she moved to Edinburgh with us and continued to look after Scott for me.

As we've said the 2013 Edinburgh run of two weeks was a great success. When we next appeared at The Assembly Rooms we decided we could risk a step up and booked the Ballroom there, which holds four hundred people. Geoffrey immediately spotted a problem. Lots of different acts were appearing throughout the day and we had just accepted the lighting and stage effects we'd been presented with. Geoffrey was furious with what he found and summoned the lighting crew.

'You've lit the stage red! The only time you would light the stage red is at an amateur dramatic production of *Faust* as he's descending into hell! And what's with all the smoke? It looked like they were coming out of f***ing Narnia! There are only two lighting cues for this show. Lights On! and Lights Off!'

Geoffrey doesn't often lose his temper but when he does it's worth being there.

He wasn't impressed with the venue at all. The first couple of performances at the Edinburgh Fringe are always a bit difficult; people who go to a first night all seem to be a bit odd anyway, including the early reviewers. But Geoffrey had spotted a problem with the hall itself; he took us aside after the first performance.

'I'm afraid there's nothing you can do. All the problems with the show are to do with the acoustics. I'm afraid this year they've brought the curtains forward. They deaden everything so that when someone in the audience applauds, they only hear themselves clapping. If they laugh, they only hear their own laugh, and after a while they start to stifle making any noise they make out of sheer embarrassment. They're all too self aware. Two feet further back and the whole room would be more echoing, but I'm afraid the venue has ruined your run for you.'

The problem was that we were sharing the space with so many other people and the venue weren't going to change it just for us.

The change over time between shows at the Edinburgh Fringe is so tight that it just isn't possible to make any more than small adjustments. For the most part people understand the concept of sharing the theatre and are very considerate towards their fellow performers: a few don't play along at all.

One of the worst offenders we came across was a man and dog act called 'Piff the Magic Dragon' who actually declared he was 'The Loser of *America's Got Talent'* because he came second. We shared a dressing room with him at the George Square Theatre in our last Edinburgh Fringe run and we didn't meet anyone who thought he was a nice person. He was unfriendly and always very bad tempered. When we arrived at the venue for the first time, we found he'd taken green tape and marked out which were 'his' parts of the dressing room.

[S: There was even tape down the middle of the mirror as though there was part of it we weren't allowed to look in.

K: His wife had been a dancer in Las Vegas and was very nice and down to earth. But he had this nasty little Chihuahua – 'Piff', presumably. If that animal had been left alone I would have been straight down to the Dundas Street Vetinerary Surgery to have it put down! I might have taken the magician too and had him spayed.]

The great thing about the Edinburgh festival is the opportunity it has given us to meet new people, and to catch up with old friends who come every year to have a good time. Even when we're not performing we get invited to lots of parties, and we are given access to the so-called 'VIP Lounges'. There's a real sense of community there. Everyone knows each other and in the days when a five star review in *The Scotsman* was a great accolade, we were on an equal footing with the best known stand-up comedians in the country. But one night we were in the Fringe Club with Al Murray, 'The Pub Landlord,' when Liz Hurley and Hugh Grant came in. Suddenly several famous people felt thoroughly upstaged. When they left, Al said:

'Phew! I'm glad they've gone. Now we can go back to being stars!'

Al had been with us that afternoon when we were interviewed by John Wilson for *Front Row* on Radio 4 in the BBC tent. Stephanie Beecham and Sofie Grabol, the Danish actress famous for *The Killing,* were on too. What was strange was how nervous Al was

```
    *** BOOK SHOP ***
    ** QUEEN VICTORIA **
1018 Jhilbert
--------------------------------
CHK 3605 13JUN'23 11:58AM
--------------------------------
    Balance due
    Sales No. 9005
    199005

 1 Entertainers Goo   25.00
   Sales Itemiser16   25.00
   PAYMENT          25.00
   Cab/Acc: 4161 1
   V315 Dr A Seet
   Guest Charge       25.00
---1018 CLOSED 13JUN 11:58AM----

CABIN:_____

NAME:_____

SIGNATURE:_____


Customer Serv +44(0)117 982 5961
 Aftersalesuk@hardingretail.com
```

before we all went onto the stage. He is used to playing his part as the nameless Pub Landlord, but this time he was there as himself. He didn't really relax until we all posed for a selfie with the audience and he could get back in character.

STEVEN

Another night we were in the Fringe Club and Dillie Keane from Fascinating Aida brought a little dog with her that kept trying to s**g me. Every time she let go of it, it ran across and started humping my leg. It could probably smell Margaret on me. Alan Davies couldn't stop laughing about it.

Another time I did my usual thing of not recognising people. I got talking to the cast of *The Inbetweeners* and asked them which venue they were on at and it turned out they were there to promote their new film. It was the same night that Neil and Christine Hamilton got really tipsy and were simulating having sex with some blow-up animals. We had to rescue them before they were thrown out.

KEVIN

Dave Gorman tweeted the next morning:

'I've got a terrible hangover and a vision of Christine Hamilton dancing with an inflatable penguin!'

We've had several afternoons and evenings drinking in Edinburgh with the Hamiltons during the Festival. They arrived at our house one Monday morning already hungover, having been away for the weekend with some of their friends who own a castle. They fell out of the car that delivered them and then just plonked themselves on the grass in our garden and lay down and went to sleep. Our neighbours' curtains were twitching, everyone wondering what on earth Neil and Christine Hamilton were doing lying asleep in our garden.

We had all been invited to The Dome by the manager Brian Crawford for one of his celebrity lunches. Alongside Neil and Christine Hamilton there was a very glamorous looking Lorraine Chase, wearing a very big hat. We all had rather a lot to drink because of the copious amounts of champagne on offer, especially Lorraine who was telling us that her real name is Lorraine Parsons. She took the name Chase because her Dad (as she put it) was a wrong'un, always the subject of a police chase and on the run from the law. At one point she declared loudly:

'I don't know why they advertise toilet roll with a little puppy. What's a puppy got to do with it? You're not going to wipe your f***ing arse on it!'

The funny thing was that when she said that everyone in The Dome turned round and looked at Christine. We saw tweets afterwards where people were commenting on: 'what a foul mouthed woman that Christine Hamilton is!'

Another time at The Dome we were with Lorna Luft, Ken Kercheval who was Cliff Barnes in *Dallas,* Craig McLauchlin from *Neighbours* and Richard Mawby, one of the world's most famous wig makers; he did all the wigs for Danny LaRue and helped Margaret Thatcher in that area too. In crowds like these it's quite fun to be the ones that no-one recognises.

Most years we would get an invitation to the Roxburgh Hotel where Jim Bowen, the presenter of the gameshow *Bullseye* hosted a birthday party during the Festival. He was a great storyteller and a very kind man. The first time we went with the Hamiltons and two mutual friends called Stuart and Stewart. Stuart introduced us all:

'... and this is my boyfriend Stewart – he's got a big willy!'

'Very nice lads, help yourselves to drinks,' said Jim, apparently ignoring what he had just been told. 'And there's some nibbles over there.'

A little later Jim brought his lovely wife Phyllis over to meet us.

'Hello lads' she said. 'Now. Which of you is the one with the big willy?'

Jim was doing a show based on *Bullseye* at Jonglers at the Playhouse. He said he knew that he was the last person to be asked to host the gameshow, and that there was a long list of people who had turned it down before the producers approached him. After the first episode the reviews came out and the programme was slated. Jim said he was sitting reading them in the ITV canteen alongside Eric Morecambe. He felt hurt by what people had written but Eric just told him not to worry about it.

'The papers are just tomorrow's chip wrappings'.

In the end he wasn't bothered what the critics thought because the public seemed to love the show and he did very well from it.

'I've got my Rolls Royce in the garage.'

We thought it must have been awful for him having to do the part of the show when the contestants who'd lost were shown what they could have won.

'Oh no! That was the best bit. The crew were always pissing themselves laughing!'

The two Stuarts/Stewarts also introduced us to another of our favourite people during the 2016 Edinburgh Festival: Lady Colin Campbell, or 'Georgie' as we know her. Stewart Nicholls was producing her show about her life called *A Cup of Tea with Lady C,* when she was trying to raise money for her project to restore Goring Castle. Rather naively she thought people make a lot of money by appearing at the Festival. People do have a lot of fun but no-one makes any money. One year we actually made £19 profit from a three week run and our agent still sent us an invoice for £4.50.

We went to see Georgie's show and it was really very good. We loved her catchphrase: 'I'm whoring for Goring!'

Then she came to see us and Stewart introduced us to her, and we went out for a few drinks with her and her two sons. She adopted two boys from a Russian orphanage as she couldn't have children herself. She is really knowledgeable about the arts and music in particular. During our show we had commented that we had been criticised for playing Scott Joplin's *Maple Leaf Rag* too fast, and it was quite reassuring when she told us that she knew Shura Cherkassky, one of the best pianists ever, and he used to play the piece very fast too.

We all got on so well that we spent several days together during that festival and then one evening we went to Bert's for dinner and found Georgie there too because she knows him as well. She has been involved in litigation just as much as we have so we have a lot in common!

One time we visited her at Castle Goring and found she had hired the building to an Indian film company. The place was awash with Bollywood actors and the accompanying technicians and film crew, but it turned out they hadn't yet paid her. We were there for a party with Bert, and after consulting him late at night on the legal position, she went down and locked all of the doors so that the following morning no-one could get in to resume filming until a bank transfer had gone through for the full amount she was due. There were dozens of very glamorous Indian people standing about in the

Sussex countryside with nothing to do, and nowhere to go. As soon as the money arrived she unlocked everything and let them in, and then made us all breakfast.

Our 2014 show was our most adventurous. We wrote a piece for eight hands called *Ziggurat* where we recorded ourselves playing with four hands and then accompanied ourselves on stage with four more.

But the centre piece of the show was even more audacious.

STEVEN

One day during the previous winter we were playing about with computer generated sounds of instruments. That evening Kevin said:

'Why don't we write a piano concerto using all those good instrument sounds on the computer? We could play along with the computer on stage.'

We had never done anything for an orchestra before, but it came to me that we didn't need a computer-generated orchestra.

'Why don't we just hire a real one, film them and then play along?'

I just realised that if we did something playing with a computerised orchestra, it was absolutely certain that someone would come along and top us by doing the same thing with a recorded orchestra instead. If we went first we had to be one step ahead and beat them all to it, and playing on stage with an orchestra everyone could see was even more spectacular than just using a tape recording.

KEVIN

I thought it was a great idea. We set to and produced what became known as *The Edinburgh Fringe Concerto* - Worbey & Farrell's Piano Concerto Number One. It is in three movements and lasts about ten minutes. All we needed then was someone to play it with us.

One of Steven's ringing friends plays the violin with the Edinburgh Symphony Orchestra and so we got in touch with their conductor, Gerry Doherty. They weren't that keen until I said we would give them a thousand pounds to play it, and then suddenly they were much more interested. As an extra encouragement we said we could arrange for them to be filmed playing another piece of their choice and they went for a Sibelius symphony.

The only suitable venue available to hire for the day we wanted to film was the Freemasons Hall in Edinburgh, and the acoustics there are a bit boomy. Fortunately we had hired a really professional recording technician from Castlegate Studios, and he was able to sort those problems out for us. Our friend Alex Hunsley hired three high definition professional cameras to film it all for us and did a great job.

STEVEN

We were there with Tommy Sheppard because he was producing our show at the Assembly Rooms and he was interested in the scheme we were cooking up. When we arrived the orchestra was rehearsing the Sibelius and it sounded wonderful. They could play that as well as any professional orchestra, and we thought it was going to be a great afternoon.

Disappointingly, when we started playing our piece with them, it was more like cats wailing! They were so out of tune that we were almost in tears. I don't think any of them had put any real effort into learning the score that we had sent them two weeks before! But they quickly got better and the end-result was more than acceptable.

By the end of the day we had a very good recording, and they were playing it well. They told us after, that the movement they liked the best was the second, and certainly that was by far the best of the three that they played. Alex's filming was spot-on for our concerto, but unfortunately, he forgot to turn on the camera that was trained on the conductor's face during the Sibelius Symphony. It was just one of those things, but at least you could see him from behind.

Now that we had the orchestra filmed we could start rehearsing how to play alongside them. It actually proved to be harder than we had hoped, because the sound of the orchestra was so loud coming through speakers on the stage that we couldn't hear ourselves playing. In the end we had to buy a system that let us hear properly through earphones. It was quite expensive, but it worked really well.

But the great trick about it all was that we didn't tell the audience that it was a film, we made out that it was a live performance. We would introduce the concerto as a world premiere and then tell the audience that we were now switching on a live feed direct from Edinburgh's Freemason Hall.

Gerry Doherty appeared on screen with the orchestra behind him and we would have a – very carefully timed – 'chat' with him.

KEVIN

I'd say: 'Hello Gerry! How are you all?'

And he put a finger to his ear as though he couldn't quite hear and say: 'Nul Points!'

'It's not the Eurovision Song Contest, Gerry'.

Everyone got sucked into believing this was a real ad-lib conversation between the two of us.

Next we got the audience to shout 'Hello!' to the orchestra, and then the orchestra all shouted back, so everyone in the hall believed they were involved in a dialogue themselves.

It was filmed so that we would look up at the conductor on the screen, and he would be looking down at us as though he could see us. We had to get our positioning on the stage just right so that it seemed as though he was looking at us through a glass wall.

Of course we had to have the orchestra tuning up, so Gerry would say:

'Can I have an 'A'?'

And Steven would ask: 'What did he say?'

'He wants an 'A'.'

STEVEN

I would run over to the piano, and play the middle 'A' a few times and then the players would all seem to pick up on that and play along as if they were tuning up to our note.

It was very convincing, even to us. We timed all of that section before the music very carefully so that we knew precisely when Gerry would be speaking and the orchestra apparently responding to what was going on in the theatre. And then when we were playing we made sure the audience could see that we were following Gerry's baton, as though he was actually conducting us as well as the orchestra in the room with him.

The first time we performed this piece live playing along with the film was a nerve-wracking occasion, partly because we were talked into doing it at very short notice. We were on a transatlantic voyage from New York to Southampton on the QM2 and the engineer on board who was entrusted with the technical aspects of our show caught us playing back the film of the orchestra on our laptop.

'What's that?' he asked excitedly.

We explained the idea, and he was so enthusiastic about it that he persuaded us to try it out for our performance on board. Paul O'Loughlin, the Cruise Director, agreed and told us about the efforts the engineer was making to stage the event. He had told all the crew that he was dealing with the technicalities of having a live orchestra broadcasting back to the ship from Edinburgh. It was in the programme as a live feed as well and the theatre was absolutely packed long before the show started.

He decided we could go one stage further with the pretence and suggested it would be even more convincing if there was a technology failure. It was a brilliant idea!

Between the first and second movements he inserted a message screen that said:

'Connection Lost'

and then there was the circle of doom going round as though the signal was buffering. The audience gasped with concern, and then the buffering message started to count up:

'10%... 20%...72%...'

And the 'live feed' came back on just in time to start the second movement.

It was very imaginative, and it worked perfectly. In fact, the following day at the ship's reception desk there were complaints that the internet hadn't been functioning properly the night before because we were using too much bandwidth.

KEVIN

An American lady stopped me the next morning and congratulated me on the show but then she said:

'Yes, it was very good, but it is a shame really, isn't it?'

'A shame? Why's that?'

'Because that's the future. Orchestras just won't be travelling to perform live now that they can do it over the internet.'

When we performed it in Edinburgh, we asked the press to keep up the pretence that it was live when they wrote about it, and we didn't let on to the audience even after we'd played it for fear that someone might spoil the illusion for people coming to the show later. Everybody tended to believe it and the chances are that there are people reading this now who saw us perform that year and still didn't know that it wasn't really live.

[S: I'm sure a lot of people went away amazed at what 'they can do nowadays.']

After the Edinburgh run we did it only a few more times, because technically it is very difficult to set up, feeding an HD film through somebody's projector and getting the sound right. Strangely no-one seemed to question the idea that a full orchestra would be available for a live feed sometimes several hours out of their time zone.

When we performed it at London's Hippodrome, Tristan Goligher, a very experienced film producer, confessed to us afterwards that he was ashamed of himself because, although he knew it was a trick, when one small thing didn't go quite as he expected, just for a second he thought - 'My God this is real! ' And then he felt stupid that he had fallen for it.

What had happened was that the film had come on a few seconds into the 'conversation' with Gerry. It didn't matter really but when he appeared, he was already saying:

'Nul Points!'

We must have looked startled by that for a second, and it was enough to convince Tristan that we really didn't know what was going on at the other end. We all had a laugh about it, and we decided not to let him in on the other 'secret', that it wasn't actually Kevin's birthday. Again.

[K: He had gone out and bought a bottle of Verve Cliquot for me!]

All in all the *Edinburgh Concerto* was a piece of theatre worthy of a magician and the deception worked really well. And we hope that if and when people find out they were deceived, they will be all the more impressed. After all it's not as though any harm came of our tricks. Unfortunately, at this exact same time, tricks were being played on us that we didn't find out about for a few more months.

Towards the end of that year, 2014, it felt like we had turned a corner again. We were at a party at Tramp in London just after the judge had made the interim award in our favour against Steven Elliott and we found ourselves discussing all sorts of business ideas with people. We were just waiting for him to pay us, and it's amazing how very differently it makes you feel when you're expecting that kind of money to arrive any day.

Our lawyers and George Clark of Quantum Claims kept up the pressure. But it was a struggle to get even the most basic information and in the end another court hearing was arranged for January. This time he did turn up but it was to tell us, quite gleefully, that we were getting nothing from him. His company, Bender Social Networking Ltd, had sold the business and had gone into liquidation. And he had gone to Brighton Crown Court the day before and declared himself bankrupt because he had no money either.

It was unbelievable.

He was the only Director and the only shareholder in his company. The accounts that had already been filed for the company showed that up to the end of March 2014 it had received more than half a million pounds from advertisers and users. In the last year alone, it had made £225,000 profit, Steven Elliott had taken dividends of £61,000 out of the company and it looked like he had paid himself a six-figure salary on top of that. And yet, just after he withdrew his defence to our claims, his company sold the Bender app business to another company called Scampbell Ltd for just £80,000. And when the liquidator drew up a statement of how much money the company had, it owed £57,500 to Scampbell and it had loaned Steven Elliott £109,000 that the liquidator didn't believe could ever be recovered. The only money it had in the bank was owed to the taxman.

The company liquidator turned out to be the same person who was acting as Steven Elliott's Trustee in Bankruptcy, and a neighbour of his. Where had all the money gone? And who was behind this company called Scampbell Ltd?

Soon after, friends of ours who still used the app said they'd had an update from Bender that moved them onto something called Wapo. As Bender seemed to have ceased to exist and this Wapo was completely new, it looked like the app had just been renamed and all the users moved over. And when our lawyers looked into it they found out that Wapo was owned by this mysterious company called Scampbell that had bought the business and which was registered in New Zealand, of all places.

Not only that, but the company seemed to have been set up by a legal firm that specialised in offshore trusts that hide the identity of the real owners and their assets. In fact, that firm was caught up in what was known as the Panama Papers scandal that featured in the film *The Laundromat*. Gavin Henderson and Andrew Smith didn't think we had any chance of finding out who was behind Scampbell.

Everyone involved with the case on our side was convinced that Scampbell was really some kind of front for Steven Elliott but there seemed to be no way of proving a connection. According to him his company had sold Bender for what he said was a fair price that someone had independently verified. It just looked too much like a trick.

We tried to think what we knew about him. When we met him, he was living with his parents and his brother in a house in Old Kilpatrick, a village just across the Erskine Bridge from Glasgow. He was an amateur musician who sometimes played in a pub with his cousin, a singer called Sian Laughland. That was about all that we had, and most of that was of no help now that he had moved to Brighton. He had blocked us and all our friends from finding anything about him on Facebook so we couldn't see if he had been talking about Wapo or had friends in New Zealand, or any connection with anything called Scampbell.

KEVIN

One night, Steven and Scott had both gone to bed and I was still up with Margaret, the dog. It was about two in the morning and I was going back over how we could make a link between Steven Elliott and Scampbell.

I decided to do another search of his family and paid about £5 for a copy of the voters list from 2004 for the Glasgow area. I knew that his Dad was called Joseph and his Mum was called Ann, and roughly where they lived and I found a family that matched those details, with Steven and his brother Andrew in the same house. And there was another person at the same address, called Ethel Elliott.

Sitting there with Margaret on the sofa, slightly drunk, it suddenly came to me that there was another member of our family who had a Facebook account that he probably didn't know anything about.

Dame Margaret de Lumiere! It would never occur to him to block her.

I had a few attempts at guessing the password that Scott had set up for Margaret and then opened up her account, and 'Margaret' started doing a search for friends in Old Kilpatrick. I found an Ann Elliott from the right area, and although I'd never met her, she did look a bit like Steven, so I thought it might be his mother. She had about two hundred friends and I went through them all and found there was someone called Ethel. But she wasn't Ethel Elliott, she was listed as Ethel Campbell, and she was sister-in-law to Ann which made her Steven Elliott's aunt.

I followed that path and Ethel only had four friends, including her daughter Sian Laughland, who I already knew was Steven's cousin. And from that I suddenly realised that Laughland was a stage name and her real name would be Sharon Campbell or S. Campbell.

I was beside myself with excitement, but I couldn't wake Steven up in the middle of the night so I sent everybody messages to say that we had broken through, gave Margaret a cuddle and said:

'Well done Margaret – good dog!'

Next morning our lawyers were so excited by it because we finally had a vital piece of the jigsaw puzzle.

[S: So we knew now that the sale of the app was not an arms length transaction at all, it was sold to his cousin's company for a ridiculous price.]

Even though he had been ordered to provide us with details of the finances of Bender it took ages for our lawyers to get access to his accounts. When they did, they started to piece together some of what had happened. Just at the point when we thought he had accepted our claim to a share of the profits (by not appearing in court to defend the matter), Steven Elliott transferred £90,000 into a bank account on the Isle of Man opened in the joint names of himself and his cousin. She had then set up the New Zealand company called Scampbell Ltd, and it then paid his company £80,000 for the business. So the money just went round in a circle.

Later Scampbell Ltd changed its name to Wapo y Wapa Ltd, and then changed its share structure so that it was owned by an anonymous trust. The new directors of the company later gave a written statement that Steven Elliott 'is not a named beneficiary of the trust', but they didn't go as far as to say he isn't a beneficiary at all, just not a <u>named</u> beneficiary.

On top of that they found out that before selling up, Steven Elliott's company had started paying large amounts of money to a another company owned by a friend of his called Amit Ratnaparkhi, supposedly for help in running the business. And this company was still helping to run the Wapo app.

We don't pretend to understand what was done (or how) in the few months before we were told that Steven Elliott had no money, but it was all very complicated. It seemed pretty obvious why it was done: to make sure that we would get nothing if we won our claim. There seemed to be no business reason why something profitable like Bender would be sold off at undervalue and the company be liquidated. But what had happened to the money that Steven Elliott had certainly taken from the business? There was no sign that he had bought anything that the Trustee in Bankruptcy could get hold of: it had just disappeared. Like a magician's trick.

Because we were his main creditors in the bankruptcy, we had the right to attend his hearing in open court, and our barrister could ask questions about his money - like why he had given his cousin £90,000 just before a decision was to be made about how much he might owe us. To which he said:

'Because I love my family. I like to give them things.'

He told the court that he wasn't going to set up another app and that the Bender and Brenda user databases were all gone. He also claimed that he had nothing to do with Wapo, but that he did help out his friend Amit sometimes, just as a friend would.

Perhaps he thought we would run out of money and wouldn't keep at it. But we had Quantum Claims on our side and George Clark and all our lawyers started taking it all rather personally. As one of them said:

'The one thing in business you don't want somebody to do is take the piss, and Elliott thinks he can make fools of everybody.'

Back to court we had to go, this time to ask the Judge to declare that we were partners in the Bender business, and entitled to 49% of the profits made by the app. And if he didn't have the money anymore we had to start a new case against the people that seemed to have been given it, so the judge was also asked to accept that Steven Elliott, his cousin Sharon Campbell, and her company had engaged in a fraudulent conspiracy to deprive the partnership of its rights.

The team at Simpson and Marwick put together the bundles and bundles of print-outs of emails and text messages again, and we had to go over and refresh the witness statements we had drawn up the first time we thought we were going to court, and he had to do the same. He was allowed to comment on what we had said in our statements: his version of the history of Bender was quite different from what we remembered and what we could point to in the emails between us.

And then we had to appear at the High Court in Edinburgh's Parliament Square in front of Lord Tyre, quite an old fashioned judge. The timing couldn't have been worse because it coincided with the start of our next run at the Edinburgh Festival (although that did mean we didn't have to cancel any engagements elsewhere as we were at home anyway).

STEVEN

I had to give my evidence to our QC first, and then I was cross examined by Steven Elliott's advocate. I think it's actually very easy being on the stand in court if you tell the truth. The only reason for worrying about it is if you're telling lies. Stick to the truth and however much they try to trick you with feeble one-liners, it is fine.

I was quite glad this man wasn't acting for us because he wasn't very impressive at all. He came across as a rather tacky performer, who had watched too many court scenes on television. He kept trying to catch me out.

'I put it to you Mr Worbey...'

I was quite surprised by how it seemed to be accepted that the 'other side' could just make things up and twist my answers to try to make them mean something I hadn't said. I almost got to the point that I started to doubt what I had told him myself. It just came across as the advocates playing a game, as though they weren't really interested in the facts or what the law says.

I find it disappointing to think that witnesses in criminal trials who might be nervous or lacking in confidence, could easily be toyed with and led into corners by tricky lawyers. It takes a strong character to go through that experience.

There was even one point when he accused me of tampering with the documents.

That was too much for the judge, Lord Tyre. He stopped the proceedings and said:

'Mr. Dunlop. Are you seriously suggesting Mr. Worbey actually altered these documents for his own benefit after the event?'

The judge was so annoyed about it he adjourned early for lunch. We all saw Dunlop pacing about during the break, storming up and down the long hallway outside the courts in a terrible state. I think he knew he'd lost a lot of points with Lord Tyre there. I was thinking: 'Why would I fake documents? Who would do that?'

Steven Elliott's family were sitting in the corner of the court. I don't know what they must have been thinking because most of the time I was talking about him in a nice way, describing him as one of our all time best friends, how bright he was, how excited we were to work with him. I never bad mouthed him once, a complete contrast to what he said about us!

The only things I said against him were that he had stolen our part in the app from us and that he had been telling lies to the courts.

I suppose his parents would have believed everything he said because he is their son. We have a friend who told us his son was having to go court after crashing his car. The story was that the first person on the scene, seeing what a state he was in, shaken up from the accident, thought they needed to calm him down by giving him some brandy just before the police arrived. Our friend seemed to believe that is what really happened: some complete stranger saying:

'Here - have some brandy, you'll feel so much better. The police are on their way, they'll understand.'

I was in the box for about five hours, and I enjoyed it all apart from being stressed about Kevin having to give evidence the following morning, hours before our Festival run opened.

KEVIN

I was exhausted by it. I told the truth of course, which meant I would say if I didn't know the answer. Dunlop would keep showing me an email saying:

'Do you remember seeing this?'

And I would reply: 'No. But I must have done.'

And then another one.

'Well, no, I don't remember it, but I must have seen it.'

'Mr Farrell this seems to be your mantra. You tell us you must have seen things but you don't remember.'

He tried to suggest that I couldn't remember anything about the meeting with Steven Elliott in Vienna.

'That night when you claim you all made an agreement, you were drunk weren't you?'

'Anybody that knows me would say that I do like a drink. However, this was a period of our lives when we really weren't drinking at all because we were performing every day. We never drink the night before a performance as a rule anyway, but in Vienna we were doing six shows a week of a play that required us play Bach's D Minor Piano Concerto. Any musician in the world will tell you that you can't be pissed out your brains the night before playing that. But on top of that we were portraying twenty-five different characters on stage.

So, no. I was not drunk!'

Lord Tyre asked me why I thought Steven Elliott talking about *The Social Network* film was important. I think he had got the measure of me by then.

'Mr Farrell, can you explain briefly what the significance was? I don't need to hear a synopsis of the entire film. I can ask my daughters for that.'

We thought the hearings had gone quite well and our case had been made by Andrew Smith on our behalf, and at one point Lord Tyre told Mr Dunlop that he thought Steven Elliott was an unreliable witness. Elliott seemed to get more and more rattled and unpleasant as the days went by and he was lashing out at our lawyers and even the judge. He put in seventeen complaints to the Faculty of Advocates about Andrew Smith, most of which were dismissed immediately.

During our Edinburgh run a series of fake twitter accounts kept highlighting the one bad review we had from years and years before. Someone (we can only guess who) was desperately trying to damage us by pushing bad news about us up the Google search list. There were more online threats and trolling but we kept our distance.

There was a lot of legal discussion about the meaning of the word 'partnership', and at the end Lord Tyre said he needed time to consider his verdict. After the Edinburgh run we went off on holiday to Gran Canaria again. It was while we were there that we heard the result.

We had lost. We were completely devastated, the worst day of our lives.

[S: It even spoiled the holiday a bit.]

And then we had *The Sun* and *The Daily Mail* phoning us wanting our reaction, and we had to suffer seeing Elliott being interviewed by these people and gleefully saying he was going to be writing a book about it all. And he kept finding ways of getting messages to us, that now the truth about us was out and everyone would know what sort of people we are, all that sort of thing.

That night Andrew Smith called us. He tried to explain the reasoning for the decision, which seemed to be very technical and, he thought, could have gone either way. Despite the email trail which showed there was 'an agreement', we had never signed a partnership agreement between us all, and that seemed to count for a lot. He assured us that there would be an appeal against the decision.

That went ahead the following year but we lost that too because we would have had to be able to prove the judge's legal decision went against what he saw as the facts. The appeal judges said Lord Tyre:

'was satisfied that an agreement of a business nature was envisaged by them during the evening in Vienna. All concerned regarded themselves as entering into some kind of business relationship. But not every business relationship entered into by two or more individuals with a view to profit is a partnership. '

Because the courts decided that there never was a partnership between us and Steven Elliott it meant that no-one had to think about whether what he had done to stop us getting any money was legal or not. In fact, it turned out that he had gone to all that trouble of liquidating his company, making himself bankrupt, having trustees breathing down his neck looking for the money he still owed us from the original case that he hadn't defended, and he had done it all for nothing. It seemed he had moved his business to a New Zealand company, closed down Bender in favour of a name that didn't work nearly as well, presumably spent thousands and thousands on legal fees just to spite us, and ended up much worse off than if he had simply kept us involved.

But the other thing Andrew Smith said that evening was that there was another way of us getting justice. The court may have decided that there had never been a partnership but there could be no doubt that we still owned a share of the registered trademark that the Bender app had been using.

STEVEN

I did the registration of the trademark. Kevin paid for it and it was registered at our address. When he moved it to his company Steven Elliott made a declaration that we had consented to it being transferred, which we certainly had not done. One of the most important things about the app had always been its name so we should be due royalties from him for using the names we came up with.

Tedious as it was to go back to court, we felt we had to keep fighting. Some people pointed out that we could ditch George Clark and Quantum Claims now that we had lost the case they had financed, and if we won anything by pursuing the trademark violation we weren't due to pay them anything. It didn't take any time for us to decide that as George Clark had taken the risk on us he deserved to win with us. We hoped that demonstrated that we aren't complete sh*ts.

[K: It's because we aren't complete sh*ts that we got sh*t upon to start with!]

Chapter 20

In which we talk about how we each approach performance, about some of our favourite places to play, and explain why you haven't seen us on *Britain's Got Talent*.

[S: I quite enjoyed being in the witness box giving evidence. It was so like being in a TV court drama that I had to keep reminding myself that it really was me standing up there and not a character I was playing, and that a lot rested on my evidence.

K: I hated it. I couldn't cope.

S: I think my theatre background helped me. I suppose it was too much like a solo performance for you. You've never wanted to do that, have you?

K: I've never been comfortable performing music on my own, not when I'm the focus. It's better when I'm playing in the background, but sitting up there playing the piano seriously? It petrifies me.

S: I've seen it. When you play a simple solo at one of Scott's informal amateur meetings in Edinburgh you are shaking like a teenager at their first performance. But you're all right when you're with somebody. I was always that kid at school who made people laugh from the back of the class. It never really occurred to me to be a part of a duo but you were always obsessed by the idea, weren't you?

K: Were you bullied at school? Is that why you went into comedy? You found they wouldn't hurt you if you made them laugh?

S: It might have been a way of hiding who I was when I was a teenager but I've always enjoyed giving a performance. And you do too. Just not on your own.]

One of the things that Geoffrey Durham encouraged us to think about is how we come across as two individuals on stage. While we are playing the music we are both contributing in equal measure to the sound, and although in some of the more 'fun' pieces we do engage with the audience a bit there is no need to think about the relationship between the two of us. Sitting on one stool, almost literally joined at the hip, we could just as well be one body with four hands. And yet, we are – obviously – two different people.

It isn't as though we are portraying characters when we are on stage; we don't adopt any kind of persona or try to distance ourselves as entertainers from the people we really are. We are the same on or off stage and we don't consciously work at showing a relationship between us in the act. But it is important that it comes over; we need to convey to the audience the relationship we have with each other in normal life. We've found that our best shows are those when we engage with each other as much as we do the audience. Having fun with them is an extension of how much fun we have off-stage.

STEVEN

We do have slightly different stage manners, but they are our real characters. Kevin certainly talks more than me and sometimes I find it hard to get a word in. It's not a competition: it just makes me laugh. He also tends to fall over his words a lot when we're on stage which can make him seem rather nervous, but it also tells the audience that he isn't just going through the motions.

There's always a danger with using a set script that the audience will sense when we are just reciting, that we've said something without really meaning it. When Kevin seems to be searching for the right words to express what he wants to say, it can actually help to give the impression this is the first time he has thought about it.

KEVIN

I've always had a problem with nerves and anxiety, even with things like getting onto aeroplanes, and I also suffer from a cough which probably comes from the same place. But I associate feeling nervous with caring and I can be quite passionate and forthright about things I care about.

It is usually when we digress from the script that things really come alive, and our individual personalities come out best. Sometimes new material, that we can use again, just pops up out of an ad-lib. We can only risk being off script for a certain amount of time and instinctively we know when it's about to go too far, and one of us will bring us back onto the page. We're also lucky in having two parts to our act because if the audience aren't very responsive to us chatting between pieces, we can just cut it out and enjoy ourselves playing the music. There will be a moment when one of us has to make the decision to leave something out.

Geoffrey told us that those apparent disagreements are magical: when we look at one another and communicate something through a face or a raised eyebrow. Apparently it brings a certain tension, a frisson when it looks like we are going to have a row on stage.

KEVIN

It sometimes happens when I launch into the story about us being mistaken for jockeys in Australia. I will say to the audience:

'Is there anyone from Perth, Australia here?'

And Steven will just look at me sternly, and say:

'No. There isn't'. And we'll move on.

Geoffrey did make the point that we really must not get bitchy with each other on stage.

'That you are gay is a given, but playing up to a stereotype, a caricature of 'gay' is detrimental.'

It has to come across that we're not in competition with each other, and we and the audience are all on the same side. Geoffrey believes this is something all double acts have to learn, that the audience need to know that the two partners really have affection for each other.

You can see the difference in the two versions of the famous Grieg's Piano Concerto sketch that Morecambe and Wise did. When they first performed it in the early 1960s, Eric was playing the piano and Ernie was the conductor. Ernie was irritable with Eric when he played all the wrong notes, which encouraged the audience to take sides between the two of them. In the later version with André Previn, Ernie is to the side being supportive - proud even - of his friend and his playing. They make 'Andrew Preview' the enemy and have the audience on their side, so much so that the conductor has to come round to their way of playing it. It is actually Ernie's changed role in the sketch that made the later version much funnier and more successful.

So many double acts over the years have had serious fallings out, sometimes even while they continued to work with each other:

Cannon and Ball, Mike and Bernie Winters, even Wilfred Bramble and Harry H Corbett who played *Steptoe and Son*. Sometimes one of the partners wants to move on into other fields, like Simon and Garfunkel and Peter Cook and Dudley Moore. But there seem to be lots of examples where a source of tension came from finding it difficult to have a stage relationship with one person, while having just as important a relationship with someone else in a marriage or partnership. There came a point where John Lennon seemed to make a choice between Paul McCartney and Yoko Ono, and we have heard of some comedy double acts where the wives didn't like each other, Laurel and Hardy for instance.

That may be the reason that neither of us has settled down permanently with someone else, away from our home. It would seem very strange having to arrange to meet somewhere to rehearse. It would make what we do feel too much like a job.

We are both passionate about ensuring the quality of our performances through being thoroughly prepared and rehearsed. Mistakes in our playing are extremely rare; the only time in our careers when we completely messed up on stage was at Scarborough Spa one night. We both forgot the words to one of our songs so it descended into chaos. We tried to start again and it fell apart again, and everyone seemed to think we were doing it on purpose. The only other time that things went badly wrong was when the piano stool collapsed underneath us. The audience loved that, lots of them were asking afterwards how we'd managed to get it to do that on cue.

When we are lucky enough to be doing a longer run of concerts, the repetition does make us much more confident of what will happen in the performance. But even for one-off concerts we have always thoroughly rehearsed the playlist. Our approach to the hours leading up to stepping onto stage can be quite different though.

STEVEN

Kevin likes to get to the theatre early but I really don't like sitting in the dressing room for too long before we go on. In fact, I much prefer to be in a hurry and get there as late as possible. It seems to make me more alert when we go on.

I noticed that Eamonn Holmes was like that when we were guests on *This Morning*. As they came out of an advert break he wanted to be chatting to someone on set, even as the Director was counting him in.

Then he would break off at the very last second and turn to the camera. He gave himself no time to think about what was going to happen; he just had to get on and do it.

My teacher Phyllis Sellick told me that the best performance she ever gave was at a concert with the City of Birmingham Symphony Orchestra in the 1960s. The audience were all in their seats waiting for her at half past seven, but she was still on a train which had been delayed. She got to the concert hall about ten minutes late, took her coat off, walked straight on to the stage and started playing.

She said she thought it was her best ever performance for two reasons: because she didn't have time to think about it before, and because sitting down to play was a such a relief from the stress of worrying about getting there. The only problem was that she was in such a state of confusion that for a moment she forgot which concerto she was supposed to be playing, and the conductor and orchestra were all looking at her expecting her to start. There are only a few popular concertos where the soloist begins without the orchestra, and Beethoven's Fourth piano concerto is one of them. So she tried that, and luckily they all joined in.

KEVIN

I don't really know what it is I want to do when I get to the theatre early. I usually just sit around sipping water wondering when Steven is going to turn up. I'm not particularly nervous at that point.

In fact, we both make a conscious effort to get the adrenaline going just before we go on stage. We remind each other sometimes as we are waiting for the announcement:

'Keep it live!'

There's nothing worse than standing in the wings feeling absolutely nothing. It's a horrible feeling; thinking that people have bought their tickets and have been looking forward to this all day, but you just can't be bothered. It happened to me at Dumfries a while back. I had zero nerves before we went on and I was really annoyed with myself, especially as the audience were fabulous that night.

Every time we arrive at a new theatre, because we are usually only there for one performance, the stage technicians are concerned about what we are going to be like. They always worry about performers that tour on their own because some of these people can be very odd, or demanding at least. It is a lonely life, and these acts aren't used to being part of a team where you have to get along.

So, although we are insistent about what we need, we are always very conscious that it is essential not to be arseholes about it. The first thing we do is calm down the technicians by joking with them.

We have a few set routines:

'Could you position the piano so no-one can see us?'

'Can you take the legs off for us?'

'We don't need the black notes because we only ever use the white ones.'

As soon as they realise we're having some fun, we all have a laugh together and they're on our side. It usually takes about ten minutes from when we meet them to the point where we're organising where we are going for a few drinks after the show.

It's particularly the younger stagehands who are afraid to ask the big names for specific instructions. It's a vicious circle: they daren't ask, so they guess, so they get it wrong, so they get shouted at, so they daren't ask. In show business there is still too much of a culture based on an idea that 'big stars' don't talk to little people.

We would hate to be like that. We will drink with anyone who is good company, big or small. One night we were out with one of the young backstage crew from the Assembly during the Edinburgh Festival. He was just starting out and hoped to make a career of it and wondered if we would mind him asking about a few things that he'd wanted to understand about show business. One of those was:

'How do you know if an audience is going to be a good one? At what point do you know if they're going to be OK?'

STEVEN

We told him you can usually tell right at the start during the applause as you make your entrance. You even get a good idea standing in the wings before you come on, just by listening to how much noise the audience make on their own. If they're not chatting excitedly amongst themselves, it's a definite that they are going to be hard work.

And the very next performance we opened the backstage door, heard the sound of the audience, and said to him:

'These ones are difficult!' And they were.

When we are standing backstage before a performance listening to the rumble of the audience waiting for our entrance, it can be quite overpoweringly nerve-wracking. I remind myself that these people have made a huge effort to be there for us. Some of them may have even had a bath!

When the stage-right door is opened for us and we walk on to applause, all of the nerves just go. There's no time to think about those anymore. Doctor Theatre takes over, and from then on it's all about the audience, and the audience alone.

Geoffrey told us how important the words of introduction, before we appear, can be. When we left it to the theatre staff to do the announcement, we had so many disasters:

'Please welcome Worbey and Farrell, with their four pianos and one hand!'

Another time there was the full blast style of a football commentator, or boxing promoter. And then there was:

'Here they are - Farrow and Ball!'

Not only should the wording be right, it has to be delivered with just the correct amount of vigour: enthusiastic, but not ecstatic.

On Geoffrey's advice we decided to have the introduction recorded for us so that we knew it would be what we needed every time. We asked a friend who has a deep and commanding voice to do the announcement, and he kindly obliged. When we played it to Geoffrey, he said:

'It sounds like a gloomy vicar at a funeral'.

He hadn't known who it was speaking or what he did. Our friend was indeed a Minister in the Church of Scotland. The solution of course was to get Geoffrey to record it, and his version is perfect and we have used his voice ever since.

Another trick that Geoffrey taught us is to leave it as long as possible after the announcement before we bounce onto the stage. It's not a precise-timing thing; we just look at each other and nod when we know the time is right to go. Usually it takes eight or nine seconds, which feels like an eternity. Just as the welcome applause starts to subside fractionally that's the time to arrive, because it makes them renew the applause. The moment their subconscious starts to think you're not coming on, it makes them extra pleased to see you.

Somehow the psychology works. Mentally they're now begging you to come on and entertain them. You give them the show they want to see, just as you would have done anyway, but now it's all on your terms. And you always start from the side with your upstage foot, because it opens your body to them.

STEVEN

The timing of this technique is the key to it and having made the assessment from backstage of what kind of audience we are dealing with helps us to get that right. We have seen at least one big star get it very wrong on a ship, assuming that the audience would give her a big reception just because she was famous.

On these ships it's quite cosmopolitan. There are guests from all over the world and it doesn't matter how famous you've become, there are going to be people aboard who don't know who you are. This performer did all the things that you would expect of a huge star. She had her music playing for a few minutes before she appeared and then suddenly there was a drum roll and the big announcement:

'Welcome to the stage...'

And then as we do, she paused. She didn't come straight on and the drum roll kept going for far too long, and then finally she appeared in the corner of the stage with an expression of faux surprise at the adulation, walking on very slowly, gesticulating:

'Yes! It's Me! Jane McDonald!'

By the time she had taken only a couple of steps the clapping had stopped. She was still doing her routine of acknowledging the applause that wasn't happening, taking her time to get to the front of the stage and doing that trick stars have of making themselves seem to grow bigger as they reach the microphone. It just wasn't working, because the theatre was in silence.

At the end of her set she swept off the stage and told the Entertainments Director:

'It's like bloody death out there!'

At the top of the show, we really make the effort to bring the people into the show with us. Just as we come on it is important to tell the audience something like:

'This is a great hall, the perfect place for us. We love it...'

It makes them feel a part of a place that we seem to want to be in. Obviously we don't have a band to strike up as soon as we appear, so it works for us to immediately establish some kind of rapport. As we've said, traditional concert pianists just make their theatrical entrance, bow and then start playing. It's almost as though they are challenging their audience to be good enough to enjoy what's about to happen.

It's just as difficult when the audience are too enthusiastic, when they're trying to give us a standing ovation by the time we've played two pieces. Those people are going to peak too early and get fatigued by the time we're halfway through. It happens sometimes when people come back a second time, having enjoyed the show before. They've been thinking about coming all week and the excitement gets to them in the very first minute. We still have to deliver, we still have to meet and probably exceed their expectations each time, but they've lifted the bar.

[S: It does feel good when they seem to give us permission to be egotistical. You know you can do anything and they will love it, but you don't really have the chance to think about that and exploit it.

K: There was one night on a P&O ship when from start to finish the show was an absolute joy. There is a feeling when it all comes together like that, that we can do no wrong. It's almost as though the audience would be really happy if we just sat and talked and didn't bother playing. It was that intimate, despite there being a thousand people in the room.]

Early in our career on the ships the Cruise Director, a very nice old-school man called Paul O'Loughlin, asked if we did encores. We had already decided that we wouldn't; we thought it was best to get off the stage and not waste anybody's time because everyone wants to get to the bar. We assumed he needed to know in order to time his return to the stage, because when we asked if he was going to watch our show he just smiled and said:

'I'd rather have a w**k with a barbed wire glove!'

We were taking our bows at the end of the show and Paul came on stage to do the close, just as lots of people were shouting 'More!'

'Really? You want more? Gentlemen would you oblige?'

So we did. When we finally came off, he said:

'If you don't do encores, get off the stage!'

Ever since then whenever we meet him, and he introduces us to anybody, he always says with a smile:

'Worbey and Farrell. They don't do encores.'

Often the meet and greet after the show is more stressful than the concert itself. Every entertainer hates selling merchandise but the truth is we can get a lot of money from it, sometimes more than we are being paid to appear. We only ever do it once on a voyage though, usually after the second show.

Whether we are on a cruise or in a theatre, we do feel it is important to let people talk to us if they want to, and for some occasions we also have to thank and spend time with the organisers and sponsors. It can be hard work, and getting the dynamics of the after-show session right is an art in itself. We keep an eye on each other to see who we have spent time with, so that no-one is left out. If we have close friends there then fortunately they understand what we have to do, and happily wait with a drink in hand until everything has calmed down.

KEVIN

If the show has gone well, that is really all I need. I actually find it quite embarrassing when people come over and say nice things, telling me how much (and especially why) they enjoyed it.

That's maybe changed over the years because I think I used to need it. Nowadays when people congratulate us it rather makes me feel as though they are putting us on a pedestal, distancing us, and I'd rather relate to people on a level with them, by talking about something neutral. It isn't that I find it patronising because it never is, it's all genuine and lovely, and I don't want to sound ungrateful, but once the show is over I just want to return to being the person who talks about any old rubbish.

STEVEN

The place where they used to make the biggest fuss over the acts was one of my absolute favourite venues: the Theatrebarn in Bretforton. The tradition there was that, after the show, the performers would be led through a garden with the entire audience applauding. Then we would be given pride of place at the front of the queue to be served food, and seated with the dignitaries of the evening.

I really didn't like doing that bit. It felt like we were extending an ovation into real life.

[K: I loved it. I was really in my element!]

The Theatrebarn is near Evesham and it is probably Britain's best kept theatre secret. It was started by James Wellman who was an actor, and his partner David Swift, a chef. They decided in the 1970s that they'd quite like to run a theatre and bought this magnificent medieval building with a long gallery, which they turned into a theatre room big enough to seat about a hundred people. James would choose the artists and David would cook a magnificent banquet in their kitchen, which everyone shared after the show. Dame Peggy Ashcroft did the formal opening ceremony for them. After a few years they bought some derelict barns behind their house and moved the theatre into the biggest one with room for nearly twice as many.

James Wellman was actually one of the Dambusters. He read in the press that the last member of that squad had died and was pleased that people were unaware that he was in fact now the last surviving one. He didn't like to talk about his involvement, hated the fact that he had been a part of it and did not want ever to be acknowledged for it.

When Scott was managing us he tried to get us a spot there, but they weren't interested in being approached like that. James used to get programmes sent to him from all around the country to keep an eye on what acts were available, and picked shows that they wanted to see. Later on they heard of us from some of their patrons and discovered that we were on at the Pitlochry Festival. James had already been booking acts like Kit & the Widow so perhaps we fitted in a bit with that style of show.

We received a very nice handwritten letter, explaining who they were, as though we didn't know, and saying that they didn't go to the theatre anymore but they very much hoped we would come and play for them in their barn.

The letter didn't really give away how big an occasion it was. The event was strictly formal dress: dinner jackets and black tie, and ball gowns andthey charged about £80 a ticket. For that the audience got a champagne reception, and more champagne, wine and canapes during the interval. The end of the show was followed by the most extravagant banquet with spectacular food, some of it quite avant-garde with things like basil ice cream. The evening would continue with free drinks in the garden, with a fairground pipe organ playing.

[S: That was my favourite bit – I loved it!]

KEVIN

We went there about six times, and the Hamiltons came once. Christine was mortified that we hadn't told them it was strictly black tie so she turned up in a pink and peach outfit and Neil was in a striped jacket and straw boater. They looked smart enough, but they stood out a mile and they were getting dirty looks. Everyone will have thought they were doing it just to be seen. I got an admonishment from Christine.

'You gave us the postcode, but not the dress code!'

STEVEN

The first time we were to play there we almost didn't make it. It was a time of big floods around Evesham and every road we came to that led to this place was closed off or blocked with the floods. Scott was driving us and we were just going round and round in circles, knowing that they were all there waiting for us. The whole thing was quite stressful and we made it with just minutes to spare.

I suppose it was a bit like Phyllis Sellick on her train to Birmingham because we went so well that night that we were invited back again and again, and we probably played there more times than anybody else.

Apart from the shows themselves we just loved going and staying in James and David's old house, and they treated their guests like royalty. They would invite some people over for Sunday lunch and David would cook for everyone and ply us all with as much champagne and wine as we could take.

KEVIN

One year I had to climb in through the downstairs toilet window. James and David had left us partying in the barn after the show, gone to bed and were fast asleep. We were staying in their house and got back quite late to find they'd locked us out by accident. We were screaming with laughter because we were trollied as usual, but we didn't want to wake these two old fellows up because they were getting quite elderly by then. Steven and Scott squeezed me up into the toilet window and I fell into the room and managed to get the front door open.

STEVEN

David just loved our bad behaviour. Staying in the house was an experience in itself, this medieval old place that creaked everywhere. It dated back to Elizabethan times.

Sadly both James and David have died, but the theatre barn is to continue because they established a charitable trust to run it after they were gone. I find it quite moving that those two old chaps are no longer around. They were such gorgeous people, and they gave so much to theatre and the arts. Because we kept getting invited back we never thought to take many photographs of the place, or them.

Another place we've been invited to several times is the Mananan International Festival on the Isle of Man. It's a classical festival started by John Bethell that has been running for years. John has done such a lot for music; he set up a world-famous viola competition there. The most 'popular' act they used to have in the festival was Hinge and Bracket, and then when they stopped it was Kit and the Widow, and then they took a chance on us.

Michael Bishop, the one who dropped us in it with the Pope's legal representatives, is an old friend of John Bethell. He used to go over to the Mananan Festival to see Hinge and Bracket who he loved. On one occasion they arrived on the island by plane but discovered to their horror that the luggage containing their outfits hadn't turned up. Hinge and Bracket without the get-up are just two men, singing as women. So Michael Bishop chartered a flight on a helicopter to go and get their spare costumes. They went on half an hour late but they had their full regalia.

For a while we were really quite keen on being asked to do *The Royal Variety Show* because we thought it would help us get noticed.

STEVEN

Kevin Bishop is a famous television director and producer who used to arrange *The Royal Variety Show* every year, for at least twenty years. He came to see our show one night and came backstage to say how much he'd loved it. I cheekily asked if he would consider us for the Royal show the next year.

'Oh. I retired from that last week!'

He's become a really good friend since and came to stay with us when we did our first Edinburgh Usher Hall show in 2017. But why couldn't we have got to know him earlier?

To be honest we wouldn't say 'no' to the *Variety Show* even now, but it's not a priority. It doesn't have the importance these days that it used to and we would find it difficult to come up with a short piece of our act that would fit.

The Grand Order of Water Rats organise another variety show and they also have a massive ball at the Grosvenor House in London every year. They are a bit like the freemasons of the entertainment industry in the UK. They invited us to play for them in 2019 and we agreed to do it. We decided we would just play the Warsaw Concerto and not include any comedy stuff because the Water Rats have heard just about everything funny already, so there's no chance of us making them laugh!

There wasn't going to be any money for appearing as it's all for charity but we were quite excited about it; it felt like a great thing to do. It wasn't the best timing as we were due to be flying in from South Africa that morning, but we said we would go. And then we asked about the grand piano that we would be playing.

'Oh, no. There's no grand piano, we're not paying for a grand piano. There's an electronic keyboard.'

So we said they could forget it. The Grand Order of Water Rats couldn't be bothered to get a proper piano in for an act? Seriously?

Over the years we have found that charity concert events are often run by people who want to feel good about themselves, but don't mind treating the people that they expect to appear for them really badly. In Cape Town recently, a woman came up to us after the show and told us that she had been discussing us with her husband. They had decided, she said, that we would do some charity concerts for them. They were going to fly us over but we were going to donate the concert for nothing. They are in the diamond business in South Africa, and they've got squillions of Rand in the bank. It was as though she thought that she owned us.

KEVIN

There was no debate about whether we had the time, or whether we were willing to do it for free. It was a deep-seated condescending attitude that some of the aristocracy and people with obscene wealth have towards musicians and actors. We should have told her our charitable fee is three times our normal fee, and the booker has to pay it but instead we just said we weren't available.

I have an analogy for charity events like that. It's the same as someone with a fridge full of Mars Bars, telling you – when you have only got one Mars Bar in your fridge - to give it away to the poor.

We did lots of charitable events when we first started out, enjoyed them thoroughly but received little in return. We did one in Scotland for the Sportsman's charity where they paid us a pittance and then announced just before we went on that they had already raised £40,000 more than they had expected. We did fifteen minutes for another charity in Edinburgh where we had specified in the contract that the piano must be of a good quality and positioned at the centre of the stage. When we arrived we found the piano was shoved hard against the wall on one side.

STEVEN

They'd put the microphone for the comedians in the centre of the stage instead. We pointed out that we'd told them exactly where the piano had to be.

'Well,' the organiser said: 'In an ideal world it would be...'

I said: 'This is an ideal world. Piano: centre-stage. Please!'

[K: It was a really nice summer's evening. I just wanted to go home and have a gin and tonic in the garden. We should have just walked out; they'd already breached the contract.]

In about 2006, Equity decided that they would establish the Blackpool Grand Theatre as the National Theatre of Variety. It was a response to the idea that variety shows were no longer viable. To launch it, they organised a massive concert night with as many variety acts as they could get hold of, and we were lucky enough to get invited on. It was stressed that we could only do six minutes, and we were finishing the second of three parts. They'd got so many acts there were going to be two intervals.

The man who had organised the whole event was one of the Grumbleweeds. He had arranged for us to stay in what turned out to be Blackpool's most notorious gay knocking shop. We arrived at the place to find there were no locks on the doors. It was quite filthy and all you could hear was a chorus of people having sex in every room. At the rehearsal he announced:

'Next up are Worbey and Farrell, they'll be in a good mood because they're staying at Trades, and so they'll have had a s**g!'

[S: I saw the Mighty Atom backstage there. She used to be one of the Roly Polys and I had seen her at a Pontins Holiday Camp in 1981 when I was a very small child, when she had an act called Mighty Atom and Roy. I told her that and asked if she remembered me.

She said: 'Of course I do, love. How are you?'

K: For some reason, my mother sat and talked to the Mighty Atom that evening about how she could save money on her gas bills!]

Jimmy Crickett was on before us. He was only meant to have the same time (six minutes), but because his act was dying on its arse he tried to get the audience back by doing some more. The more he died, the more he wanted to get them back. The more he tried to get the audience back, the more he lost them. Everyone had had enough and were desperate to get to the interval by the end of his set. It's a golden rule in variety that you never go over your allotted time and he had been on for twenty five minutes. We had to follow this nonsense, and we went on at ten to eleven!

Before him, Bernie Clifton had appeared. He was another client of Michael Vine; famous for his act with a stuffed ostrich but at the time he was reinventing himself as a singer. He'd been going through a period when audiences were confused as to why he didn't have his ostrich with him, but that night he gave a lovely energetic rendition of *You Raise Me Up*, proving he really does have a very strong voice. We know how hard it is to reinvent your act and change people's expectations.

At the end, well after midnight, a tubby man from Equity, dressed in a sparkly suit came on to announce:

'I think we've proved Variety is not dead!'

[S: It had been a lovely evening and everyone had had a good time, but we were exhausted and felt like shouting back: 'Yes, it is.']

KEVIN

When we finished the show we went back to my room at The Trades and opened a bottle of wine to wind down. It must have been at least one in the morning by the time we got there. Suddenly the bedroom door flew open and there was a man with a wide moustache dressed all in leather, complete with leather cap with chains, looking as though he'd just escaped from the Village People.

I said: 'Is this your room?'

'No'.

'Well then, f*** off!' And I slammed the door.

[S: The bar downstairs seemed to be open all night so anyone could walk in off the streets, open any door in the hotel and expect to get what they wanted!]

We've been back to the Blackpool Grand a couple of times when Paul Iles, (who was involved with the plan for us to tour *Two Pianos, Four Hands)* was running it. One year he had us there during their pantomime season and we did our show on the one night of the week that *Dick Whittington* wasn't playing, but with all the scenery in place. The star of the show that year was the Australian actor Ray Meagher from *Home and Away* and he came on as our special Christmas guest and read some poetry.

STEVEN

I was late coming on for the second half because I was chatting with him backstage about *Prisoner Cellblock-H*. I was a big fan of that show and I told him that I knew he'd been in it twice as two different people. He said I was the only person that he had met who had spotted that.

And then we were enjoying a conversation about my favourite character (known as 'Vinegar Tits') when I realised that Kevin was out on stage in the middle of Sarah the cook's kitchen, wondering where I was.

Sometimes the nature of our act is not suited to the venue or the audience, rather than the other way round. When we played at the Dora Stoutzka Hall at Royal Welsh Academy of Music and Drama in Cardiff, we found that the acoustics were perfect for the Steinway piano, but were useless for us trying to do any comedy. It really is the most beautiful music venue, but their set-up was designed around the sound of the music and it just wasn't so good for the spoken voice.

Michael Vine always had a big problem fitting that mix of comedy and serious music into something he could sell; he never really got to grips with identifying what it is that we do. For a while after we had left him we toyed with the idea of setting up our own agency to promote ourselves, because no one has a better idea of our act than we do. We tried phoning up theatres pretending to be somebody else recommending that they book us.

KEVIN

We even invented a character to use, to make the calls. We called the fake agency 'Hope and Glory', and I would phone people telling them that I was a man called Peter Land.

It was just so that they would remember the name. I would answer the phone saying:

'Land, of Hope and Glory!'

I'm afraid I imitated Michael Vine's voice when I did it. Steven had been trying to get us a booking at the Newbury Corn Exchange because it's a great venue and we'd been at their Spring Festival there once and sold out. We thought we should try to get back there but they weren't returning the calls. I phoned them, as Peter Land.

Someone called Ruth answered. I said:

'We've been looking round the venues and choosing the best theatres in the UK... who am I talking to? Ruth? Let's face it Ruth, between you and me, there's an awful lot of crap out there, places are basically booking dreadful tribute bands. Now what we're doing, we're giving good classy places like yours the opportunity to book the lads. Now I haven't looked in detail at what availability you have at the moment, but I'm assuming you wouldn't want to miss out on their tour for this year?'

It had to be presented that way. When we were phoning them before we were asking them to consider booking us but this time we were giving them an opportunity not to miss out. The trouble with a lot of these venues is that they don't disclose the name of the person who does the booking of acts. That's where an agent earns their money in knowing exactly who to call, and also by the quality of the acts they offer. Of course if the venues did give out the name of their booker, they would just get inundated with calls and wouldn't know whether what they were being offered was any good. What we've learnt is that the best way is to phone the stage door, and then apologise profusely to the person who answers:

'Oh, I'm terribly sorry. I didn't mean to call the stage door. I was wanting the bookings department. Could you put me through or give me their email address?'

People on the stage door are treated like sh*t by so many egocentric actors and artists, but we've discovered if you just phone and chat to them they're so happy to be treated nicely that they'll give you all the information you want. Either that or they haven't got time to waste and just put you through to get rid of you. It usually works but keep that trick to yourself!

As long as it doesn't cost us too much we'll accept any chance to promote ourselves. We're always happy to appear on the radio and on TV if anyone will have us; we've even been guest reviewers on BBC Scotland arts programmes. And over the years we have been lucky enough to have features about us printed in newspapers and magazines.

STEVEN

We've had a lot of support from the magazine, *Pianist*. It's edited by Erica Worth, who is a friend and plays the piano herself and she's been good enough to publish a few articles about us and our shows. We were really pleased when Erica first gave us a feature article in the centre pages, and I phoned home to tell them the good news.

'We've been given a big article in the *Pianist* magazine'.

'What?' said my father in an irritated voice.

'The *Pianist* magazine have featured us. Kevin and I are their centre-page spread!'

Dad sounded a bit confused and said, in a tone of disgust:

'Well... that's really nothing to do with me!'

I couldn't understand why he wasn't happy for us, and it didn't occur to me until some time later that he had misheard the word 'pianist'.

There was one 'opportunity' that we resisted. Most years since it started, we would get a call asking us to appear on *Britain's Got Talent*. From what we can gather, the show has talent scouts who spend most of their year phoning professional and semi-professional acts trying to persuade them to go on. They would dangle a carrot in front of us, saying that we wouldn't have to queue with everyone else and all we had to do was turn up and we would be put straight through to the televised stage in front of the judges. What the public don't know is that there are many rounds before you get to the main judging panel, and the queues of hopefuls that you see on the television are really used by the scouts to look for the entertaining nut cases to be made fun of. Ben Elton exposes this brilliantly in his book *Chart Throb*, describing the three categories that the producers are looking for: 'Mingers, Blingers and Singers'.

We were getting work all around the world, so we were not really interested in doing a TV talent show or reality TV. We knew we wouldn't even be gaining access to better venues than the ones we appear in already. When we had our concert at the Usher Hall in Edinburgh in November 2018, the pianist Tokio Myers, winner of *Britain's Got Talent* in 2017, was performing at the Queen's Hall in the same city, a venue less than half the size.

Simon Cowell used to criticise people auditioning on *Britain's Got Talent* or *The X-Factor by* saying:

'You're like a cruise-ship act!'

Ironically, most of his winning acts soon find themselves working on cruises (with the notable exception of Susan Boyle). On the QM2 we saw one winner of *American Idol.* He didn't start well because the audience were mostly British and hadn't seen the show he'd won, but then he lost his voice two songs into what was supposed to be a forty-five-minute set, and his backing singers had to take over for him. He'd been given no training in how to protect his voice, how to put together a show or how to deal with a slightly hostile audience. These aren't things you can just pick up while at sea.

A recent winner of *Britain's got Talent* is a fellow cruise ship entertainer, another piano act. He has been around a long time and he was appearing when we got our very first cruise contract on the Brilliance of the Seas. We were quite nervous about our upcoming shows and he stopped by to introduce himself. He had heard we were also pianists and seemed a bit defensive. He wanted to know how many different shows we had prepared and we replied that we had two ready.

'Well. I've got at least twelve.'

He was obviously trying to belittle and unsettle us, but there might have been another reason why he wanted to know about our act. We went on to discover that he is notorious amongst entertainers for stealing other people's material.

But that happens. A few years ago we were promoting one of our shows, and our PR representative Sarah Harris thought it would be a good idea to send a video of one of our comedy routines to the producers of Ant and Dec's *Saturday Night Takeaway* show with an offer to go on and perform it. We never heard anything back from them but strangely, a few weeks later we were watching television and were surprised to see them do a sketch almost exactly the same as ours. An almighty row broke out on social media with people saying the routine had been stolen. Our management asked us if we wanted to take legal action, but we preferred to stay out of the argument. We can only guess that Ant and Dec had already been working on the idea and so didn't need us to perform something so similar for them!

So we had decided there really wasn't anything to gain by going on shows like *Britains Got Talent*, and quite a bit to lose. Apart from anything else we thought we would have to sign a contract with Simon Cowell, allowing him to take a large percentage of our income for a period after our appearance. But then one year we were going through a lean period and promised the talent scout who called that if we felt we hadn't furthered our career in the way we wanted to over the next twelve months, then we would think about going on the following year.

KEVIN

I never imagined for one moment that we would ever talk about this. It is probably the only dark part of our career and we really wished that it hadn't happened.

A year after that call, we weren't having a fruitful time so we said yes, we would do it. The one thing that we kept on telling the production team was that we were not prepared to sign any contracts with SyCo, because we were already with Michael Vine's management company. They assured us that this was fine.

After some discussion Michael came round to the idea, and suggested that we didn't wear anything too showbiz, and told us to sort out three different routines for the programmes we would be on.

STEVEN

Geoffrey kindly offered to direct us for a few days at Steinway Hall to get everything right, and this gave us great confidence. We also rehearsed what we would say if the judges were really horrid to us after we had finished; we wanted to prepare ourselves for anything.

We only told a few people that we were going on as we knew that our close friends and family might see it as a sign of failure. No one really supported the idea, and perhaps we should have listened.

All of the contact with the production team was incredibly positive though. It was clear from their phone calls that we were going to stand a really good chance; we were being treated very well. You would think, from the way the the show is presented, that the acts come as a big surprise to the producers and the panel. In fact we were regularly phoned by the people that worked for the television company and they advised us what we should play. We sent them some recordings, and between us the routine took shape.

They liked the idea of us doing a medley of well known pieces including Coldplay's *Viva la Diva*, the theme to *Murder She Wrote* and the Liszt *Hungarian Rhapsody*. We decided not to do *Murder She Wrote* as we thought it was a bit old fashioned, but then the show's producer came back and asked us to put it back in as she thought that would go down well.

The day of reckoning arrived. We were told to get to the Birmingham Hippodrome for half six in the morning. The building has a vast auditorium decked in gold with red velvet seating, and it is the biggest theatre in the country. There weren't many people around that early, certainly not the queues of hopefuls who appeared later.

We were taken for a coffee, and then started the day with a series of interviews with some really positive people who made us feel that we could win this competition. And then the production team took us out and filmed us walking around Birmingham, and then making our way into the Hippodrome, as though we were just arriving. We were wired with microphones the whole time, and they even told us what we should be talking about. And then as the rest of the crowds turned up hoping to be a part of the circus, someone would be constantly asking us to comment on our surroundings. Everything we did that day was on record.

Later we were taken down to meet Stephen Mulhern who was hosting the *Britains Got More Talent* chat show. He seemed to be nice, and said he had heard about us before and that it was about time this show had more solid talent.

STEVEN

But when the cameras went on he became aloof and unfriendly and was doing his best to make us feel uncomfortable. In particular he focused on us being gay, and asked if we were together sexually. When we told him that we aren't, he asked Kevin what type of man he would look for.

Kevin replied: 'One with a pulse'

The conversation had turned a bit bizarre, so I asked Mulhern if he had a pulse.

And then Kevin continued: 'Or one with a bottle of wine'

And I asked Mulhern if he had a bottle with him. He clearly didn't like the way we were shifting the focus onto him.

KEVIN

We were taken back to the Green Room. The place was now packed with every am-dram oddity imaginable. There were dance schools with young children with tightly permed curls who seemed to have been dipped in glitter, practising their shuffle-off to buffalo tap steps. Several magicians were exercising their sleight of hands with brand new packs of cards.

Looking back, the whole thing was a hideously cruel well rehearsed exercise in winding up hopefuls and dreamers. There was little or no hope of any of these people escaping as a star from this vaudevillian concentration camp.

When it was announced that the judges were about to take up their positions, the production team went into something of a panic and everyone had to get out of the way. All the corridors had to be cleared in case anyone should make eye contact with them. It felt like the imperial entrance of Nero at a gladiatorial slaughter of the innocents.

We were ushered to the back stage area where we could hear Simon Cowell sounding thoroughly irritated as he talked to the audience:

'Let's just try and find some decent talent.'

One of the production team came over to us with a message from the producer:

'The whole team loves you guys, and everyone thinks the chemistry between you both is amazing, but could you play down the professionalism as Simon is going to hate it.'

There was no time to think about what that meant because the cameras came over to us along with Ant and Dec. We were both aware that this meeting was going to be interesting, because of the Twitter-storm that blew up over them doing a routine similar to ours.

The one on the left said: 'Hi - who are you and what do you do?'

We told them, and immediately and simultaneously their arms crossed and their whole body language changed as they remembered they knew our names.

The one on the right said: 'Oh! We did a piano duet on our show. Did you see it?'

We had prepared for this moment, and told them we had watched it and enjoyed their performance very much. And then we asked them a series of questions about their careers, and whether they were going to be learning any other new skills, as the public clearly love them trying out different things. They relaxed and answered our questions: we all understod that none of this footage was ever going to be used.

We stood and listened to the acts on before us. Everyone was getting buzzed off, and in most cases there seemed to be no reason. We have since been told that the judges have little choice about when they press the buzzer: it's all dictated in advance. The singer on stage before us was brilliant, but she got three buzzes and Simon launched into a character assassination that reduced her to tears, begging for a chance. Then it was our turn.

We walked out on to stage to a thunderous round of applause. Simon asked for our names.

'Steven Worbey and Kevin Farrell.'

'And your act? What's it called?'

'Worbey and Farrell.'

Simon rolled his eyes.

KEVIN

I panicked slightly, and said:

'Yes, but we used to call ourselves Katzenjammer until we realised in German that means misery and depression.'

The audience laughed. Simon glared at us:

'I'm sorry guys. I'm getting a really bad vibe from you both. I don't like the chemistry between you. In fact I don't think you really want to be here. You look as if you've just walked off the street, you both look terrible'.

We didn't respond but we were shocked that we were being criticised before we'd done anything, other than saying our names. It was especially strange that our 'vibe' was being being mocked, when we had just been told not to seem too professional.

STEVEN

We went over to the piano, believing our talent would save everything, and as soon as we played the opening bars to *Viva la Diva*, the crowd started to go wild.

For a second it felt good, but then Simon pressed his buzzer, followed immediately by Alesha Dixon and David Walliams.

Simon started to hurl abuse at us, saying it was just a medley of cliched numbers. We could have said that we were playing precisely what the producers had asked for, but instead we didn't respond to anything.

KEVIN

We just froze. Alesha told us she couldn't imagine anyone wanting to watch us (even though the audience had clearly enjoyed what we did). David Walliams kept on saying he wanted to see Steven in a dress, an idea he seemed to find very funny. The comments were humiliating, and standing there in front of nearly two thousand people and millions more at home, we could see our careers ending in disgrace.

As we walked off the stage, we turned to each other with the cameras still on our faces. Fortunately, we had rehearsed this moment.

Steven said: 'I'm very proud of you'

and I replied: 'I'm proud of you too.'

'What a wonderful day we've had!'

'Weren't the audience gorgeous?'

We both felt awful, but we remained upright, dignified and professional. We kept the positive comments going, determined not to give them anything negative to use against us. The cameras kept following us as we turned into the corridors back towards the Green Room, but we gave them nothing but sheer eccentric happiness.

Then they took the mics off, and told us to wait where we were until someone came along to take us to be interviewed by Stephen Mulhern about our disappointment. As we stood there feeling wretched, one of the production team suddenly remembered that we hadn't signed our release forms yet, and went away to get them.

As soon as they were out of sight we grabbed our bags, kicked open a fire door and ran for it!

STEVEN

Kevin phoned his Mum and she was absolutely horrified that we'd gone on the show at all. But she assured us that they probably couldn't show anything as we hadn't signed the forms. Then Geoffrey called us, and we told him what had happened. The first thing he said was:

' Oh - I've had to escape through many fire doors in my career. I hope you resorted to sex and drink as soon as you got out?'

'Don't worry. If they do show this, it will take us six months to recover, but we will be ok.'

We suspect that as soon as we said we wouldn't be signing a contract with Simon Cowell's management company we were destined to fail, just as much as the queues of amateur hopefuls. All of the negotiation about content of the routine and the advice to not be too professional was designed to make us look like failures. They were constructing an entertainment show that has to have winners and losers, so they have to cast a few people to be those losers. Whether they knew or cared that they were also potentially destroying our careers, we can't tell.

We were worried sick for months that our humiliation would be exposed to the nation. A couple of our friends noticed that in footage of people sitting in the Green Room there were two people who looked remarkably like us, but the episodes went by and our audition didn't appear. We were actually sitting on QM2 watching a friend singing when we got the call from home that theauditions were over and the semi finals were about to start. We were so relieved that at last we could relax that we bought a bottle of champagne. We told our singer friend that we were celebrating her marvellous performance, but really it was because we could look forward to the rest of our careers.

There is one funny thing about this whole story. Because we were never shown on television, or maybe because we didn't sign any forms, the talent scouts who find acts for the show don't know that we were on. So every year we get a call asking if we would consider going on *Britain's Got Talent*, with a guarantee that we'll get through to the televised phase.

Chapter 21

In which we choose our three favourite performances and we return to the beginning and Kevin's birthday party.

If you have read this far you will have got an idea of how much we have enjoyed our life: touring the world, meeting lots of interesting people, having the odd drink or two, but most of all having the opportunity to do what we love, play the piano and make people laugh.

There have been so many good times and we have made so many good friends that it's hard to choose any that seem like the best, but here are three examples of what it means to us to be Worbey & Farrell.

In terms of pounds per hour, the most lucrative engagement we ever had was also a fantastically fun experience. We were asked to do a three week run at the 'Secret Cinema' in Stepney. 'Secret Cinema' started in 2007 and has grown to be something of a cult in London. They show a well known film in a secret location in such a way that the audience is completely absorbed into the action. The venue is usually somewhere like a massive warehouse which has been made into a film set and the idea is to recreate the atmosphere of the film so that people think they are actually living it. The audience members have to dress up as characters from the story and they are free to roam the 'world of the film', surrounded by actors and entertainers who make it seem like they are really there. It is a huge piece of theatre, so much more than just a showing of the film.

The film we were booked to be a part of was *Who Framed Roger Rabbit?* It's the story of a version of 1940s Hollywood, where live actors and cartoon actors (known as 'toons') exist side by side and regularly interact. As the audience were queueing up there were gangster-like characters coming round saying.

'Are you toons?'

Then they would be invited into a lavish artdeco set and see Jessica Rabbit up above them on screen, getting dressed up. The whole thing was very clever and just huge fun. If you know the story, we were there to re-enact the scene in the film where Bob Hoskins comes into a theatre and finds Donald and Daffy Duck duelling on two pianos. There were lots of sequences of that kind recreated during the evening but that was our only bit, just acting out that one short scene in the film. The producers of the experience didn't want to have to set up two pianos for the performance so they needed a four-hands/one-piano act and that is where we came in. Fortunately we weren't required to dress as ducks: just full evening dress, black tie and tails. It was only a six-minute spot.

Most of the other performers were acting students who were paid peanuts, but Michael Vine negotiated a very good fee for us and arranged that, unlike everyone else, we were to have our own dressing room. Somebody had to collect us from there, take us down to the stage five minutes before we went on and then escort us back through the throng of people after we had done our bit. We were the only ones getting special treatment and we didn't have to interact with anybody else.

We could turn up at the venue at about ten to seven, get ready, go on, do our piece and then leave. Each night we would be out of the building by ten past seven and on our way to the bars of Soho. We would have been perfectly happy to do that for the rest of our lives.

[K: And I've still never seen the film!]

One thing about that experience was that we were free of any worry about how many tickets were being sold. The shows did fantastically well anyway but it wasn't something that we had to be concerned about. Touring our own shows, it's always there at the back of the mind: how are ticket sales going? You might think that when we perform on ships, because the passengers are likely to turn up for whatever entertainment is provided for them at sea, then we don't have to think about how many people come or how well we go down. In fact, on cruises, as soon as we finish our performance, someone is sending an email back to let the booking team know how the show was received, and that dictates whether we get booked again.

Just recently, nearly fifteen years into our partnership, we had a long run of shows where it felt like we could do no wrong.

Early in 2019 we were going in and out of South Africa on ships a few times. It's a country we've passed through often and we spent that week in Johannesburg when we were on our way to Namibia. We've always loved Cape Town and one of the cruise engagements was finishing there.

KEVIN

I don't know whether Steven did this deliberately or 'accidentally on purpose', but he booked us to have a few days in Cape Town as a holiday. In order to kid ourselves that we were working and not just having a good time, we put a message on Facebook announcing that we were going to be in South Africa and asking whether there were any agents or bookers that might be interested in our act who we could meet while we were there.

There wasn't a lot of response from the Facebook message, but Dillie Keane from Fascinating Aida sent us a private message saying:

'I'll get in touch with my friend Pieter Toerien for you if you like. He runs The Theatre on the Bay in Cape Town and produced our show when we were out there.'

We waited to hear back but nothing happened. On the last evening of our stay in the Cape we wandered along to have a look at The Theatre on the Bay and then sat in the Mantra Café a few steps away, enjoying a bottle of local wine. The next morning we caught the flight back to London.

As soon as we switched our phones back on after we landed at Heathrow, we found a message from Pieter:

'Just heard from Dillie K. Any recommendation of hers is good enough for me. When are you coming to South Africa?' We called him back:

'We just left last night! We were sitting right outside your theatre!'

Just as Canadians and Americans used to come up to us and tell us about *Two Pianos Four Hands*, a lot of South Africans would catch up with us on ships and say, 'Have you heard of *A Handful of Keys*?' It was a piano based revue that ran for years with a variety of different cast members and for a while it was Africa's most successful show. We didn't actually see it before came to an end, which was a pity because by all accounts it was very good. It turned out Pieter had been the producer of *Handful of Keys* for years, and although it wasn't happening anymore, he knew his audience still wanted to see a piano show: we were just what he needed to satisfy that demand

He had done some research into our act and was quite keen to get some dates from us when we could do some shows: two weeks in Cape Town and two more weeks in Johannesburg. He wanted us for October and November 2019

We didn't understand what an important man Pieter Toerein is until we got there. He is to South Africa what Andrew Lloyd Webber and Cameron Mackintosh are to the United Kingdom: he virtually is theatre! In fact if Lloyd Webber wanted to take *Cats* or *Phantom of the Opera* out to South Africa then Pieter Toerien is the man he has to go through. His theatre in Johannesburg is more famous than the shows he takes there.

He is a quite incredible person and very ambitious. When he was still only twenty he was so desperate to get Marlene Dietrich to go to South Africa that he camped out on her front step and sat waiting for her to come out. Eventually, intrigued by the young man sitting outside, she invited him in and he managed to persuade her to tour his homeland. After that he got other big stars of the sixties to follow: Alma Cogan, Russ Conway, Cyd Charisse, Maurice Chevalier, Marti Caine and even Judy Garland just before she died. Then he started to stage big West End productions too.

Pieter runs his companies with an iron rod and people rather tiptoe around him. But he really looks after his staff and he even houses some of them. In Cape Town we were put up in a very nice and fully staffed house rather than a hotel, and that meant we could indulge our passion for baking. Because we didn't quite understand how famous he is we couldn't see the aura and we didn't have the same level of fear that others have around him. We would be bursting into Pieter's office every morning with a tray of parmesan and rosemary biscuits or millionaire shortbread that we had just fetched out of the oven. We think he found it quite amusing that we could be so naïve about his status.

Of course his apartment was fantastic: a huge open plan space with a swimming pool in one part of what is effectively his living room. Both the décor and the artwork on the walls were incredible, and he has Noel Coward paintings that were done especially for him. If we had to pick one item out of the fantastic furnishings it would be the white piano that was given to him by Johnny Mathis.

KEVIN

We had only just met him when he was showing us around this fabulous place, but modestly underplaying it. I stood and looked at the view and then turned to him and said:

'Do you know? I think you've done quite well.'

There was a moment when he was obviously a bit non-plussed but then he started laughing; he realised I was being ironic.

Pieter had a gut feeling that we were going to go down well: it's the reason he hired us. On the first night he declared the show was going to sell out, and it did. The audiences in Cape Town are reputedly quite reserved and at the end of the performance we walked off, intending to come back on for an encore. But the applause started to die away even though some of them were shouting 'More!' When we went back on they all stood up and burst into applause again.

We realised that over there, if you leave the stage they think that's the end of the show and start to let the applause die down and shuffle out. They expect you to stand there, take the bow and milk the applause. If they stand up and keep applauding, give them more!

After that Pieter organised a press night and stepped up the promotion. He said to us:

'You're not famous out here yet, but this show is going to run so we need to get you up to that level'.

We found ourselves getting up early to go on breakfast TV and then he arranged for us to go on South Africa's equivalent of *Desert Island Discs*. Within a couple of days people were recognising us when we were out walking the streets.

STEVEN

It's a very different culture there. People just love going out to the theatre in the evening and wouldn't dream of staying in to watch *Ant & Dec's Takeaway*. They are really happy to go and see a new production, even though it isn't cheap!

We did two weeks in Cape Town, flew home for a couple of weeks and then went straight back out and did another two week stint in Johannesburg. In all, that was twenty-eight shows and every single one ended with a standing ovation. We got to the point where, before we went on each night, we were getting nervous that we might not get the same response. It was just an amazing feeling going to work every night for two weeks – twice – and knowing that we were selling out and really reaching our audience. We will happily play at Pieter's theatres for as long as he wants us to.

KEVIN

It's a very nice feeling being able to relax during the day and just concentrate on the music, and not worry about the numbers of tickets that have been sold. There was one night on stage when I looked out and realised how different it feels when you can accept being successful.

There was a time when we probably wanted to have that kind of fame everywhere, but lovely as it is to be so appreciated we aren't looking for such adulation anymore. That isn't because we've come to accept that it's not going to happen (although we probably have). It is because we see how it affects the life of those who achieve it. We saw how small and claustrophobic Mickey Rooney's life really was and we know how Lorna Luft has to live with constant intrusion into the lives of herself and her family.

More than anything we want to be able to go out and enjoy a few drinks with friends after our shows without having to be careful in any way. What we do is all about having fun with our music and giving people a good quality show.

KEVIN

In 2011, just after the run at the Edinburgh festival that didn't go so well, we were booked to be the soloists at a concert for the Young Musicians' Symphony Orchestra. Over the years since the incident in the bush (hiding from Yehudi Menuhin) I remained good friends with James Blair, and it was at his invitation that we were to be playing; he was conducting us in a concert at St John's Smith Square in London. I had progressed from being the musician booker, to being one of the soloists all those years later.

This was one of our first concerts since we had rebranded ourselves from Katzenjammer to Worbey and Farrell, and at Geoffrey Durham's suggestion we were now concentrating on the musical arrangements rather than the sketches and songs of the previous few years.

We were asked to perform our own arrangement of Saint-Saens *Carnival of the Animals*, but we also had an idea to rearrange a rather special Malcolm Arnold concerto. This one was specially written for Steven's piano teacher Phyllis Sellick and her husband Cyril Smith, for them to be able to play together after he had had a stroke that meant he lost the use of his left hand. They performed *Concerto for Two Pianos (3 Hands)* at the Proms in 1969 and it was such a hit that they had to play the final movement again as an encore because the audience loved it so much.

Steven knew about the piece from Phyllis of course, and introduced me to it soon after we first met. We had wanted to do an arrangement of it for years: converting it from three hands, two pianos to four hands, one piano.

[S: It still adds up to five!]

We were told we probably couldn't get permission because of problems with the Malcolm Arnold estate. He left the rights to some of his music to the man who had been looking after him for the last twenty years of his life, and his family were still disputing the will. We were trying to think of ways to make contact with someone who would have the authority to allow us to adapt the piece. I approached my friend Kenneth Hesketh, who is now Composition Professor at the Royal College, and asked him if he knew who we would have to get to know, to even <u>ask</u> if we could do some work on the concerto. He put us in touch with Fiona Southey, who was Malcolm Arnold's personal manager until his death.

It turned out Fiona Southey was aware of us. She knew we did comedy songs and sketches, and she wasn't at all happy with the idea that people like us could make fun of the Malcolm's work. I went to meet her and we had a lovely time together and I assured her we would have the utmost respect for the piece, especially as Phyllis had been such an important part of Steven's life. After that she told Faber Publishing that she gave her blessing to us doing an arrangement.

Faber agreed to it but, as is usual with these people, they wanted control in the form of a copy of the sheet music that we were about to create. To which we replied:

'No, we won't be writing it down. We never write anything down.'

They couldn't be bothered to fight about it and gave us permission. So that was that.

STEVEN

The first performance of our rearrangement was at the Young Musicians' Symphony Orchestra concert at St John's Smith Square. The concerto went down far better than the well-known Saint Saens' *Carnival of the Animals* everyone had come to hear.

This was just after we'd met Geoffrey Durham for the first time in 2011, and he came along to see us that night with his partner Helen, to start to get to know our work. The following evening, we were doing a concert in Benslow and we spent the day working on *Carnival of the Animals*. Having just performed it alongside a full symphony orchestra, this time we would be doing it without accompaniment. Geoffrey was quite impressed that we could get the transition done so quickly. On that second night it was the first time that he took full notes, and we met him for coffee the following day. He gave us a long list of stuff to work on; it was really the beginning of our working relationship.

For years people have been performing *Carnival of the Animals* using the Ogden Nash poem. Fabulous as it is, it has become a bit dated so we decided to rewrite the script. We really enjoyed doing it and Geoffrey gave us some suggestions for further improvements when we performed it again later. He was a great help because he is such a wordsmith. We used to call him 'Dictionary Corner' because he appeared so often in that role on *Countdown*.

In our version all the animals are irritated about the adverse publicity they are getting because of the spread of diseases: Mad Cow disease, Swine Flu, Avian Flu. They arrange a big party with us there to help relaunch their image.

I noticed in yesterday's *Daily Express*,
That apparently animals suffer from stress.
In the past, their worst problems were worms, ticks and fleas
But, alas, now it's swine flu and mad cow disease.

We made some of the references more relevant for younger people.

The pert kangaroo is directly designed
With the Blackberry, Kindle and I-pad in mind.
Her pouch is just perfect to hold them. And maybe
She might even manage to fit in a baby.

We even found a way to explain why the tortoise's music is a slowed-down version of *The Can-can*.

The tortoise was once a seductive young belle
But for years now, she hasn't come out of her shell.
She sits reminiscing with ciggies and booze,
About dancing *The Can-can* at Le Moulin Rouge

When it was finished and we tried it out on stage, it went brilliantly!

Fast forward a few years to 2018. We were working on a recording of some of our pieces for a new CD at Sir Henry Wood Hall, one of the main venues for orchestras to rehearse and record. We got speaking to Ian Brignall who runs the venue and we happened to mention to him what we had done with the Malcolm Arnold 'three hands concerto'. He knew the piece and absolutely loved it.

'I run the Brighton Philharmonic Orchestra. You could maybe come and do it with us. Let me speak to Barry and see if he's interested.'

The 'Barry' he was referring to is Barry Wordsworth, one of the world's leading conductors and Conductor Laureate at the Brighton Philharmonic. For years he was the visiting Principal Conductor with BBC Concert Orchestra and is the Music Director of the Royal Ballet Covent Garden. He is a very important person in the music world and amongst many recordings he has conducted, there is a very good version of *Carnival of the Animals*. He has conducted this Malcolm Arnold concerto as well and was definitely a man we would want to work with.

KEVIN

The last time I'd seen Barry was when he was conducting at the Royal Opera House and I took my Mum with me. It was amazing to think we were going to be put forward to him and I really didn't think it was going to happen. But then we got a phone call to say that Barry had looked at what we do, and he would be interested in taking us on for a let-your-hair down end of season concert at the Brighton Dome. It was going to be their equivalent of the *Last Night of the Proms*.

We were quite nervous about the prospect of doing this so on the day of the rehearsal with Barry, we decided to go early and practise before he arrived. We were working away at the piano and became aware that there was a man standing behind us, applauding what we'd done. And because Barry was so enthusiastic even before we started we weren't so nervous, and it all went well.

He cut the session early because he was completely happy with it and called across to Ian Brignall:

'Have you seen what these guys are doing?'

He said he really couldn't tell the difference from the original Malcolm Arnold version of the concerto, even though we were both on the same piano and using an extra hand. That was exactly the result we wanted because he knew the piece really well.

We were meant to be going on to the Steinway Hall to continue rehearsing but Barry said:

'Let's go to the Union Café.'

We thought he meant we were just going for a cup of coffee somewhere; we didn't know that it's actually a Gordon Ramsay restaurant.

[K: When we arrived at the restaurant I said to Steven: 'I think we may have to cancel the booking at Steinway.'

S: I said: 'No, no, no. We'll get there on time.'

K: 'No. Barry's opening a bottle of champagne, and I get the feeling it's not going to end there.']

We phoned Steinway to say we wouldn't be coming and they were quite disappointed because we were meant to be picking out a piano for them to send to Brighton for the concert. The wine selection went from champagne, through a rosé, a white and then on to a delicious Gewurtztraminer from Alsace. Barry suggested that:

'If you drink a lot then it really is important to have periods in your life when you stop altogether.'

We were quite disappointed with this theory because we've never been ones to stop. But then he said:

'For instance: if you've been drinking at eleven in the morning and then stop, don't start drinking again until one!'

It was one of the best afternoons of our lives: it was a seven hour lunch. The bill must have come to an absolute fortune because we got through so many bottles of really good quality stuff, and in an expensive restaurant too. We were staying with our friend James Hurr, the electronic music producer, and as he wanted to go out with us that evening we decided it probably wasn't a good idea to go back to his place and sleep it off – the chances were we wouldn't wake up. So we waited until James came home and then went out clubbing. We were on such a high, and finally finished drinking that day around three in the morning.

With a conductor of Barry's calibre, and a knowledgeable and appreciative audience, it was inevitable that the concert in Brighton would go fantastically well. We were completely in awe of Barry because of his status and what he's achieved, but he was equally admiring of our work. After the concert he was good enough to say it was the best end of season concert he's ever done, and gave us a quote to use on posters in the future:

'Worbey and Farrell have an astonishing ability to convey the joy and fun in making music.'

Which is pretty much what we are aiming for!

STEVEN

We actually got him to take part in the *Carnival of the Animals* verses. The audience were amazed that someone like him would get involved in the fun because he's such a serious conductor, but he obviously enjoyed himself. We got him to recite the verse about pianists.

Pianists are notoriously the biggest pains,
According to the immortal Mr Saint Saens.
I've composed a small section to give them their due
But they're the one animal I'd cage in a zoo.

What was especially good was that he asked us to perform a couple of our usual routines at the end of the concert. Instead of just leaving us out there on stage, he came and sat right next to us and he and the orchestra were howling with laughter at our nonsense. It was so nice that the audience could see another side to these celebrated musicians: really enjoying themselves and not being constrained as they usually are by the formal nature of a concert.

Our friend Bert Kerrigan, the QC, came down to Brighton to see that concert. Afterwards we were all driving to Lady Colin Campbell's castle to stay the night. Bert remarked:

'In life, one is constantly trying to get to the level that you remember your teachers and professors seemed to be at when you were a student. What you don't realise is that you have probably reached their level or gone past them.'

The Brighton Dome will always be very special to us and it was great to get the chance to go back there a second time early in March 2020 as part of the Sunday afternoon concert series. We were performing our *Rhapsody* concert, on our own without an orchestra. It was also a significant day.

[S: Having joked so many times that we were there on Kevin's birthday, it felt a bit strange when it really was – his fiftieth.]

Bert was there again with a large group of our friends and family. After the show we had a party upstairs in The Cricketer's Arms, one of Brighton's historic pubs.

KEVIN

It was a marvellous evening with some of the people who have been with us for years. My mother and sister were there, and Steven's sister Dawn. One of my oldest friends from my schooldays had put together an album of photographs and invited people to write memories in it.

Someone put something about how I wrote 'SH*T' on the vicar's shed wall and Dawn laughed and said:

'Steven did worse than that. He used to draw pictures of houses on the wall of our outside toilet, IN sh*t!'

And then she went on to complain that every time she comes to visit us, she has to check the bed because Steven always hides a plastic turd under the duvet!

STEVEN

I looked around at one point that evening and realised what a strange group of people we have collected over the years.

Chapter 22

In which we somehow get through lockdown, help to make Mr. Trump famous and look forward to new opportunities.

And then when we got home from that trip, the pandemic descended upon us and like everyone else we were confined to our home.

When the lockdown was first imposed, it actually felt a bit like having a holiday away from the constant travel, the hours sitting in airports, the not as glamorous as you might think taxi trips through tropical rainforests to join ships, and leaving the house before dawn to get to the airport. A holiday in Edinburgh, what could be better than that?

Like all creative people half of the time we are working at home. When we aren't performing, or travelling to an engagement, we are in our own house in Edinburgh practising several hours a day and working on new arrangements for future shows. As we've said some of these pieces can take a year or so to get right, so in some ways being stuck in the house is what we do anyway,

Then came the really depressing part. Over the course of a couple of weeks, absolutely all of the concerts we were booked to do in 2020 were cancelled one by one. Cruise ships stopped sailing and the planned return to South Africa was on hold. It became increasingly clear that it was going to be at least a year before we might perform again, and it is very dispiriting to work on something not knowing when, if ever, we would get a chance to perform it. Being self-employed we weren't eligible for the furlough schemes and the government seemed to be very slow in finding ways of supporting the creative arts through the crisis. We were facing an enormous financial loss. We had some savings but with a mortgage to pay they wouldn't last much more than a year.

[S: We had to apply for Universal Credit. It was quite an exciting day when £409 appeared in my bank account.

K: I'd never claimed benefits in my whole life, and now I was suddenly one of those 'scabby dole scroungers' that *The Daily Mail* talks about.]

Normally our outgoings are substantial but then we realised that they weren't going to be during lockdown as there was nothing to spend any money on: no hotels, no flights, taxis or trains, no meals outside the house. And no socializing and drinking with friends. It was actually quite a shocking revelation when we realised how little we could live on comfortably. It calmed us down and made us take stock.

We felt lucky in so many ways. For months it felt similar to the time back in the 1990s when we kept hearing about close friends being diagnosed with Aids, only this time it was hearing of theatres closing (perhaps forever), of friends in the same business losing their homes and having to move back in with parents. Many had trained for years in the arts and now they had to get a job stacking shelves or working for UberEats. We could send sympathetic messages but saying 'Sorry to hear that' to someone who has had to abandon all of the dreams they have worked towards, was so like saying the same to a friend who had newly tested HIV positive.

This pandemic is a great leveller of course in that it touches the lives of everyone. No matter how privileged or wealthy we have all had to deal with it, and the chances of succumbing to it are pretty much the same, whoever you are. But living in the shadow of a deadly disease is something that one part of the community has had to do before, and we went through it last time largely unseen and unsupported. That hasn't made it any easier but maybe it helps with understanding that we just have to get on with life as best as we can.

Like many, in the early days of the pandemic we wanted to believe it was an over reaction, that it couldn't be as serious as we were being told. But then people started to die. The first person that we knew was Andrew Watt, a very talented harpist who died shortly after the first lockdown aged only thirty-two. And then in April we heard that Rick Unterberg, a legendary pianist in New York, one of the inspirations for our act, had also died from Covid-19.

KEVIN

I first met Rick when I was doing some work for Liberty Radio with Sadie Nine. I mentioned to Sadie that I was going to go to New York for a few days and she suggested that I do a report from there about the New York piano bar scene. I talked to quite a few players while I was there but Rick was easily the most interesting.

For thirty years he was resident pianist at the Townhouse on the upper east side, starting there when it opened. His playing was virtuosic and flamboyant and he had the most infectious smile ever. He used to do some incredibly acrobatic things at the piano and it gave me the idea for one of the routines that Steven and I were putting together for our first appearance at the charity concert with David Soul.

Years later we went back to the bar together and he noticed us immediately. He was really showing off and fired up, pulling faces and calling over to us:

'Get me to London!'

STEVEN

He was a real character. We would go and see him each time we went to New York and I filmed him playing there: it was quite magical. He was really quite keen to get a chance to play in the UK and if we had done any agency work he was the one person we would have loved to introduce to London.

The Townhouse is quite an exclusive gay men's night club. A lot of very wealthy old queens go there with good looking young boys, suited and booted. It's an elegant cocktail bar that people in London would love to have near them. It's never going to be the same now because Rick was just stunning.

KEVIN

I remember him saying that he was always susceptible to any flu or cold that was going. He probably knew this new virus didn't bode well for him. When he got symptoms of Covid, the hospitals wouldn't take him because he was still breathing freely and maybe they didn't understand why he was so sure it was going to be serious for him. He went on a ventilator in a hospice and died quite quickly. I am really upset about him having gone.

I still have the recording of the interview that I did with Rick. It lasts about forty five minutes and it's going on a website that his friends are setting up as a memorial to him.

Luckily, we haven't lost anyone in our families or any of our really close friends, or their families either. But we have seen some of the friends who we always believed had the most intact mental health, struggling and buckling under the strain. In some ways however the two years of the pandemic have been good for us.

We've spent a lifetime making things up as we've gone along, so having to stop and just live in the moment has probably been the best thing that's ever happened. And if that sounds a little selfish we are very aware that for many this has been simply horrendous.

STEVEN

To start with, Kevin was a bit more at a loss of what to do but we kept ourselves surprisingly busy and the situation gave us an opportunity to think about what we would like to do in the future. We know that we won't stop performing because we love it so much but we may find that the cruise ships won't be such a good source of income for us after the pandemic. So many jobs in that business are being lost that the cruise lines will inevitably want to concentrate on the entertainment that will cost them less.

We were fortunate to receive some commissions for composing piano music: one of them for tap dancing exams. And we also started working again with the dance music producer James Hurr, composing short pieces that could be used for TV and film music, a very popular genre of music.

We met James through Michael Topping. He's very creative and becoming one of the country's most significant music producers. A few years ago we worked with him on converting a piece of bell music called Stedman Caters into a dance track. It was a fun thing to do, bringing out how complex the music of campanology can be; this piece was twenty-one beats to the bar. And we only used bells at the very end.

Early in the first lockdown James called a big company that sells music to the producers of adverts, television dramas and game shows and asked them if they would like to work with him. Normally they commission what they need and don't answer the phone to anybody but they took his call just because of the reputation he now has. They certainly wouldn't have listened to us if we had made an approach.

What they look for is composers who can do music for things like crime series, the minimalist style of music that Brian Eno and Phillip Glass write that produces the right feeling without the viewer even realising. What is interesting is that so much of this music isn't written with a specific film or show in mind. Instead, the company builds up a stock of different pieces in a variety of styles that film and TV producers can then fit to the emotion they want to invoke. These are styles that we are very comfortable writing, but James, and people like him, just aren't. We don't have the musical production abilities that James has so working together has been beneficial to us all and we have gained an immense amount from each other.

STEVEN

Kevin has a background in this sort of work, because he used to write music for Screen Partners. I don't really count myself as a composer but I'm really pleased with what I've done so far. When James heard them he seemed to think they were on a level with the best of what he's been working with up until now. We forget sometimes that we actually know what we are doing in music.

Over the year we have been putting pieces together and making them into albums. We think that sort of thing could lead us to a bigger audience; a market has grown up with people seeking out the background music for Scandi-noir shows like *The Bridge* to listen to away from the series. We released our first collection in the autumn - *Evocations* - an album of beautiful, relaxing and inspiring piano pieces which is available on all platforms. Geoffrey Durham listened to it recently and suggested that we play some of the pieces in our concerts. If that succeeds and gets us a bigger audience, then perhaps it will give us the chance to introduce people to some of the more serious stuff we love playing.

We realised that we suddenly had the time we needed to do some detailed work on our ideas for musicals. We have had a few ideas through the years, and we started working on one with the tentative title of *Gentlemen*. It is a full length show, an affectionate look at a world that is disappearing: the gay culture around men's toilets. It's based in the early 1980s, a time when many homosexuals had nowhere to go to meet others and were forced to live in denial.

What inspired us to think about that as a subject was witnessing the public conveniences near the St James Centre in Edinburgh being closed down. So many older gay men who don't use the modern apps like Grindr, Bender and Gaydar, would rely on places like that for their sex lives. We never went there ourselves but we knew people who did, and if we ever stopped at the traffic lights outside that building, it would make us smile to see the old fellows walking along and then feigning surprise that they had discovered a toilet. They'd probably walked two miles to get there but they would make a great show of having noticed it, as though for the first time.

'Ooh that's handy, I'll just pop in there!'

On the day that this toilet block was bulldozed we saw a group of little old men standing by, practically holding a funeral for the place. Their long faces forlornly betrayed that they knew a sexless future was stretching out ahead of them. We would like to honour their happy memories in music.

We approached our old friend Patrick Wilde, who is a brilliant writer, and he has joined us on the project and has written the story and the script: what is known as the 'book'. We fed him our initial ideas and he has come up with some brilliant characters and a superb compelling synopsis. Most importantly for this project, he has not gone too far along the sleazy route. It is going to be a comedy, but we all want it to have real warmth and touch on the politics and climate for gays of the time – such as Margaret Thatcher's law against 'promoting homosexuality'. We have even managed to set the words of the infamous Section 28 to music, in a parody of the style of Gilbert and Sullivan. It's a period of history that was starting to be forgotten about until Russell T Davies' wonderful series *It's a Sin* was broadcast, and we would like to keep its memory alive in music.

The show is finished, and our old friend John Stalker came on board as producer and arranged for a cast of eight professional actors to spend a week at the Charing Cross Theatre in London going through the script and the songs to iron out any wrinkles, before we look to raise the money for a full scale production.

So we managed to keep ourselves busy. As a diversion in the first few months of the lock-down, we got a bit more serious about writing this book and made some progress, recording our memories with our friend Simon, who then went away and tried to make something coherent out of what we had told him. He probably knows more about us now than we do.

And then some other things happened, which improved our lives considerably.

We have a friend called Craig who lives on an alpaca farm in Lochmaben, in the south of Scotland. He let us know that his West Highland terrier was about to have a litter of puppies and wondered whether we might be interested in having one of them, to replace Margaret. So we took him up on his offer and now we have Beryl, a playful bundle of fun who seems to love everybody. She is the complete opposite in character to the rather severe and disdainful Dame Margaret de Lumiere.

We were expecting the resolution of (what we hoped was) the last round of litigation over Bender and Brenda, but we knew that in the circumstances the courts would be delayed in making decisions so we really weren't holding our breaths that there would be any news on that until the pandemic was all over.

Quite out of the blue a letter arrived. Steven Elliott had decided to give up all claims to the trademarks and just walk away from the whole thing, after all the years of fighting! He wasn't giving in graciously though. Despite it being near certain that the court would rule that the trademarks are jointly owned he was suggesting some conditions on him giving up his rights. At one time he was boasting about writing a book about the whole saga and now he was asking us to not talk to anyone about what happened between us, except in repeating the legal judgements.

On top of wanting us to be gagged about the whole affair, he expected us to fire his trustee in bankruptcy (we are his main creditors) and withdraw our financial claims on him. Our lawyers sent him back a fairly short response and assured him that we have no interest in doing anything other than telling the truth.

The first hearing about our claim to the trademarks had gone the way our court cases usually do: we lost. It was a complaint to the Intellectual Property Office that Steven Elliott had illegally transferred the rights to the Bender mark into his company. He had signed a declaration that we had consented to that happening and we had done no such thing. In fact, by the time we got to the IPO he had gone a step further and moved it on to another company called Totally Outsourced Ltd, owned by his friend Amit Ratnaparkhi.

It was always going to be an uphill job to get the IPO to admit they had allowed something illegal to happen so it wasn't really a surprise that they found against us. The long game was to take a review of that decision to court and it was quite clear, even to Steven Elliott, that we were going to win this one at last.

KEVIN

The judge we had this time looked at the whole thing again and said he couldn't really understand why the matter had got that far. He was even finding fault with Lord Tyre's decision even though the Court of Appeal had agreed with it. At one point he became quite irritated about the other side still trying to argue the technicalities.

'Can we just stop? Are we not all in agreement that three people invented a 'thing', and that these three intended to make money from this 'thing' together? Did these two people not believe they were a part of this 'thing'? Seriously, Gentlemen, are we not all in agreement about this?'

It was then that I knew we were finally going to win. It didn't matter what percentage of any partnership we might have thought we were entitled to, it didn't even matter whether there was a partnership or not. This judge understood that when Steven registered that trademark, and I paid for it, from our address, the three of us all knew we were doing something together. And the intention was to use it to make some money. On that basis we were each entitled to a third of whatever came from that registration and Steven Elliott couldn't just take our two-thirds away for himself.

We still don't really understand why it all went so wrong with Steven Elliott. Thinking back to the start of the whole episode it's sad to remember how excited we all were when Bender started off so well. Our app was launched only about six months behind Grindr and it was on course to be just as successful. Grindr has just been sold for $608 million so we could all have done very nicely out of Bender.

[K: That's an awful lot of Boozy Pianist cocktails.]

Maybe he was egged on by friends, but we feel he became the author of his own downfall and he didn't recognise what we had brought to the app. He was right in thinking that he was doing all the programming and making the thing function but that wasn't all that Bender was.

We always thought that he didn't understand how crucial the name was in making it succeed, how the two-syllable 'er' name has been repeated over and over because it works: Qrushr, Tinder, Tumblr, Growlr... The great thing about 'Bender' is that it is cheeky, as well as fitting in with the psychology of a brand that will sell really well.

KEVIN

> The app that was 'Bender' mutated into something else and it's not done nearly as well under the new name which is why he's been fighting to keep hold of the trademark. We suspect that there was a plan that eventually the name could be changed back once we had lost any rights to the trademarks, but now we own those and the domain names as well.

When Andrew Lloyd Webber writes a song, if someone changes one word of the lyric they become part of the composition team. Quite often he gets someone else to do the orchestration and that process will often take far more time than the original composition of the song, just as Steven Elliott put in thousands of hours working away at programming Bender. But no Lloyd Webber orchestrator claims the composition is all theirs; they are a part of it just as much as anyone else who has contributed. Steven Elliott maybe didn't recognise this because in his eyes he'd done most of the work. To those of a technical mind, the visionary contribution of the creative person is often dismissed as 'easy'. You hear the contempt in people's voices as they stand in front of a piece of modern art, a Tracy Emin bed, or a Damian Hirst pickled shark:

'Well! I could have done that!'

To which the answer is: 'Yes. But you didn't.'

Now, after all the years of litigation over the Bender and Brenda apps, they are ours and they have returned to a smart phone near you. We have new investors, real business people who are totally trustworthy and who insist on proper legal agreements being drawn up, including one with Steven Elliott that prevents him from saying bad things about the new version. Our new partners have put a lot of money behind making it work as well as it possibly can, and we have found an excellent software development company that has a large team working on the app for us.

Scott has joined us on the enterprise, and his work has been vital to getting it off the ground; he has the understanding of IT matters that we lack so he's a good link between us and the developers. The cost is immense, but there are features that we are implementing that other dating apps don't have and that gives us much confidence in its potential success.

The market is far more competitive now than it was when the original Bender was released, and the technology much more advanced, so we all know that it will take longer than last time to establish Bender as a market leader.

STEVEN

There are so many dating apps out there - not just gay ones – and that has put a lot of pressure on us to come up with something new. Our new investors don't know anything about the gay world and its apps, so the creative side has been all our responsibility. But they are definitely people who know how to run a business, and we're very lucky with the people we have got with us. The way they speak, it feels like they don't know anything but success.

After so many years of worrying about the legal wranglings over Bender it is so refreshing to be able to think of it as something new and exciting again.

The other good thing that happened to us in 2020 was that we suddenly became huge media stars! We appeared in a ten-minute item on the main television news and became famous throughout the country. If you think you may have missed that happening – or have suspicions that we entered a drink induced fantasy state for a while – we have to admit that the country in question was Estonia so it's quite likely all the coverage passed you by, but this is what happened.

The story started in June 2009 on a cruise through the Baltics on the QE2. Scott was there with us. When the ship came into Tallinn in Estonia one evening we all got off and went out for a few drinks, well several drinks.

[K: I seem to remember I was so rat-arsed at the end of the evening that I bought a cheeseburger and dropped it straight away.

S: It was a jacket potato, and we had to stop you from scrabbling around on the ground to salvage it!]

The following afternoon we went out for a walk in the pouring rain to try to shift the hangovers. In the corner of the main town square there was some sort of music festival going on, so we wandered over and listened for a while. There were two girls singing a rather beautiful song in Estonian as a duet. It was one of those moments when you hear a melody and you realise that it isn't just a 'tune', it's something really very special. The chorus was enchanting, and Scott was particularly mesmerised by it. We took a recording on a phone and wandered on.

After the cruise we thought of the music as something we would like to work up as an arrangement for our concerts, but we couldn't find out what it was. We assumed that it was a traditional Estonian song, but if it wasn't we would need to get the composer's permission. We tried using Shazam – the software that recognises tunes – but it didn't register at all so we got in touch with some Estonian friends we had met years before on another cruise, and they had no idea what it was either. They passed the recording on to some more people but no-one could identify it. That made it less likely that it was something in the public domain that we could just use.

[S: Then I lost the phone – it was just an old Nokia - and with it we lost the recording. And that was that. We forgot about it for over a decade.]

A couple of weeks into lockdown we were trying some things out on the piano and thought of the song again. We decided it might be worth having another go at locating it, especially as everyone in the world was stuck at home with not much to do. Only once before have we had any success with making things happen on Facebook.

KEVIN

I got into a taxi in Edinburgh one night and the taxi driver started singing in the style of Barry Manilow. He desperately wanted to be famous and wanted to meet Barry (we do have a connection there...) but I didn't get his name. I had filmed him singing so I put the clip up on Facebook with the comment:

'Who is the singing taxi driver?'

And then because Steven copied it onto his YouTube channel, the *Daily Mail* picked up on it and suddenly thousands of people were a part of 'the search'.

From that experience it did seem possible that if we could get enough of our Facebook friends to share a search for the music, eventually someone might be able to tell us what it was. We thought the best way to do it would be to make a video of us playing what we could remember of the song and then ask for help.

STEVEN

To be honest I wasn't that keen on the idea, but Kevin said we could make it a bit funny. We dressed up and put on our cravats and swigged from glasses of what looked like champagne (but was actually ginger beer) and talked about having cocktails later – all the sorts of things that our followers would expect – and put it out. Eleven years down the line we could really only play the chorus from memory, but we hoped there was enough there for someone to recognise it if they'd heard it before.

Most of the funny clips we put up are shared by just a handful of friends and eventually only reach about four hundred people in total, but within twenty four hours this short clip of us playing an Estonian song had got to more than ten thousand: the response just got crazier and crazier. Lots of people started sending us things that sound a bit like it, but they weren't what we were looking for. There was one person that we know who used to work at the BBC who shared it with the correspondents in Eastern Europe, and through that link it reached a lady called Siri.

Siri sent us a message: 'I think I know what it is'.

[S: I lay in bed one morning running through the messages before I got up and Siri's looked like another one that was going to take us up a blind alley. But when I looked at what she'd sent I immediately knew that this was it. I ran downstairs and woke Kevin up and played it to him.

K: I couldn't believe that we'd found the song, especially so quickly. Siri seems to be one of those people who collect obscure pieces of music and she recognised it from an old CD. She could tell us that the composer was someone called Juhan Trump.]

We googled a photo of Juhan Trump and from there found a Facebook account. It was obvious he wasn't in any way active on social media, but we could see that he had a son, and so we sent him a message explaining the story of our search and asked if he could pass it on to his father.

He replied: 'I just looked at your video on your FB page and yes this piece is composed by my father. He dedicated it to his mother (my grandmother) and to be honest, it's one of my favourite songs of all time. So simple, but yet so beautiful. I spoke to my Dad and he wanted to thank you for spreading his music! Additionally, he wanted to share the recorded version and sheet music with you as well.'

When we received the music we realised that we must have misheard or misremembered one of the notes because it wasn't exactly as we'd played it on the clip.

[K: That was a bit disturbing! I always tell people I only need to hear something once to get it perfectly!]

We made another recording of the whole song and put it out again and the clip had seventy five thousand views in the first week alone. Juhan Trump was suddenly very well known in his home country and his music was now in demand. He was completely overwhelmed with good wishes from all around the world and then the Estonian media picked up on it as a charming feel-good story for troubled times. Estonian TV interviewed Juhan and his son and showed our video clip in a ten-minute broadcast to about 1.3 million people. We thought maybe the press in the UK would be interested but when our publicist told the story to some journalists the response was the same everywhere:

'We're not interested in anything to do with Eastern Europe, our readers don't want to know anything about that part of the world.'

The whole episode was very moving and we definitely have a future career in Estonia because we are now better known over there than in our own country, and they hail us as heroes for making their music famous. As soon as we can organise it we'll be off to play some concerts in Estonia and Finland.

A couple of days after the broadcast an Estonian girl got in touch with us and said she thought she knew when we first heard the song.

'Hi. My name is Siri Kolka. Were you in Tallinn on June 9th, 2009? My mother's theatre school were singing some songs in the city square that afternoon and we have got a recording of it.'

She sent the recording through, and it was indeed the two girls we heard all those years ago and that was the perfect end to an enjoyable week. Even better: when we played it back, there they were singing the wrong note exactly as we'd remembered it.

Epilogue

It is a cool autumn morning and we are back in Chelsea, the part of London that we know so well from our student days. It is Sunday 10th October 2021 and it is Steven's fiftieth birthday The eighteen months of not being able to do what we enjoy most - performing in front of a live audience – is finally coming to an end. It seems quite appropriate that our pandemic started immediately after the concert and party in Brighton on Kevin's birthday, and here we are emerging from it with another big concert - and another party, of course.

We are at the Cadogan Hall, one of London's leading music venues. It is just a couple of minutes' walk from Sloane Square and only a mile or so from St Peter's Parsonage where Kevin lived in the bohemian commune. In those days this place was a derelict church that Mohammed Fayed wanted to convert into his home, but now it is a grand concert hall seating nearly a thousand people and home to the Royal Philharmonic Orchestra. After the Royal Albert Hall, it is the second venue for the Proms season. We have played here before, but we want this afternoon to be as special as that day in Brighton. And that feeling is adding to the usual nervous excitement of going through our set-up routines.

Only a couple of days ago we weren't even certain that the concert could go ahead despite it having been planned for weeks. Last Friday we held the launch party for the new Bender app in a bar in Edinburgh. It was a wonderfully busy evening of handing out shots and T-shirts, and showing everyone there what the app can do, and how it has features that they have never seen on any other gay dating app. Our friends were there to support us, but unfortunately one of them got in touch on Sunday to say that she had just tested positive for Covid-19. She was fine and had no symptoms, but it means we have been testing ourselves all week and thankfully we are both clear!

These past few weeks we have been concentrating on rehearsing our new material. There is so much in this new show that we have never performed before that we are conscious that this could be the most demanding programme we have ever put together.

STEVEN

Last night we were at the Lighthouse in Poole, a concert that was almost a rehearsal for today. It was lovely to be performing again and the show went really well apart from one mistake. We started to play Liberace's *Boogie-Woogie*, a fun piece we have performed hundreds of times, but only a couple of bars in it sounded all wrong. Kevin broke off:

'Am I playing this in the wrong key?!'

'You're playing in F, It should be in C.'

The audience started to laugh. They thought this was another one of our silly routines. So I gave Kevin a hard shove along the keyboard and said:

'There! Now you're in C'

That got such a big laugh that we have decided to keep it in the show today.

The sound check is all done, the screen is in place, the camera is working and there is nothing left to do but get into our stage clothes and wait for the audience to file in. The special occasion means that there will be as many friends and family out there to see us as there were last March in Brighton. Steven's Dad is going to be here watching us for the first time in years. He hasn't seen us perform since those early days when we were still playing to half filled theatres.

And then as we sit in the dressing room scrolling through our phones, we find a really special message:

'We've managed to get over for your show!! We are here!!'

It is from Siri, the Estonian girl who sent us the recording of her mother's theatre group Bel Canto singing the song we fell in love with in Talinn a dozen years ago.

And then we are striding out onto the stage to a rapturous welcome from the audience. There is emotion in the applause; most of these people have not been to a live performance for such a long time and people tell us afterwards that in that moment they felt the camaraderie, the sense that we had all pulled through together and a joyous relief that at last we are coming out the other side.

In the first half we play the premiere of a piece by Mary-Ann Ephrave, and we tell the audience about her and what she has done for us over the years. It is a stunning composition that is well received and, very reluctantly, Mary-Ann stands and takes a bow. And then we tell the story of how we became famous in Estonia, of the singing we heard, and the research that we did to try and find the music. We play our arrangement of this lovely song, and then surprise the audience by introducing Siri.

The second half includes our new arrangement of Littolf's *Scherzo*. It has been so difficult to put together that we nearly gave up on it. And then we launch into a new composition: *Variations on John Lennon's Imagine*.

KEVIN

We are very pleased with what we have done with this, but there is one person in the audience we really want to impress. Our friend Sandra Clay is a proud Liverpudlian, and fierce defender of The Beatles. When we told her we were working on *Imagine,* she told us in no uncertain terms that:

'You can't improve on perfection!'

Our composition starts on a single note – middle C – and then builds through a full set of variations until it transforms into the original song before falling back to the single note again, gradually fading away.

The audience join in enthusiastically with the song and we can feel their passion as they rise to:

'You may say I'm a dreamer...'

And then too soon the show is over and we are exhausted, but happily greeting people in the foyer, including Sandra who admits to the tears in her eyes.

Later, upstairs in the Antelope pub in Belgravia, there is a slight concern that we have exceeded the maximum capacity of fifty and that the floor might give way. There is the usual eclectic mix of people, some the same as were with us in Brighton, some different.

There is Steven's sister Dawn, and his Dad beaming with pride at having witnessed his son in such a buzzing show. There is Christine Hamilton telling anyone who will listen that some of our jokes don't quite work. There is Patrick Wilde, who has finished the book for *Gentlemen,* talking about taking it into the workshop stage. There are the major investors in Bender. And the usual collection of transvestites, and church bell-ringers, with a *Newsnight* journalist and a nuclear physicist.

Eighteen months ago we were confident that the next year would be spent busily touring the world, performing in big theatres and concert halls. What was going to be our most financially lucrative year, ended up being exactly the opposite. And yet it turned out to be our most creatively rewarding year. The time of the pandemic was our most productive yet.

There may be more lockdowns, more cancelled appearances. Who knows? But there will also be more concerts, cruises, and parties. At last it feels as though we can look forward to having our social lives back and being able to see friends again.

As long as there's wine and music and laughter - and an audience - Worbey and Farrell will be Well Strung, and ready to play!